# THE HOUSE OF PAIN

# THE HOUSE OF PAIN

## The Strange World of Monique Von Cleef *The Queen of Humiliation*

AN AUTOBIOGRAPHY AND A MESSAGE TO ALL HUMAN SLAVES

*by*
MONIQUE VON CLEEF
*with*
WILLIAM WATERMAN

LYLE STUART INC. / A Maurice Gerodias Book •
SECAUCUS, NEW JERSEY

Library of Congress Catalog Card Number: 71-190771

ISBN Number: 0-8184-0163-X



Queries for rights and permissions should be addressed to Lyle Stuart, Inc., 120 Enterprise Avenue, Secaucus, New Jersey, 07094

A MAURICE GIRODIAS BOOK
published in association with
Lyle Stuart Inc. and Maurice Girodias Associates Inc.

Printed in the United States of America

# THE HOUSE OF PAIN

# PART I

*The Hague, June 1971*

'You ridiculous slave!' says Monique, tapping half an inch of cigarette ash on the pale blue Chinese carpet. 'Worthless specimen of shitbagginess that you are—crawl to the kitchen at once and come back when I call you.'

The president-director traces two clearly visible grooves in the carpet pile with the knife-sharp creases in his trousers and vanishes into the hall. Even his hind parts make a humble impression.

'He is having the time of his life now,' Monique says. 'In the meantime we can go on with our talk. I get all sorts of clients. There's the type that's always in a hurry and they want their kick fitted in between business appointments. This one is the sort that wants to drag it out. What were we talking about?'

I don't reply at once. I am half lying back in one of her enormous armchairs, a half-filled crystal glass in my hand.

She asks: 'Are you thinking about something?'

'About you, my dear. About the human phenomenon Monique von Cleef.'

She shoots me a vaguely suspicious look, and I add: 'There must have been a time when you were just a little girl, taking her first hesitant steps. With or without a pink bow in her pigtail. Was it predestined, when that little girl was born, that she would become the legendary Monique von Cleef? Or have circumstances forcefully twisted that little girl's life course around?'

Monique is certainly intelligent. Although that in itself does not signify much, since there are so many different types of intelligence. Put it this way: she has a natural gift for understanding, with lightning swiftness, what someone is driving at. And that ability can take you a long way.

'Of course I've asked myself that question. Suppose at that hour of that day I had not met that person, or had not written that letter—would I now be the official wife of a businessman, boring myself to death with a lot of jabbering women in a beauty parlor? I had a talk about that with my father during the period when the trial was pending against me in New Jersey. I was living in California at the time . . .'

'Yes. As far away from Newark as you could get.'

She makes a gesture of irritation: 'Yes. It wasn't all that funny, with those arrests and all that puke-publicity.'

'The remarkable thing about you, Monique, is that you have become a living legend as The Pitiless Mistress, and thousands of men may wet their pants when you so much as frown at them, but in certain respects you have remained a vulnerable girl.'

She won't buy that. She gives me a dirty look. The amusing thing about talking with Monique is that against certain unexpected angles of attack she has no defense at all: she just evades or dodges. Perhaps she originally built up that armor of 'Pitiless Mistress' because she needed it as protection, just as a tortoise needs its shell. The trouble with armor is that its weight may become so colossal that one's speed gets cut to almost zero.

While I (sagging in her chair) sit looking at her, she slides back to that talk with her father: 'We were sitting on the terrace of my house in San Francisco, drinking coffee. In front of us a fantastic view of the Golden Gate Bridge. I asked him, "Papa, was I difficult to handle as a small girl?"

' "Not particularly. But you were very forward. Before you were a year old you walked underneath the dining room table, for you were very small and as straight as a stick. And if we tried to help you with anything, you beat our hands away, muttering angrily. You were too young to be able to talk, of course, but you made it clear that you didn't want to be helped. You wanted to do everything by yourself."

' "Were you and Mother happy together?"

' "Jesus, no," he said. "I was a damned unhappy man. Your mother was a beautiful woman with flaming red hair and skin like gleaming porcelain. From the first moment I saw her I was sick and gone about her. I simply had to have her, no matter how. I never understood that we could never form a workable partnership. An American could never understand that, for here in the United States there are no hard and fast class distinctions. But in Europe, it is damned difficult to marry into another class than the one you were born in. I came from a large working-class family in Amsterdam. My father was a mason who worked with his hands. That in itself, before the Second World War, branded me irrevocably.

' "Then there was the problem of drink. My father drank up four-fifths of what he earned. My mother was a pious churchgoer who worked herself into an early grave trying to raise eleven children on what she found in my father's pockets after he staggered home.

' "Your beautiful mother was a qualified nurse, from a solid middle-class family. Why she finally consented to marry me, I never found out. When I asked her she merely smiled in a mysterious way. But I worked hard, went through school, and refused to give up. So I finally got her. We got married and ten months later your brother Jan arrived. From almost the first week we had quarrels. No matter what we said or did, we always wound up at loggerheads. I worked morning, noon, and night, but your mother was incapable of handling money in a reasonable way, and she simply detested housework. She had the idea, I think, that after marriage her only function was to keep on looking beautiful and desirable. Well, to be fair, that's what I had married her for. I soon found out that straight sex bored or irritated her. Thereafter I had to conquer her anew each time, acting out all sorts of games and scenes. I would have to act the role of a knight in a castle who kept trying to seduce the governess—your mother. She would run around the living room, wailing, 'Oh, no, my lord! Please don't touch me! If my lady finds out I'll be kicked out and then what will I do!' When she finally allowed herself to be captured, she was completely caught up in the game; in that kind of mood I could have her. But those moments were few and far between. And unpredictable! To be honest, your mother could not get rid of the idea that she had married beneath her, and I think she refused to forgive me for that."

'Papa sat looking out at the Golden Gate Bridge and then went on: "When you were two years old we gave you a very big, expensive French doll with eyes that could open and close. I had a better job then and times were getting a bit better, too. But you hid that doll in a dark cupboard, stamped your little foot, and said: 'I don't want a doll! I want a dog.' " '

I say: 'Well, you certainly got that,' looking at the two magnificent boxers dozing at Monique's feet.

'Yes. That idea . . . I never let that go.'

I ask: 'What girlhood experiences do you think made the deepest impression on you?'

She gets up and does something with a glass and an ash tray. Sits down again, pulls her short skirt down chastely. I ask myself what our industrial tycoon can be doing in the kitchen. But that's Monique's business.

'I had a younger sister, Claartje, with red hair and blue eyes. I didn't mind her at all, she was almost as good as a dog. When one of those eternal quarrels between my father and mother would begin, Claartje used to creep into bed with me and then I would tell her all sorts of stories to divert her attention. By that time I had more or less immunized myself against their rows and quarrels. I had withdrawn into a world of my own.'

'Isn't it still that way with you?'

'And what's so special about that? Isn't that pretty much what everybody does in one way or another? I know lots of people who have been married for twenty years who hardly know what each other is thinking or daydreaming.' She nods her head in the direction of the hall. 'Take all those people who come here because they simply have no place else where they can go and be really understood. Their sexual idiosyncrasies are not the cause of their loneliness . . . it's usually the other way 'round. And once they are that way, they don't dare go anywhere else because so many of them are in prominent positions and can't afford to run the risk of slander or blackmail. Most of them are quite solidly married, and have kids. Married to beautiful women or nice women or rich women who don't understand the first thing about the men they married, or their work, or their ideas. Nothing about what interests motivate their husbands; women who aren't even remotely interested. I've often asked myself —for now and then you cannot help but sit back and think—' she stops.

'What have you asked yourself?'

'Whether I, because as a young child I myself had to live internally and by myself . . . have perhaps become conditioned that way . .. whether because of that training in loneliness I haven't developed quick understanding of men—and of women, too—who have become sexual deviates because of the burden of loneliness.'

'That's not such a bad theory, Monique. It's very difficult to recognize anything in someone else which one doesn't carry in oneself. How often do you hear it said that all psychiatrists are crazy? That is a generalization, of course, but you can certainly see it regularly demonstrated. It may be, in your case, the fact that your father and mother lived together like cat and dog.'

Monique begins to laugh: 'I think I'm perfectly in the clear with myself, thank you. All right . . . there was a time when I still dreamed of a pleasant, uncomplicated marriage, and some degree of comfort, luxury.'

'You must earn money like water. You think money and luxury are that important?'

'In themselves? Not particularly. But . . .'

'They mean security? Defense material?'

'That too, yes. Look here—I am not a girl of nineteen anymore. And the sort of man that I had vaguely in my head as a possible husband—I just never met him.'

'Are you quite sure you really wanted to? There's no doubt about it, Monique, you do have a strong and willful personality. If you try to associate yourself, tie yourself to a man with the same characteristics, you are heading straight into a civil war. And the sort of man who meekly does what you decide to decide . . .'

She smiles ironically. 'That's the type of man I like.'

We sit looking at each other, grinning a bit. She gets up suddenly, walks to the half-open door, and shouts: 'Bas! Bas! You hear me? Come here at once.

There is a sort of muted bark. Monique steps aside as the president-director comes crawling into the room. I half expect him to get a rewarding pat, but this shows how little I understand of this weird emotional world.

'What fool thing have you done now!' Monique shouts, furious. She rises to her full height, wrists on her hips. 'Have you wetted yourself again, you stupid beast?' Go back to the kitchen and make it fast!'

The president-director makes frightened, yelping noises, turns rapidly around, and at that instant Monique hits his posterior with a well-aimed, vicious kick, calling after him: 'And don't try to piss against the doorjamb like you did last week!'

She leaves the door nonchalantly open, walks back to her chair, lights a fresh cigarette, and nods her head in the direction of the hall. 'All this is part of the build-up. This type has to work up a tremendous need to relieve himself. And I refuse to let him go outside, until he almost explodes. I give him lots of strong tea with lemon as soon as he gets here. In a couple of minutes you'll hear him begin to whine and bark that he needs to be taken for a walk. I take no notice. Then, when he can't hold it anymore, he lifts his leg, opens his fly, and lets go against the doorjamb or the newel post of the staircase. Then I have to discover it, and as punishment he gets a terrific spanking. That makes him come. He can then go home perfectly pacified and content.'

'To be the successful businessman and reliable father?'

'I have that impression, yes. And he probably is both those things. He is a nice and decent man. I don't suppose anyone in his family or his office has the vaguest inkling of the deviation that sends him here.'

'Men like him don't go roaming around red-light districts do they?'

Monique considers this. 'I . . . sometimes ask myself whether it has anything to do with the fact that I am a trained nurse. Of course, those women in houses and bordellos get their share of weirdos . . . But still, it's not the same, I think . . .'

'You get a superior type of kook here?'

'That sounds so snobbish, put that way. But there is something in it. My kind of client generally has a private girl friend, a mistress, or a special call girl. But some of them specifically do not want that, for those relationships can become troublesome or threatening. With me they pay a set fee per treatment, and no strings attached. Still . . . that's not the main point. I think I really understand these people. There's a word for it: empathy. They sense that, and these relationships are highly sensitive. You have to be and stay tuned to a very narrow wavelength. I often know, intuitively, more about the people who come here than they know about themselves. And they don't want to have to explain . . . I have to smell out their deepest and most secret wishes. That's what really gets them. And here they can blow off their own particular steam without damaging anything or anyone. If they didn't have me, they might wind up in institutions or start taking drugs, or cause serious accidents . . . or worse.'

'You never fuck with your customers, do you?'

'Generally no. As a matter of fact, almost never. Even when I started out. With boy friends, yes. But not in the . . .'

'In the line of business?'

'Precisely. I was in the massage scene from the very start. In a short time I had my own circle of sado-masochists and that kind. They just came flocking to me.'

I begin to laugh. 'Build a better cock-trap and the world will beat a path to your door. You must be a natural. Perfect pitch.' I drink some more whiskey and sit looking at her. What has she got that other girls haven't got? I don't really know. All I see is a not-so-young girl from the sticks who made good, learned a hell of a lot, and now knows which side her bread is buttered on. But the legendary 'Pitiless Mistress' escapes me. I must be tuned to a different wavelength. To me the girl doesn't emit unadulterated sex appeal. (Perhaps that's why we get along so well?)

'Monique, do you dislike men? I mean, do you have contempt for them?'

'Lord, no. I mean—look, of course we all run up against freaks, windbags, shits, and bullies. But there are women like that, too. Goddammit, they write about me in those lousy newspapers as if I were a cross between a sadistic amazon and an avaricious bulldyke. Look at it this way: I have a special stable of unusual clients, or particular patients, or whatever you want to call them. I am a specialist in my business. Like a brain surgeon or a TV repairman. And it makes me goddam mad when some ignorant sensationalist makes me out to be a deliberate sadist who can only reach an orgasm by beating up some poor freak with a cat o' nine tails or a nail-studded slat. In many cases it's not even a question of inflicting physical pain, humiliation is the main thing. Of course, that often implies and goes together with being hit on the buttocks or other sorts of physical punishment, but that's only because that treatment is the *summum* of humiliation for an adult. Even for a child, being put across the knee and spanked means little in terms of pain; very few children are really afraid of the physical pain. It's the emotional humiliation that's the real punishment. And *punishment* is the right and operative word. All my cases, they all want punishment.'

'In the sense of guilt, and, uh . . . penitence?'

'Look, don't push this too far. Sometimes early sexual experience is simply associated with punishment. With a loved and desired person like Mother, or with a hard-handed governess or servant girl. And that association sticks. Those feelings become irrevocably tied up with the person's emotions. Punishment is linked to sex and sex is linked to humiliation. These people can only get their kicks when that chain is ignited. Any other ignition does not light, or at least gives much less satisfaction.'

'As a child, were you ever humiliated, Monique?' I half expect her to become angry, but no, she begins to seriously consider this, or acts as if she is.

'That's not so easy to answer. I have done a lot more thinking in my life than most people suppose.'

'And you are not stupid, Monique.'

'No, I am not stupid. But it's damned difficult to judge and decide precisely what incidents from your childhood have left the deepest and longest-lasting impression. The things that you laughingly shrug off . . . who can say whether those weren't truly the vital ones? The fact of Roman Catholicism, for instance. When I was eight years old, we moved to a better part of town and we were sent to another school, a Roman Catholic one. Something had happened at our former school, but of course no one told us children exactly what. We caught some whispers about the headmaster having done dirty things with some of the girls, but that was all. In any case we now went to that Catholic school. That disrupted my life, for as a non-Catholic and a child of North Dutch parents (the difference between the Dutch above and below the Meuse and Rhine River delta is enormous), we were rapidly known as those "Hollands" children. Talk about discrimination! We simply didn't belong. When all the other children went to first Communion in their long, white dresses with flowers in their hair, I was deeply and desperately unhappy. My mother tried to compensate by buying me a new dress, but that did little to take away the hurt. Also, when the other children went to confession, they whispered among themselves all day, but I was excluded, for I was not a Roman Catholic. I remember vividly one day how I asked my father why we weren't Roman Catholics, but I can't remember his answer. He probably just grunted. One day, a procession went by in the street. We had to stop because everybody around us kneeled and made the sign of the cross. I pulled my father's coat and said: "Papa, let's kneel down like all the other people." '

' "Under no circumstances", he said curtly. "That has nothing to do with us. We are not Catholics."

'Children have the strangest fantasies. Some of them stay in your mind for the rest of your life. I remember going to mass with some of my classmates. That was quite something. I, a non-Catholic, being taken to their mass! In their own church! I did exactly as they did; now and then I looked very hard at the statue of the Virgin Mary and then closed my eyes very tightly and thought: I am going to count up to ten now. When I open my eyes I will be a Catholic, too.

'In other respects also we never belonged anywhere. We never fitted in with others. Not on my father's side and not on my mother's. One day a large troop of singing boys and girls passed us in the street. They belonged together, that was clear at a glance. They all wore light blue uniforms with short white socks and sandals.

' "Mamma, look at all those children! Don't they look nice? Who are they?"

'I was dragged along at a trot. "Don't you get involved with that trash! Those are Reds. Children of socialists. Common workmen who want to get rid of the queen."

'My mother's voice was so violent and full of contempt that my immediate reaction was that maybe we weren't Roman Catholics, but it must be even worse to be a socialist.

'It was around that time that I discovered books and began to read like mad. I simply submerged myself in the imaginary world of animals, travel, and fairy tales.

'At school we had one nun who was always especially nice to me. On Wednesday afternoons I was allowed to stay on and water the plants and clean the blackboards. After I was finished, I sometimes sat on her lap and she read to me, or told me stories. I felt perfectly happy then, completely and serenely happy.'

'We lived very close to the German frontier and across the border everything was a lot less expensive. That is perfectly clear to me now —Hitler had to have hard currency and any foreign money was welcome. So Mama and I regularly took the tram to Aachan to buy German clothes with Dutch guilders. That must have been late 1938, early 1939. Papa used to warn Mother, "Now listen, Letty, I don't want you to buy in Germany, because you're helping the Nazis, and those ruffians are only biding their time until they can overrun us."

'Mother would just smile, nod and say: "Sure, sure". Then she went on doing what she wanted. How can a small child understand the implications of such discussions? But then, suddenly, something happens which leaves an indelible impression.

'It was a lovely spring morning and Mother, Claartje and myself were shopping in Germany again. In the strong, bright sunlight I saw myself reflected full-length in the plate-glass of a shop window: a little girl with a serious face and freckles. I was twelve years old. Excitedly, I took my sister's hand and pointed at the window: "Look, that's us, that's me!" Claartje nodded and smiled but didn't quite see what there was to get so worked up about. Perhaps that was the moment that I found and realized my own private identity. You see yourself with your mother and your sister—full-length, head to foot. I have watched young babies moving about in their beds and all at once you see how such a small creature, moving its hands in front of its eyes, begins to realize that the moving things are its own hands . . . that is, its own self.

'And perhaps, on that spring morning, I entered the second phase of self-realization: the little girl who always did what Papa and Mama told her to do saw herself reflected in a sheet of plate-glass and came to understand ."I . . . I am, and I have a distinct, separate *I*."

'Shortly afterward we were standing along the curb with a lot of Germans, watching a troop of young men marching by, singing loudly. A tall, blond boy brought up the rear. He gave us a sharp glance and we were probably lacking in the quality of our admiration, for he suddenly left the ranks, shouted "Damn foreigners!" and spat. It hit me straight in the face.

' "Ach, you poor child", Mama said. "Come to me." She wiped my face clean. "Take my hand, come along and don't think about it any more. We'll go to a toy shop and buy you something nice." Typical of mother. She had a firm conviction that buying "something nice" was a universal anodyne against any and every kind of hurt or humiliation.

'But that same evening, at home, my younger sister guilelessly said: "Cripes, Daddy, Mummy bought new coats for us in Aachen and one of those Hitler boys spat in Monique's face".

'My father jumped up and smashed his fist down on the table with such a bang that the meatballs jumped all over the floor. "You goddam stupid piece of trouble! Didn't I forbid you to go shopping in Germany? You and all those other brainless housewives! You keep fattening Hitler's bank account, but I tell you the day will come when they'll attack us and then it will be too late to start weeping and wailing!"

'My mother shrugged her shoulders. But I could not help wiping my face again at the place where that boy's spit had hit me.

'From that day on we did our shopping surreptitiously, and my sister was absolutely forbidden to never again open her silly mouth about it.

'Now, many years later, I cannot help asking myself whether my mother did not make a serious mistake by systematically undermining my father's authority. Later, of course, it was amply proved that my father had been right all the time. But by then our characters, or perhaps I should say our personality structures, had already been formed. I'll have more to say about that later. Talking about incidents and impressions from my early years, I can tell you one thing for certain: there were damned few sexual impressions or influences, if that is what you are so patiently fishing for.'

'My brother Jan was serving with one of the Dutch frontier guard battalions. My father had left for a three-day visit with his family in Amsterdam. But on the afternoon of the second day we saw him coming up the garden path, looking quite upset.

' " Letty, a man can take only so much. My own sister's children, members of the NSB (National Socialist movement in Holland)! For the sake of family peace I kept my mouth shut last night at dinner until they started to pass around fake railway tickets, 'Single Trip Palestine', and gloatingly told us how they threw them into the faces of Jews in the streets of Amsterdam. Right here in Holland—my own sister's children! God, Letty—what is the world coming to?"

'My mother said nothing.'

'On the tenth day of May, 1940, my father worked the early shift; he left at 5:00 a.m. to move the first streetcar out of its shed. How do I know that so exactly? Because, years later, when I was a big girl, he told me many things in detail. When I was in trouble in the United States, it was my father who crossed the Atlantic to come and help me. On that historic morning in May he didn't even get across the Heerlerbaan, for the Germans were marching down it. At home, we heard a lot of noise and the roar of planes overhead.

' "Mummy, come and look!"

'She said in a funny, strangled voice: "Jesus Christ! Those are German planes! Look at the swastikas! Your father was right!"

'My father came home with a chalk-white face and sat at the table, weeping into his hands. "Come, come." my mother said. "I'll make you a nice fresh pot of tea." I had never known her to be so gentle to him.

'How my father managed to survive the Occupation is still a mystery. One of those inexplicable mysteries of human existence and cosmic fortune. Nowhere did he ever take the trouble to keep his mouth shut. The Dutch have a famous saying: The impudent own half the world. It certainly was true in my father's case.

'At 9:00 that same May morning my mother took practical measures. She took us on a shopping trip for shoes. After all, no one could be quite sure how long a war might last. I got a pair of sturdy walking shoes with thick rubber soles.

' "They are very expensive", I was told, and they were. "You have to take good care of them." Mother also bought five pounds of tea and after that we went back home. Mama said gaily, "That's that. That will keep us for the time being." '

'Later that summer long rows of Belgian and French prisoners of war began to stream past. We prepared loaves of brown bread with butter and cheese. Sometimes the German guards allowed us to hand them over, sometimes not. But my brother Jan was reported missing in action. My mother was depressed and wept a lot. Perhaps mainly because my father had been right. But suddenly there were hardly any quarrels in our house any more.'

'My sister Claartje was playing in the garden in the sun and came running inside. "Mummy! Jan is coming home!"

'We all rushed into the hall where my mother collided not with my brother Jan but with one of my Amsterdam cousins who resembled Jan. He was still wearing his Dutch army officer's uniform, but with German jackboots. He greeted us boisterously.

' "Hello, Aunt and Uncle. I'm just dropping by to sat hello. I'm on my way to Germany to volunteer."

'My father exploded. "You lousy NSB traitor! Who gave you permission to enter my house, and in Dutch uniform, too! While my own son is still missing! Get out of here—fast—or I'll kick you out!"

'My cousin Hans was really frightened. Not for himself, but for my father. "For God's sake, Uncle. Be careful what you say! The Gestapo is everywhere!"

'But my father interpreted that as a threat and lost control of himself. He grabbed my cousin by the collar, threw him outside, and kicked him down the garden path.

' "My dear man", my mother said, "that boy came all the way from Amsterdam and the trains are not running with all the bridges blown up. Perhaps he was hungry."

'My father growled: "Then let him go and feed at the German cook wagon".'

*The Hague, June 1971*

I am sitting in Minus Verheyen's pub on the Noordwal, downing gin for gin with a former Royal Air Force flight commander, Ricky de Paula Lopez. Sometimes we go pub crawling together, when we both feel an urge to get professionally drunk. There are a lot of things Ricky doesn't like to talk about, but now and then he lets something drop when he's had enough to drink.

He suddenly begins to talk about the day when he was ordered up, on a crystal-clear morning, to take aerial photographs of the city of Magdeburg which had been bombed the night before.

'I came flying in and I didn't even need my compass. There was no wind at all and the only thing I could see was a column of smoke going straight up thirty thousand feet in the air. You can't help wondering, you know . . . what was happening down there.'

'Meaning what, old boy?' (I knew that he had been part of the pathfinder fleet: the machines that flew out at night, located the targets, and dropped the flares and markers for the following fleets of night bombers. He was one of the few who had survived.)

'Now listen, Ricky, war is war and *Befehl* is *Befehl*. What could you have done in '42 or '43? Desert? Become a conscientious objector? Let the others go ahead with the dirty work? Apart from that—who started the game? As far as I know, the Germans began with gleeful terrorist bombardments on Rotterdam and Coventry. An eye for an eye, a tooth for a tooth. In the long run there are only two possibilities: either you never start, and capitulate at once, or once you start you have to win else the whole thing is senseless in the first place.'

'Of course, of course you're right, old man. But even so . . .'

'You talk too much. What you need is another snootful of gin. Let's drink to the living.'

'Yeah. Let's have another gin. To the living.'

Once again I am at Monique's place, drinking Pernod with ice-water. Her Pernod.

'Listen, pearl, what percentage of your clientele, as far as you know, is troubled by conscious or repressed feelings of guilt? I don't mean because of things like war crimes. I mean this, Monique: because I am a writer I know the most diverse types of people. Americans with Congressional Medals of Honor; ex-SS-paratroopers who were in on the kidnapping of Mussolini; women who survived extermination camps; Frenchmen who fought with the *maquis* and feel violently disappointed now. Many of them have a lot in common. For instance, some of the men who worked on the Burma Road and survived live burdened with guilt because they are still alive while their comrades, colleagues, or friends have long been buried there.'

'You mean that they keep asking themselves why the others were picked to die and not they?'

'Yes. They wonder what, oh . . . can be so good about them that they deserve to go on living. They cannot tolerate the hard truth that it might be just a matter of sheer, stupid luck, or wayward fate. Perhaps it is preordained by a cosmic system, ungraspable by the human mind. Why did the neighbor's daughter become the victim of the drunken driver when my son, who was walking next to her, escaped without a scratch?'

Monique sits gazing at me for some moments. She slowly puts down her glass and beckons with her head. 'Come upstairs with me for a moment.'

'Give me a hand with this,' Monique says.

I am squatting, a cigarette between my fingers, watching her open an old steamer trunk and unload its contents on the floor. A Japanese samurai sword, some battered military mess tins, handfuls of brownish, human bones, three or four bundles of dried sticks that can only be firewood, and last of all, a fat, flat bundle of painted cloth.

It's damned heavy, painted on cotton, and not painted badly. Unfolded, the whole thing is about three yards high and five or six yards long. Along the top, a row of curtain rings have been sewn, with a string running through them. We stretch the cord between two hooks in the wall, evidently placed there for that purpose. I step backward. A bright spotlight flares, making the painted scene come vividly alive as if under hot, tropical sunlight. The spotlight has been expertly placed, in such a way that the shadows of huts, palm trees, and fences slant the correct way. In the center of this painted backdrop, a bearded, raggedly dressed man is kneeling, his hands tied behind his back, his bowed head awaiting the final stroke of a Japanese with high, raised sword.

Monique stands by my side and we look at the thing for a long minute.

'Yes, yes,' I finally say. '*A la recherche du temps perdu.*'

'What?'

'A book by Marcel Proust. *Remembrance of Things Past.*'

'There are a lot of them like that,' Monique says. 'Some of them have nightmares every other night for the rest of their lives. Others wind up as drunks. Quite a few become regular psychiatric customers, or get periodic attacks of madness.'

'And those who come here?'

'Shall we put this stuff back?'

When we are sitting downstairs again, I say, 'Take ten people of about the same age, all of them reasonably healthy and with roughly the same background. All receive the same violent emotional shock. All of them assimilate that experience, cope with it in quite personal and completely different ways.'

'Yes,' says Monique, pensively. She gazes out the picture window, across the spotlessly clean and orderly Bezuidenhoutseweg, with Her Dutch Majesty's Forest in the background. 'And some of them never assimilate it or manage to cope with it. They have to live with that indigestible, traumatic memory until they die.'

I silently ask myself what shock or traumatic memories she herself has not managed to digest. Aloud I ask, 'Who was he?'

She gives me an astonished look and after a moment I spot the misunderstanding: 'No, no. I am not asking who your client is. I mean the man in the painting. The bearded man on his knees.'

'I really don't know,' Monique says. 'I never asked.'

Monique is getting impatient with me; I keep trying to get hold of something in her early years that could give some explanation of her later meteoric sex career. She suddenly bursts out:

'What the hell are we trying to do? Commit amateur psychiatry? I keep telling you that nothing happened to me either during the war or during the Liberation that is in any way relevant to my later adventures.

'It all started when I decided to leave home and go to work in a hospital as a student nurse. Perhaps if I had gone to work as a stenographer, my life would have taken a different course. I really don't know, and frankly I am not much interested. That's all theoretical and academic. One last thing I'll tell you about: my defloration.

'Living so close to the German border we of course had Allied soldiers billeted on us, who later moved out and on across the Rhine. We had a whole succession of them, as division after division came rolling up. They belonged to the Second American Tank Division, I think.

'One night around two or three o'clock there was a loud ringing of the doorbell and lots of shouting and banging. We all got out of bed and there were three of the Americans who had earlier roomed with us, loaded with bags and suitcases.

' "Hello, Pappy! Surprise! Can we come in?"

'In our living room they turned their bags upside down and the floor was strewn with fur coats, table silver, fine linen, silver candlesticks, and antique clocks.

' "All this stuff is for you, Pappy and Mama." A few days earlier, they told us happily, they had liberated, or conquered, or occupied a castle in Germany and this was some of the loot. Only some of it. They went out to their truck again and came staggering back under loads of Persian and Chinese carpets and rugs. "For you, Mama." I began to crawl around among all this fabulous treasure and my mother stood speechless, staring down at it with big, childishly yearning eyes. But my father sternly shook his head.

' "Sorry, boys. I want no part of it. Stolen stuff."

'The Americans slapped each other's backs and laughed wildly. That was the funniest thing they'd heard in months. Dutch deadpan humor at its best. The Germans had robbed Holland bare and it was only fair to pipeline some of it back to the right kind of people. That's the way Mama and I saw it, too. But my father stubbornly said no.

'My mother, with tears in her eyes, pleaded: "But Frank! Use your common sense for a change."

' "No!" said my father. "I refuse to have stolen stuff in my house. Even if it's stolen from those bastard Germans."

'Our Americans finally grasped that he really meant what he said, and vanished back into the night with their booty. Next day they were a bit curt with us. They said they had thrown the whole lot into the Meuse River.

'That incident may have had more to do with my leaving home than anything else. Even my defloration left far less of an impression, I can tell you that, man!

'You hear and read a lot about the powerful influence her first lover leaves on a young girl. Pooh! For some girls that may be so, but for me it was more like the first time I got burned by a hot water bottle in bed.

'One of the last GI's billeted on us was a short, nervous boy of Italian descent. His name was Tony: I remember that much. He had the room next to mine and sometimes at night I heard him groaning or sobbing softly. That had been going on for more than a week and all of a sudden I took pity on him. I slipped out of bed, cautiously turned his doorknob, tiptoed inside and turned on the lamp by his bed. I had a vague idea that perhaps he was afraid in the dark. Some sort of a childish idea mixed with maternalism. What could I know about a soldier's experiences then?

'I was surprised to find that he was asleep, but sobbing and groaning at the same time. I gently shook him awake. "Tony, it's me, Tony." I wiped his tears with a corner of the sheet. He woke up, saw me, and at once was more or less himself again.

' "Oh, hi, kid—I must have been dreaming."

'I slid into bed with him. "What were you dreaming about?"

' "Oh, just war", he said, flicked off the light, and pulled me close against him. After a time he told me that they would have to move into Germany very soon and that he was afraid. Desperately afraid. While he was talking, he snuggled up to me, kissed my cheek, began to stroke me. I struggled a bit, but not very much because he was so nice and gentle. Even when he slid my pajama bottoms down I let him go ahead. for he held me very close and I was suddenly far more afraid of my mother finding out that I was in bed with him, than of Tony himself.

'After a while he got on top of me and I felt something pushing against me down there and it hurt. But I was caught firmly by then, and yelling or protesting aloud was out of the question. We struggled silently for a while and suddenly everything was quiet again. He rolled off me, and dammit, he pushed his head into the pillow and started sobbing all over again: "Oh, Monique—Jesus, Monique, I'm sorry".

'I angrily got out of his bed and went back to my own room. If he thought I would ever comfort him again, he had another guess coming. He had hurt me, too. I lay awake for some time and didn't understand much about it.

'I got up very late the next day and heard that our Americans had already left. Mother gave me a thin bundle of papers.

' "Tony asked me to give you this."

'I unfolded a map of the United States, with a red circle around Chicago. There was a penciled letter, but I didn't take the trouble to read it, for I didn't care if I never saw him again. I later heard that he was one of the very first to get killed when they ran up against the Germans in some forest or other. And that was that. I was fed up with home, fed up with father who threw away a fortune in furs and silver, fed up with billeted, sobbing soldiers. I just wanted to get out and away, and said so.

' "Might not be a bad idea", my mother said. "I was a trained nurse myself. And they need nurses very badly. Why don't you apply for a student internship at a hospital?"

'I was accepted, and that's how it all started.'

'Those were wild times and we student nurses were a wild bunch. When we weren't getting into trouble with those gray bitchy supervisors, we were catting around. You can read about that sort of thing in hundreds of books about doctors, nurses, and hospitals. We had our fair share of lesbians, nymphomaniacs, and mad masturbators. Compared to most of the others, I must have seemed like a professional virgin. Now, don't get the idea that I am repressed, for I certainly am not and I never was, but for the most of those girls, sex was the main thing in their lives. With me, it was the other way around. Sex fascinated me, but I was never the victim of my own urges. At least, not my sexual urges! Perhaps that was why so many of those young nurses picked me for their confidante. They told me the damndest stories and whenever they got in any kind of trouble, they came running to me for advice and support. What I learned in that hospital about nursing and medicine is nothing compared to the insights I gained about sexuality.

'One of the first things I discovered was that there appeared to be a tremendous difference between men and women in the basics of orgasm. I'll tell you how I learned this.

'We student nurses were housed, two or three to a room, on the top floor in one wing of the hospital. I shared a room with a girl called Nora. Nora was really lovely; slender and lissome, with shiny dark brown eyes surrounded by that special eye-white that is not pure white, but rather a light porcelain blue.

'Nora and I had both had dates with army men. We went drinking and dancing, but we had to be back at midnight. Around half-past ten my date paid the check and announced that he would walk me home. That always went by way of the park or a dark street, with some heavy necking or more. By that time I had already found out that being straightforwardly fucked did very little for me, it didn't excite me much. But I had more or less come to expect that; from the remarks the more experienced nurses occasionally let drop I had come to the conclusion that fucking was fun for the man only, and a girl's duty was to spread her legs as "payment" for an evening out, or later, in marriage, for bed and board. I came to regard my cunt as a sort of potential life insurance.

'I was late that night and found the front door locked, so I used the secret system we had rigged up: a piece of string passed through a small hole in an upstairs window. One of us would then creep downstairs to open the door. That meant, of course, that we had to sneak upstairs with our shoes in our hands. For the same reason we all kept our locks and hinges very well oiled. I had our room door half-open when I froze in my tracks, not knowing whether to go forward or back. Two straight-backed chair had been placed in front of the washbasin, about a yard apart. Straddling the chairs, her legs spread and without a stitch on, stood Nora. She was roughly sideways from where I was standing, and there could be no doubt about what she was doing. She was masturbating in front of the washbasin mirror and in order to see herself, she had to stand on the chairs. Her head was thrown back and her long dark hair was hanging loose down her slender back. She was using both hands; one stimulating her cunt from the back and the other in front working on her clitoris. But that was not what made the shivers of excitement run up and down my back and my legs: it was the sounds she made and the language she used that really got to me. Panting and groaning, it went something like this:

' "Look at me, Harry . . . do I excite you, Harry? . . . Look at my lovely hairy little cunt, Harry. . . . Do you have a big prick, Harry? . . . Look at me, Harry. . . . Say you are looking at me, Harry. . . . Is your prick getting bigger and bigger, Harry? . . . Do I drive you mad, Harry? . . . Let's do it together, Harry. . . . I want to see you spurt, Harry. . . . Tell me when you feel it coming, Harry. . . ."

'It was absolutely impossible for me to do anything but stand there with the doorknob in my hand, and look, feeling a mixture of horrified fascination and hot, violent excitement, watching that beautiful, abandoned girl on top of those chairs, using the filthiest and most outrageous (as it struck me then) words and sounds until the moment when she and the imaginary Harry reached their climax together. She stood there on the chairs, with clenched teeth, masturbating like a lunatic, her knees bobbing up and down. I remember fearing that one of the chairs would slide sideways and land her on the floor with a torn ligament or a sprained back. But nothing like that happened. Her tempestuous explosion of sexual lust—sheer, unadulterated lust—slowly ebbed away and left her standing there, one hand gently stroking her flat belly while her head came slowly forward to its normal position. Perhaps I made a slight noise (it may well have been my own excited breathing) or else she had some sort of intuition, for she suddenly looked sideways toward the door. She gave a violent start, but when she recognized me she stepped down to the floor, stood looking at me for some seconds, shrugged, and walked over to her bed to put on her dressing gown. She lay down and lit a cigarette. All this without a single word.

'Well, if she wanted to act cool about it, it was all right with me. I undressed as I did every night, went to the basin to have my pre-bed wash, and ran up against those chairs. I put them back in their places and began to wash. Then she said, in a quite normal voice: "Did you have a nice fuck?"

'We had never talked about the intimate details of our dates before, but by that time I had my wits about me again and went on washing between my legs. "And what if I did?"

' "Don't bite my head off. I'm just curious. Whether you let him into you or not is none of my business, of course. But if you did, did you enjoy it?"

'I dried myself, hung up the towel, and turned around: "How do you mean, enjoy it?"

'She rolled onto her side, her head partly raised on one elbow, and lay there, smoking and looking at me: "You must have noticed that the only thing a man wants is to get that thing of his straight into you and then plunge away until he's shot his load of porridge."

'I sat down on the edge of my own bed and started brushing my hair. I really had no idea what she was driving at. Vague ideas about lesbians began to float around in my head, but they did not particularly horrify me. Even at that age I had already found out that one of my main motivations was a sort of adventurous curiosity.

' "Isn't that the way a man is supposed to be?"

' "Yeah", she said. "But what does the girl get out of it?"

'Of course I understood perfectly well what she was driving at then. After the demonstration I had so recently witnessed I would have been a moron not to understand.

' "You mean . . . when you are fucked by a man you, uh . . .?"

'She interrupted me bitingly: 'You are theoretically supposed to reach your own, female peak of ecstasy. But these egotistical maniacs are conceited enough to believe that the very fact that a woman gets that stiff piece of sausage pushed up her front hole drives her mad with pleasure. With nine out of ten women it just doesn't work that way. Now be honest and tell me: did you fuck tonight?"

' "Yes, I did."

"What did you feel?"

'Frankly—not one bloody thing.'

'The girl fascinated me. That lovely, sensitive face and those beautiful eyes were in sudden and complete contrast with the way I had seen them when she was in front of the mirror and with the harsh, direct way she was talking now. As if a mad, violent soul was secretly alive within that tender slender body.

' "Now listen, Monique. Tell me straight. Did you ever masturbate? Or don't you know that word? Ever make yourself come? Ever play with yourself in bed?"

'I stopped brushing my hair and slowly shook my head.

'She gave a sort of grunt, put out her cigarette, and said: "I thought so. If you ever want to know anything, you just ask me." A faint note of bitterness crept into her voice. "I am a real expert at knowing what not to expect of men. They have their uses, but hardly in bed. A man is completely different from a woman, not only in the way he is constructed physically, but even more so in the way he acts and reacts sexually. Emotionally, I mean. Once a man gets his prick stiff and up he can excite himself until he shoots his wad any way he damn pleases. He can do it with his hand. He can put his prick into the neck of a milk bottle; he can shove it up the asshole of another man, or he can plunge it into a woman's front or back hole. Most of them prefer a woman, because it gives them some sort of conquering idea that they have had you. That's the biggest joke of all time. Blindfold most of them, tie their hands behind their backs, and they can't even tell what they put their prick into. But a woman is completely different."

'I sat on the edge of my bed, playing with my hairbrush, but it did not make much sense to me. I finally ventured: "Yes, but . . . if you blindfold a woman and tie her hands and keep her legs spread apart and . . . she has no sense of smell . . . would she . . . could she tell the difference between one stiff prick and another?"

'Nora lay looking at me for a couple of seconds and suddenly broke into a charming, impish grin.

' "I'm really beginning to like you. You may be horribly innocent, but you're not stupid. What I am driving at is simply this: a woman has very little feeling in her vagina, very little feeling at all. There's the rub, sister. And now listen to me: don't get the silly idea in your head that I'm a frustrated lesbian, for I am not. You needn't be afraid of that. But will you do me a favor?"

' "Yes, why not?"

'She suddenly got up from her bed, threw off her kimono and stood there completely naked and completely sure of herself.

' "Do you think I am beautiful?"

'God, she was. Like an elegant, fragile, porcelain statuette. Everything about her was beautiful.

' "Yes, you are", I said with sincerity. "Anyone who says you are not is either jealous or a bloody liar. Man or woman."

'She nodded with some satisfaction, sat down on the edge of the bed, and spread her legs slightly, leaning back on her arms.

' "I'm an exhibitionist," she said. "I want to be admired. If there is no one to admire me, I have to admire myself. That was why I got on top of these chairs. To get a good look at myself while I was doing it. You interrupted me, you know. I can do it three or four times in a row and it gets better and better all the time. Now I'll show you how a woman does it with herself. I am not going to touch you, ever. And I shall never ask you to touch me, you can depend on that. But will you sit by my bed and just admire me?"

'I swear to you: she looked at me quite anxiously. "In exchange I can teach you a lot, Monique."

'I got up and fetched a chair. "Well, why not?"

'She let herself fall back on the bed and spread her legs, both hands gently stroking the insides of her thighs. I sat on that straightbacked chair, straight-backed myself, and then she started talking like someone who is hypnotized or is trying to hypnotize himself:

' "Look at me, Monique. . . . Aren't I nice to look at? . . . I'll open my elegant little cunt for you . . . see my rosy lips? My frail and tickly little clit? Look at me, Monique. Tell me that I am lovely, Monique, that excites me so . . . I want to hear you say it, Monique. . . ."

'My voice sounded funny to me as I repeated what she wanted me to say. And dammit, she DID look lovely. And the whole scene was so strange and weirdly exciting that I would have done far more than that to see how far I could get her to go. It was not only a fierce, fascinated curiosity that welled up in me—what I felt was far more complicated than that. What surged through me was a sense of power. I mean that: a wonderful, surging realization that just by looking at her, by using my voice, by saying certain things in a certain tone of voice, I could charge her, move her hands faster, and then see her get those orgasmic spasms.

'I think I made her come three times more that night. She was a damned clever, bewitching girl. For you see it is hardly possible for anyone to develop a sense of guilt in that kind of situation. After all, nothing is expected of you. You need not do anything nor let anything be done to you. Just by looking at a lovely girl's body and egging her on, you manage to give her an immense amount of ecstasy. And, obviously, the act in itself is highly provocative.

'Oh, yes, she was a witch, all right. But not the only one.'

'No, not the only one.

'Without any real lesbian inclination I seemed to be predestined to be picked up and coached by women. Nora told me a lot and taught me a lot. But there were two other women who entered my life about the same time: Marina and Gonda, and the funny thing is that I met both of them in the most ordinary and innocent way; one through my brother Jan and the other through my father.

'I was on duty on the second floor when I was called to the telephone: "Von Cleef? There's a visitor for you down here. You know you may not have callers during duty hours. but she is from out of town and I told her that for once I would make an exception."

'A female visitor from out of town? Yes, obviously a female visitor, a man wouldn't have a chance of coming within a mile of any of us on hospital grounds.

'When I entered the reception hall, a smiling Indonesian girl rose from the visitor's bench.

' "Hello, Monique. I heard that you were working here and I thought you might like it if I looked you up."

'I suppose I must have stared at her rather stupidly.

' "Don't you remember me? I was in your brother Jan's underground group. I spent the night in the cellar of your house many times."

' "Oh, of course. I'm sorry, but I really couldn't place you, you are a totally different girl."

'She gave me a brilliant smile. "Yes, I suppose so."

'I said spontaneously: "You were a thin, scrawny girl then. In thick boots and pants and a bulgy coat. You . . . you are beautiful now." Which she truly was, with her almond-shaped eyes and blue-black hair, high-heeled shoes and dove gray tailor-made suit. At that time good clothes were still hard to come by. Europe did not really get back on its economic feet until after the Marshall Plan was put into operation.

' "Look, I can't talk long. They made an exception for you because . . ."

' "Yes, they told me. What time are you off duty?"

' "At eight."

' "Then I'll pick you up here and we'll get a bite to eat and have a nice long talk, all right?"

' "Lovely", I said.

'All afternoon I felt vaguely puzzled. I wasn't as green as I had been. Nurses, like doctors, are a tough lot. Gradually, past observations and small incidents began to fall into place. There had been a direct air of intimate friendliness about this . . . what was her name again? . . . Marina. . . . That had something disquieting about it. By now I had learned to recognize certain signals and signs. I recalled some of the remarks my mother had made to my brother during those war years. "Jan, what is that creature downstairs? A boy or a girl, or what?" Until my brother gruffly explained that she was one of the most courageous and reliable workers in their group. Yes, there had been something strange about her in her men's clothes and unwomanlike bearing. And now, after this stunning metamorphosis, she looked completely feminine, but there was still that quality of essential boyishness about her. Five to one she was an out-and-out les. But so what? Half our nurses were lesbians and my lovely roommate Nora was a narcissistic, exhibitionist masturbator. By now I was an expert masturbator myself, and no longer a sexually frustrated female. So what could happen to me?

'And nothing did happen to me. At least not that evening. I got a damned good meal out of it and some funny reminiscences.

' "I am a social worker in Amsterdam now", she told me. "With my own flat. Why don't you come up to Amsterdam when you get your next leave? You can stay with me and you'll hardly need any money. Just train fare. I'll give you my address and telephone number."

'She lit my cigarettes for me, poured my coffee, and practically helped me into my coat. Oh, she was a les, all right. But a nice les. So what the hell.'

'By this time Nora and I had developed a curious sexual symbiosis. In the main, there are two types of masturbators: the solo workers always do it strictly on their own and would rather die than admit it or let anyone else see them doing it. Often they get a tremendous kick out of it and in this group you find the most incredible way-out practices. The biggest advantage of solo masturbation is that you are entirely independent. You can do it whenever you want it or need it, whichever way you want it and as often as you like. At most, you only need some simple implements like mirrors, table tennis paddles for self-spanking, brushes for stroking between your legs, etc. The main drawback is that solo masturbation is a lonely and lonesome activity. Therefore all solo masturbators, without exception, need vivid fantasies. They have to imagine being with someone or the thing simply won't work. The only exceptions are the truly narcissistic mirror-masturbators, who are completely in love with their own bodies and watch themselves doing it. I've known some who put complete programs of dirty talk on tape and then masturbate to the stimulating sound track. But that's only a mechanical substitute. Solo masturbators are, as human beings, on their own. To use a comparison: you might as well buy a show-window mannequin, put her in a baby-doll nightgown, arrange her in your bed, and imagine you are married. It may save a lot of wear and tear, and a lot of trouble and money, but you lead a lonely life. You get what I mean? I am not talking about this for nothing, for basically my whole later business, and everything I do with and for my clients now, is a ramification of the fundamental principle of loneliness and . . . How To Come.

'The second group consists of what I call duo or public masturbators. Nora and I very quickly grew into a team where she did the masturbating with me in voice control.

'If you happen to have the sheer luck to be married to someone who rides the wave in unison with you when you copulate in the orthodox way, so that you climax at the same moment, then for

God's sake, don't start monkeying around with yourself. You don't know your own luck. There is a rumor that those couples exist, but of course in my line of business I am not likely to run into them. But even so, I haven't spoken to anyone in years who was on speaking terms with such a happily matched couple. The last pair tracked down—near Uppsala, Sweden—proved, on closer observation, to be a satyr and a nymphomaniac, secretly brought together by their mutual psychiatrist.'

'I never wanted this book to be just a succession of dirty scenes. I maintain, and have maintained for a long time, that I know and understand more about this whole sexual business with all its variations and ramifications, than did Messrs. Freud, Adler, and Jung combined.

'I mentioned the element of power inherent in making another person climax. You may have gotten the idea that Nora and I were completely dependent on one another for our sexual kicks. You couldn't be more wrong.

'During all the time I roomed with Nora we of course had many talks. She was one year ahead of me in her training, but she was three years ahead of me in age, and certainly about twenty years older in insight and experience. She was rather tight-lipped about how she had managed to cram all that experience together in so relatively short a time, unless she had started as a baby on her crib, of which I judged her not entirely incapable. She came from an upper-middle-class family and was amply supplied with money. Her family name meant nothing to me, but that was not surprising, for I had been brought up in social isolation combined with the four years of German occupation and I hardly knew anyone outside my own family. She taught me practically everything she knew about the sexual handling of men when they saw us home after an evening out. I can summarize her whole system in one paragraph:

' "They pay for the food and drinks, so they expect you to be a good sport and give something back for their time and money. Well, they can have it, but not what they expect. As soon as they have you in a secluded place, in a car or a dark side-street, or a corner of the city park, don't let yourself be messed up by kissing unless you really like them. That can happen. Sometimes I really like the guy and then he can kiss me. If his breath doesn't smell, and his teeth are right, and he isn't too rough for my tender liking. Right away he'll begin to feel you up—above or below the belt. The poor, primitive bastards expect you to get so excited that you'll lose all control of yourself and spread your legs for them so that they can go ahead and plunge right in. That's where the poor goons get tripped up. Just start wriggling and groaning and right away they'll get enthusiastic and believe that they've copped themselves a really hot piece. It's the easiest thing in the world. As soon as they've got that idea in their skulls, go straight for their fly and pull out the works. That really drives them nuts. Grab them by the balls with one hand from below and start moving up and down with your other hand. Now comes the big trick. As soon as you start playing around with their cocks, you run the risk that they'll try to take you by force, and if there's anything I detest it's a wrestling match with torn clothes and bruises. You have only to say in a panting, admiring way: 'Oh, darling . . . how stiff and big you are . . . I want to see you. Let me see you . . .' and they're absolute goners. They let you go immediately and sit there like the conceited apes they are, showing off their pricks, giving you the chance to toss them off with no further nonsense about it. Just take care that they don't spurt their porridge all over your clothes, for some of them will always try to do that. I suppose they feel that in that way they leave some sort of signature on you . . . just as a dog has to piss against a tree to prove that he was there. And that's easy to do—when he comes, just cup the hollow of your hand over the head of his prick and his juice will run down into his own pants. It's very, very seldom that they get over that shock. Ten to one you'll have no further trouble, and will get taken straight home. If ever you should get the sort of virile ape that goes for you immediately afterward and this time really tries to get in, just say you're unwell, or afraid of pregnancy. I once said that I was recovering from an infection. That always does it. And the beautiful thing about it is . . . at least with me, Monique . . . I get an absolute charge out of making their pricks spurt that way. I like to do it. And then I want to get here, to this room, as fast as possible, while I am still all steamed up, and masturbate like a witch. It gives me a sense of power. Sheer, straightforward power over them. Not only the sexual excitement of seeing them spurt and hearing them pant, but also the power of not giving in, and having them by the balls, in all senses of the word." '

'By now you have a pretty good idea of what made my beautiful

Nora tick. After a couple of months of her training, we were the most popular team of nurses in the hospital. We got flowers and boxes of expensive chocolates practically every hour on the hour. I confess that at some point I began to wonder whether I had not let myself be indoctrinated too much by my beautiful friend. I decided to try some experiments of my own. I waited until I got the right date: a young, amusing, handsome officer. I felt I could really go for him, and that evening, when I felt really like it, really felt like giving him his way, I relaxed and let him take off my panties.

'I was never so disillusioned in my life. Not even the night of my defloration, for then I expected nothing and got nothing. This time, knowing all about the pinwheel pinnacles of the gorgeous Come, the let down was so colossal that I nearly slapped his face. He charged ahead, spurted inside me, and pulled out immediately afterward. Then he buttoned his fly and said, very manly and contented: "God, you're good, girl. You are wonderful".

'I was so angry I refused to say a word. I got out of the car and walked home. He came after me and kept asking what was the matter. He actually had the sheer gall to trot along and ask me what the matter was, old girl!

'Part of my fury, of course, derived from the fact that Nora had been only too right and that I myself had proved her right.'

'Let me tell you about Mister Mustache.

'I was a junior nurse and Nora senior to me—not only in age, but also in training. The junior nurses were not thrown "cold turkey" into the men's ward. We began with the women and children and the usual menial jobs; to break us in, so to speak.

'But Nora worked in the men's ward, and one evening she entered our room with a smirk on her lovely face, which I spotted at once. She sat down on the edge of her bed, her hands folded, and looked up at me.

' "Monique, while you are on duty try to figure something out. You're good at that. Listen: in a first-class room in the men's ward we have a patient who has recently come back from Indonesia. He's a civilian who got mixed up in the fighting there and the doctors are picking a handful of shell fragments out of him, piece by piece. He's in his early thirties and he sports a mustache you could sweep the floor with. And he paints."

' "Paints? Pictures, you mean?"

' "Yes. He's bored stiff." She grinned evilly. "That's not the only stiff thing about him. He has boxes of paints with brushes and canvases and some sort of rig to keep the canvas upright, so that he can paint in bed. He seems to have money. You know how horny the patients get when they've been here for a while. You know about the rule that male patients in private rooms may only be washed when there are two nurses present?"

' "Un-huh."

' "When I came in this afternoon to bring his tea he was lying back with his hands under his head, looking me up and down while I arranged his tea things. I felt something brewing. Suddenly he said: 'Nurse, of course you know that you are a beautiful piece. Just thinking about you gives me a prick like a tent pole. I know you must have a cunt that is lovely to look at. I want to paint it. And I will pay you very well.' "

'Nora and I sat looking at each other, and both of us began to laugh.

'I began to strut up and down our room: "What do you do for a living, my dear?"

' "Oh—I'm a nurse."

' "Isn't that a prosaic occupation for a girl as lovely as you, my dear? I would have thought . . ."

' "Oh, but in my spare time I model. As a sideline."

' "Really? Hats? Skirts?"

' "Oh, no. I model cunts."

'When we had stopped howling, Nora sat looking at me, a mad glitter in her brilliant, dark eyes.

' "I stood there, demurely, with my hands folded in front of me. Inside I was having the time of my life, but I didn't show it. The bastard knew, anyway. He was quite sure about me. I said, quite coolly, that even supposing, my dear sir, that I would seriously consider such a lunatic proposition, how did he propose to pull it off within the confines of a hospital?"

' " 'That's not so difficult as you might think,' he said, lying there with his hands behind his head. 'I have no intention of painting you completely nude. That is precisely what I do not want. What I want to catch is the fascinating contrast of that chaste, starched nurse's uniform with that lovely, serene face on top, and below, your hands lifting up your apron and skirt, so that your lovely little bush is displayed. It would make a really great picture. And, as I said,

I will pay you well. There is a second motive, dear nurse, and I confess quite frankly that there is something about you that drives me to distraction. When you are in the room I need all the self-discipline I can muster to keep my greedy paws off you. Last night I masturbated twice, thinking of you. Once I have painted your cunt, I'll always have you with me. Think about it.' And with that he took up a book he was reading and stopped talking."

' "Then what did you say?"

' "Say? I said nothing, of course. I picked up his waste-paper basket and went out."

' "That gave you time to think?"

' "Yes. You must admit an approach like that would tip any girl slightly off balance."

' "Would he really pay you?"

'That really set Nora off. She howled with laughter, slapping her thighs. "I've noticed that about you, Monique. You have a horribly practical mind. But that's exactly what I need right now."

' "Are you going to do it?"

' "You bet your right tit I'm going to do it. I would do it for nothing." She jumped up from her bed and waltzed around our room with wildly excited, slightly mad eyes. "Imagine standing there—exactly as he expressed it . . . how did he say it again? Something about chaste and demure?" She made a wild gesture with her hands. "Oh, I know exactly how to stand and look. Like this."

'She bent down like a flash, took off her sensible nurse's shoes, reached under her skirt, and ripped off her panties. Then she stepped into her shoes again, took the hem of apron and skirt, and lifted them in front of her, slightly above the dark patch of her pubic triangle. The contrast between the serene, angelic expression on that virginal face and the perverse aspect of that displayed pudenda was really something. While I still stood drinking in that pose, her expression slowly changed to one of sinful glee, and then she said, dreamily: "Do you suppose he could paint me masturbating?"

'I said coldly: "Your imagination is running away with you, sweetie. He is not producing movies."

' "Why, Monique . . . you're not jealous, by any chance?"

' "Don't talk shit", I said, but realized in a flash that she was, as usual, precisely right. And I realized, just as fast, the danger I was gradually getting into. We did not have a lesbian relationship, but I saw then that there are other ways of tying someone to you, of getting under their psychological or sexual skin. And I had no intention of getting too far under her bewitching influence. Oh, no. Not Monique. She had made a mistake . . . she was too sure of herself and in the excitement of this new gambit had overplayed her hand. I turned to the mirror, began to comb my hair, and asked, coolly: "So what do you need me for? Hurry up, I have to go on duty."

' "That's obvious, my dear. I have to pose for him with my skirts lifted."

' "You can drop them in a hurry, can't you?"

' "I can even stand with my back against the door—someone coming on would bump the door against my back. That's nothing. But I don't know how long I'll have to hold the pose. It's not like taking a photograph, you know. And when you're assigned to male patients in private rooms they watch you like hawks. If you stay inside too long, they give you another assignment."

' "Then what do you need me for?"

' "To figure out something, darling. I need your practical mind."

' "What you need", I said waspishly, "is a practical cunt. You always let your clitoris do your thinking." '

'Waspish or not, I was right there. I didn't even try to find a practical plan for her crazy scheme. She kept pestering me, but fortunately we were on alternate shifts, and it was fairly easy to keep out of her way. And by the following day everything had already arranged itself. When I came off duty, Nora was lying on her bed, smoking a cigarette, her eyes smoldering and a smug look on her face. Smug and impish. Her mood had completely changed.

' "Hello, darling. Surprise! Look what's on the table."

'Held down by our ashtray was a hundred-guilder bill. That doesn't sound like much today, after twenty-five years of continuous inflation, but at that time, for a hard-working, underpaid nurse, it was nothing to sneeze at. I looked at that bill, and back at Nora. She tapped the ash off her cigarette and stretched like a lazy cat.

' "A present for us. Fifty for you and fifty for me. From my artist friend with the mustache."

' "But . . . what for? Did you tell him he could paint my cunt too?"

'That made her laugh. "We found out it's impossible to do the painting here. I showed him my pussy and he realized immediately it would take him hours and hours of painstaking work to do it justice.'' The crazy girl fairly squirmed, wriggled when she said that. "We did it together, he and I . . . a quickie. God . . . you should have seen him spurting! About a yard straight up in the air."

'I slowly sat down on the edge of my bed. "So the painting . . ."

'She waved it airily away: "We'll do that in comfort at his studio as soon as he's discharged. In the meantime we can have all sorts of fun. The three of us."

'That mad glitter in her eyes again. Once again I understood in a flash. Only this time my reaction was a positive one. I asked: "You mean . . . you and he . . ."

' "He's a masturbator, darling. An out-and-out looker and talker. At long last, a real man with a beautiful penis, who does not want just a stupid fuck, but who wants to do it to himself and see a girl doing it. A great many artists are that way, he told me."

'I said drily: "You must have had a busy couple of days. All that talk."

' "Oh, you don't need much talk when you understand one another. You and I didn't need much conversation, did we? Would you like to join us in a threesome? What we always did together, with him joining in? Must make it a hell of a lot more exciting. That's something, a real kick . . . seeing a man tossing himself off while looking at your dripping pussy."

'Then it began to get to me too. I've always had a vivid, creative sexual imagination. I felt myself getting hot and prickly down there. I had often tossed my dates off, but I had never seen a man quite openly and unashamedly tossing himself off. While Nora and I were doing it and watching him and him watching us . . . Nora lay watching me.

' "Like the idea, darling?" She had already seen that I did. "Now you figure a place where we can do it." She slipped off the bed. "I'm going to take a shower. Those hundred florins are a present. To buy candy or flowers with." '

'It didn't take me but an hour to figure it out. The main problem was how to get me into and out of the men's wing, where I was not allowed to go. Once that was solved, the rest would fall into place. The time factor was variable. I mean, you can do your masturbating at midnight and at three o'clock in the afternoon; horny is horny. Even if one of us should be unwell, that need not necessarily be an impediment. Nora always masturbated in front. I mean she never put things inside of her. She was an orthodox clitorian. As Nora once said, while pissing in the washbasin: ". . . and the clit moved over the waters. . . ."

' "Nora", I said, later that night, "we have to arrange for you to get a telegram."

'Nora was doing something to her face in front of the mirror. "Easy."

' "You arrange to be on duty in the men's wing, and when a telegram comes for you, it is sent up to our room here, no?"

' "Oui."

' "We arrange for me to be off duty then. I get the telegram here and a sudden panic comes over me. I get the telegram here and a sudden panic comes over me. It says that someone near and dear to you is desperately ill."

' "My mother", said Nora, clicking her teeth together and baring them at herself in the mirror. "I hate that bitch."

' "That's just in case something goes wrong. Serious illness always disarms them, even in a hospital. As long as it's not one of the patients. In this state of spontaneous panic I rush into the forbidden men's wing to bring you the telegram."

'Nora flicked around, rushed at me, and gave me a hug. "Ah, the beauty of simplicity. The elegance of it! If you're not caught everything is fine. And if someone stops you . . ."

' "I show them the telegram . . ."

' "And of course . . . under the circumstances . . ."

' "I'll be excused. And when I go back . . ."

' "You have just delivered it. Oh, you cunty mastermind, I love you. Let's work out the details."

' "Wait. If we are both in his room, that's the vulnerable point . . . nothing much can happen either. For I'm in his clothes cupboard, with the door open."

'Nora began to whirl around the room: "Oh, Monique! I can already see you standing there, watching Mustache and me in the throes of self-inflicted lust, and us gorging our eyes on the unforgettable spectacle of you riding the scene. If anyone should try to come in . . ."

' "I pull the door shut."

' "And I do it with my back against the door. Yes."

'I said: "Don't wear nothing under your apron. Anything to save time."

‘ “Done. I’ll compose the telegram.” ’

‘Oh, we had a fine time, and everything went off without a hitch. That telegram arrived on the dot. No one saw me entering the men’s wing and no one asked me any questions, coming or going. For some reason the secrecy and the risk lifted the whole scene to a higher plane of excitement. In later years I was to see this demonstrated often. Men and women who are married, but have an illicit liaison, experience a rising tide of tension and longing until the moment of hasty reunion with the clandestine lover. Once they have been found out, and everything is out in the open, they tend to discover that without the planning and plotting, a large part of the sexual fascination has also mysteriously vanished.

‘We did it just as we planned, with me in the open clothes cupboard; Nora leaning back against the door, her legs spread wide and her apron raised, and our Mister Mustache flat on his back, feasting his eyes on her hands and pussy, while stimulating his vertical penis until his eyes began to bulge and he spurted straight up in the air, making a deep, animal groan. I felt a hot flame of wild mania coursing from my excited brain and then I came, my eyes on his sweating face and hearing Nora’s soft, keening cries as she felt her own orgasm welling up.

‘ “Oh, God!” she panted. “Go on! Let’s go on! Let’s do it again!”

‘ “The hell with you”, I said. “Let’s get out of here fast.”

‘She didn’t listen to me, I don’t believe she even heard me. She hurried over to the bed, grabbed Mister Mustache by the balls and began to roll them around in her hand, like Captain Queeg in *The Caine Mutiny*, palming his steel ball bearings, hissing at him: “Let’s do it again. Let me see you spurt!”

‘And they were off again. I went over to the door with pumping heart, opened it an inch or so, listened, opened it wider and peeped outside. The corridor was deserted. I closed the door again and said: “I’m getting out of here.”

‘Mustache had his prick up again, pumping away like a piston engine. He panted: “Come here, nurse. Let me see your lovely blonde pussy.”

‘ “Next time”, I said, opening the door again, peeked out and did a smooth vanishing act, leaving them to do it.’

‘I don’t mind being quite frank about this: it was not so much the fear of discovery that prompted my fast departure. I needed time and quiet to assimilate the violent sensations that were still milling around inside me. I still to this day cannot explain why seeing or making someone come should excite or satisfy me so much. Perhaps it does have to do with a sense of power. And, of course, people pay me for it. They pay me a lot for making them come in the right way, and under the right circumstances. But why that should be so still beats me.

'I was lying on my bed, smoking a cigarette, when Nora came in ten minutes later. She stood looking at me for some moments, walked over to the mirror, and began to comb her hair.

' "Before I forget—we get some more money."

'I blew smoke into the air: "That's nice. When?"

'She glanced at me sideways. "Did you like it?"

'I didn't reply at once. For some private reason I did not want her to know how deeply moved and shaken I had been by that scene of a man masturbating. "Oh, yes. But the risk is colossal. We were just lucky. If we go on like this we'll get caught as sure as sin. Especially when you lose all sense of . . . I've told you that you let your cunt do your thinking for you. I want to get my diploma, even if you don't. If you got kicked out of here you would just grin and try something else. I sometimes wonder why you started working here at all."

'She said nonchalantly, without any further explanation: "Well, I feel safe here. You know what he told me?"

'I tossed around on the bed: "Oh, God. What now?"

' "He wants me to get on the bed with my knees spread and my cunt over his face, and when I feel myself coming, he's going to take my clit between his lips and finish me off that way."

' "Try and explain that when the head nurse barges in," I said.

'She didn't pursue it.'

'Our Mister Mustache had left the hospital and Nora never did get her cunt preserved in oils for posterity, since he didn't take the trouble to leave an address. Nora didn't seem very surprised, she took it in her stride. Not long afterward she suddenly announced that she was moving in with another nurse in another room. My reaction to that was somewhat blasé, for by that time I was moving on to the next stage in my rapid sexual evolution, and that stage was set in Amsterdam.

'The only person I knew in Amsterdam at the time was the lovely

Indonesian girl, Marina, who had invited me to look her up. And now, unexpectedly, my father had written, saying that he would be attending a conference in Amsterdam; that my mother refused to go with him, and would I be willing to take her place? Yes, I was very willing, for to me at that time Amsterdam was what New York would be for someone living in Amsterdam today. I arranged for two days off and on the appointed date, met my father at the railway station.

'The first evening we had cocktails at one of the largest hotels in Amsterdam. At dinner afterwards, we were seated four at a table. Our table partners were a long-standing friend of my father's, who was accompanied by a tall, willowy strawberry blonde in a black evening dress that must have cost a fortune. She impressed me very much. Her name was Gonda. During dinner all four of us engaged in conversation, but I was struck by the extreme attentiveness of my father's friend to Gonda. It was more than just good manners, but she never gave the slightest sign that she noticed his attentions, much less appreciated them. After dinner the men began to circulate. Gonda, who sat smoking a cigarette in a slender gold holder, said to me: "Let's go and sit somewhere quiet. I detest business talk."

'She led me to a table half hidden behind some potted palms. I couldn't help noticing how she caught the attention of every man within shouting distance, she walked so straight and completely self-assured, like a princess, a demi-goddess. She was not what you would call a beauty, but there was something indefinable which seemed to radiate from her, and that, welded to her air of unapproachable self-assurance, made her dominate the living space around her. I was so impressed that I didn't dare ask her any personal questions. Instead, she made a point of drawing me out: asking about myself, my family, my work and ideas for the future. She had a languid, slightly lisping way of speaking which added to her fascination.

'Quite suddenly she leaned forward, took her cigarette from that long holder, put it in the ashtray, and said in that bored voice of hers:

' "I'm getting out of here. I'm fed up. Listen, Monique, I like you, and I never say things I don't mean. I don't need to. I have an apartment in Amsterdam. Here is my card. If you come again to Amsterdam—and you must, soon—don't forget to ring me up. Don't be shy. You can call late at night if you want to, for I have my telephone by my bed." She smiled in a mysterious way. "And don't complain too much about that hospital. Your training as a nurse may be very advantageous for your future career. Be seeing you." And she sailed out without looking back.

'Later I said to my father: "This friend of yours, Daddy—does he have much money?"

'My father scratched his cheek, grinned a bit, and said: "Well, he's certainly done better than me. He doesn't talk about it much, but as far as I could find out—hearing this and that—he had the luck of arresting a couple of important Germans immediately after the capitulation. In one of their cars they had two trunks full of diamonds and cash. Something like that." He shrugged. "Well—that's his personal responsibility."

' "That wife of his . . . Gonda—he must love her very much."

' "I should have told you. She is just his big girl friend. He has a legal wife in Doorn who looks like a bad-tempered witch and five children."

' "You mean he . . . she . . .?"

' "Don't look so shocked, you're a big girl now. No doubt he would love to marry her, but Gonda wants no part of that."

' "You mean . . . he pays her?"

' "I think we can safely assume that, little girl."

'This was the first time in my life I had run up against "a kept woman". It confirmed an idea that had been developing in me for some time, that there was something to be said for a life of sin. With increasing speed, certain impressions and ideas began to fit together, forming a pattern: the violent fascination of seeing someone in the throes of orgasm; getting a hundred-guilder bill for watching a man masturbate; walking through a hotel dining room like a haughty princess on the Wages of Sin. I was determined to go to Amsterdam as soon as possible and find out more. There was no conscious planning behind it, just an almost compulsive curiosity and the feeling that I was being drawn to that city as to a vibrating magnet.'

'Exactly what is the nature of Amsterdam's strange magic? Long ago it was nicknamed "The Venice of the North", but there's more to it than that. When you stroll along those semi-circular tree-lined canals you become aware of—impregnated by—a sense of tension within harmony. It's like listening to good jazz; the melody varies, soars, tries to escape the tight stricture of the beat. The greater the contrast between the strict measure of the beat and the inventive variation of the melody, the greater that inner tension. Amsterdam has that in several polarities. The architecture of the old inner city; for instance. As you walk along those canals you are all at once struck by the superb artistry of design and building in those thousands of houses, one beside the other. Some large, some small, some broad, some narrow, but no two alike, each unique in its own way, and yet each managing to be part of one harmonious whole. There never was a master plan, the city simply grew that way.

'A second polarity is the violence, madness, and infinite variety of the city's people. No single class or character dominates, but each is defined and delineated by the unwritten tolerance and democracy of the people as a whole. It is not easy to describe but a feeling radiates, from the city and is felt instantly by each newcomer.

'I took night duty for four weeks in a row, and that gave me four free days. I telephoned Marina, who was enthusiastic: of course I could stay at her flat, though I would have to amuse myself during the daytime when she was out doing her social work.

'She met me at the central station and picked up my suitcase as matter-of-factly as if she were my boy friend. The streetcar brought us to a house on one of the canals where she had one room and a kitchen, cozily furnished, with Indonesian art objects on the walls.

'She teasingly asked me: "Do you drink sherry, or are you still too young?"

' "Pooh!" I said. "We drank straight whiskey with the Canadians and Dutch paratroopers." I began to tell her funny stories about all our tricks for getting in and out of the hospital. When she went into the kitchen to prepare dinner, I followed her.

' "By the way," she said, "here's a key to the front door. I work from nine until five, so during that time you'll be on your own. Now, let's eat. I'm expecting company."

'We had hardly finished when the bell rang and a fragile-looking girl came in, wearing a tailored dark blue dress. She had a shy, subtly sensitive face. Like a cameo, I thought.

' "Jeez, Marina. Aren't you ready yet? You know how I hate to be late."

' "I know, darling, but I had an unexpected visitor. This is Monique, one of Jan's sisters. Jan in our group 326. Remember him?"

' "Yes," she said darkly. "For heaven's sake, can't you leave those dishes until later?"

'I noticed that her eyes were darting to and fro between Marina and myself. I said, jumping up: "You go along, Marina. I'll do the washing up."

'The new girl was surprised. "What? Isn't she coming with us?"

'Marina seemed to hesitate. "Uh . . . I hardly think we can do that, Jackie."

' "Why the hell not?"

'I began to notice now that there was a distinct discrepancy between Jackie's fine, sensitive face and her rough language, voice, and behavior. Marina took her into the other room and closed the door. I wondered what the mystery was all about. I finally decided that they were probably spiritualists or members of some sort of Asian mystical society.

'They came back into the room and Marina asked: "I don't particularly want to leave you here on your own, but . . . how old are you?"

' "I'm twenty-one and three months," I replied. "And if you are going to some spiritualist or witches' session I'd love to come along. I promise not to make a fool of myself."

'They seemed to find that very funny and erupted into bursts of laughter.

'They took me to a ramshackle building whose ground floor was a small converted theater. The stage was still in its original shape, but the floor had no chairs. It was filled with an odd collection of variously shaped tables with seats of all sizes and conditions: beer barrels, boxes, benches, and stools. There were between a hundred and two hundred people there, many of whom had brought their own bottles. I sat looking around in amazement, but it didn't take me long to tumble to the fact that I was in the midst of a group of male and female homosexuals. Well, I had had my private suspicions about Marina all along, so I was neither shocked nor surprised. I saw Marina and Jackie glancing at me sideways, but they got no reaction out of me. I simply sat there, downing sherry after sherry, gazing around me with an amused party smile on my face. Which was not difficult, for nothing unusual happened. After a time the stage lights went on and some sketches were performed that produced gales of laughter, but most of the allusions escaped me. Girls and women dropped by our table, sat chatting for a while, and moved on again. I kept up my polite front, all the while secretly checking myself for stirrings of a sexual nature. I felt no lesbian inclinations. There was one girl, though, who reminded me vaguely of Nora, and I did feel something for her. I wondered whether she would be like Nora sexually. The girl seemed to sense something alive in me, for she leaned toward me and started talking. But as I noticed her avid looks at my breasts and thighs, I froze up and after a while she went away with Jackie. That left me with Marina and around midnight we left together. I had downed a fair number of sherries and when she put her arm through mine, our hips pressed together. After all, she had taken the trouble to put me up. Quite apart from that, I had been conditioned to the idea of paying for evenings out with my male escorts. Paradoxical as it may sound, there was something girl-scoutish about my idea that it is unsportsmanlike to accept food, drinks, and fun and give nothing in return. What puzzled me was how to satisfy, or at least pay back, a genuine lesbian. I had a rough idea, of course, and being slightly drunk and inquisitive too, I didn't protest when she told me we would have to sleep in the same bed, as there was no sofa or camp bed.

We put our pajamas on and got into bed with a fresh bottle of sherry. Then she began to talk. It didn't take me long to catch onto the line: story after story of the terrible things she had to see and take part in during the last years of the Occupation. (I later found out that a lot of it was not true.) At some stage she began to weep and shiver and put her arms around me. She had a nice, slender body so I relaxed, closed my eyes, and let her do what she wanted: some sucking of my nipples and stroking of my thighs. But when she slipped her fingers into my wet slit, I sat up, tore my pajama pants off, spread my legs.

'She wouldn't leave me alone the rest of the night. The more she came, the more she wanted. The girl was insatiable.

' "You drive me nuts . . . completely mad!" she panted, during a short pause, lying curled up with her eyes closed. "Your cunt is electric. There's magic, some bewitching chemistry you've got down there."

'I am recapitulating those incidents and remarks that have a direct bearing on how I later became what I became. Some of the scenes that I have recaptured are just as vivid to me today as they were the moment they happened. And each and every one of these incidents is marked by a *hervorragendes*—an outstanding new element in my sexual evolution. If there is any one special characteristic about my sexual awakening and rise, it is that its development was never a gradual one, but came about in distinct leaps and bounds. Suddenly something happened and I saw or realized: "That's it! That's the way it should work?" And from that moment on I operated on that level. I am aware that in this book I am saying certain things that have probably never been written before. What I said about the element of power in making somebody come, for instance. Do you have any idea how true that is? Clever psychiatrists spout booksful of sentimental nonsense about the element of "generous giving" in love. A lot of that is pure, unadulterated shit. A lot of women open their legs to a penis only because the knowledge that their hairy mousetrap has the sheer POWER to make an arrogant man yelp in ecstasy is a kick in itself.

'The same goes for masturbating a man or a woman. And it is this pure, undiluted feeling and love of POWER that makes me an ideal Merciless Mistress. Of course, I have clients who pay money just to sit opposite me in an overstuffed chair while they masturbate.

'The essential element of that first night in bed with Marina was not that it was my first straightforward lesbian experience. No. It was that mysterious remark of hers: ". . . your cunt is electric. There's magic, some bewitching chemistry you've got down there." I immediately knew that what she said was true. I just knew it. Of course, you can pay any stupid girl a compliment and she'll begin to think she's Cleopatra. But later experiences proved only too clearly that she was right. What the secret is, I don't even know myself. But I do know that some women radiate something through their skin, secrete something that is highly exciting. This is not always a desirable thing to have, for a variety of reasons. I once had a client who was married to a very sexy woman. His reaction to her cunt was so electric that his orgasm exploded a few seconds after he had put his penis inside her. With other women he had no trouble at all. He told me: "Monique . . . the whole of her cunt is charged with a sort of exciting fire. The moment the head of my penis touches the outside of her cunt my ecstasy is so unbearably intense that I erupt." I advised him to use a condom; that would avoid direct contact between their mucous membranes, and, you know, it worked! In a lesbian relationship such as I had started with Marina, her tongue reacted the same way as the man's penis.

'After Marina had left to go to work I snoozed for a couple of hours, then got up to make myself some coffee, and found a note on the table: "My eternal darling, please be home when I get here after five. I'll bring you the loveliest things to eat."

'Yeah, yeah. I dressed with great care and spent some wonderful hours roaming around the streets and canals of Amsterdam.

'I had heard stories about the old Jewish quarter, and I wanted to see it. After the Germans had deported most of its population, around September, 1944 (the Battle of Arnhem), the Dutch emigré government in London ordered the Dutch Railway to strike. It happened overnight. The next morning not one switch worked, not one train ran. The Germans had to bring in their own personnel to keep their military trains running. In reprisal they stopped all transportation of food and fuel for civilians. The following winter, when gas and electricity also began to fail, people in the larger cities began to cut down the trees, and like an army of ants attacked empty houses and buildings to get at the wood. But wrecking a house in secret and in the dark of night is a hazardous undertaking. Scores of people died under piles of rubble as roofs or walls collapsed. But that didn't stop them. When Holland was liberated in May 1945, the entire ex-Jewish quarter was one colossal level plain of tiles and masonry. There was not an inch of wood left. Termites could not have done it more efficiently.

'I wandered around that district, wondering why, here and there, an isolated house had been left, untouched and intact in that sea of ruins . . . trying to imagine the reason.

'About two o'clock I went into a coffee shop to do what I subconsciously had known I would do: ring up the fabulous Gonda. I immediately recognized her lazy, slightly lisping voice: "Whoo's theeere?"

' "This is Monique. I don't know whether you remember me. I . . ."

' "But of course I remember you! Where are you? In Amsterdam?"

' "I am staying with a girl friend, and . . ."

' "But you must come and have tea with me! I insist. Let's say half-past three. Just take a taxi and I'll pay for it. No, I won't hear of it. You do as I say. Right! See you at half-past three."

'I bought a couple of newspapers and had a bite to eat. I think I went looking for a taxi and had to kill time wandering around, an unexplainable excitement slowly mounting in me. Exactly on time, the taxi delivered me in front of an old building, once a private mansion, now converted into apartments. I paid for the taxi myself, pushed the bell, and there she was, standing at the top of the stairs; every bit as statuesque and impressive as I had remembered her. She was dressed in black satin house pajamas with a wide, gold belt. She greeted me with outstretched hands, her long gold cigarette holder in a corner of her mouth.

' "Ah . . . how lovely you look, my dear."

'In her large living room all the curtains were closed. She had screened lamps lit in the oddest places. Everywhere you looked were Chinese, French, or Dutch antiques; persian rugs and vases filled with flowers.

' "Sit down on that couch, my dear, and we'll have some tea."

'My eyes followed her as she floated through the room and I believe that had she asked me, I would have gone down on my knees and kissed her cunt there and then. But it soon became clear that she was quite different from Marina. She sat in the other corner of the couch, gesturing with her gold cigarette holder, pouring tea and chatting away quite happily. I had never, ever met anyone I liked so much, with whom I felt such a complete and direct affinity. She showed me around her apartment: three large rooms in a row. In the middle one was a colossal canopy bed with wing mirrors. The third room was a dining room with a gothic table, monastery chairs, silver candelabras, and an enormous sideboard. And then a tiled bathroom, too. And that in a time, not long after the Liberation, when entire families were living six to a room!

'Back on the couch. I said tentatively: "I . . . I hope this won't make you angry, but my father told me you are not married."

'She laughed gaily and gave me a sideways glance: "Is that the only thing he told you?"

' "Well, uh . . ."

'She made a sweeping gesture around that splendidly furnished room: "All this is loot, darling. Paid for in cash and bought in my maiden name. Men have their uses, you know. If you know how to handle them. That man you met me with, didn't you notice how nicely I have him trained?"

' "Trained?"

' "To do my bidding."

' "Oh, that? Lord, yes. He was really most anxious to anticipate your wishes, I thought. He must be very much in love with you."

'Her laughter made the crystal chandelier tinkle. "He is a slave, darling. I can pretty well make him do any damned thing I want. And he loves it."

'I had no idea what she could possibly mean. A slave?

' "What does he love?"

' "The whole situation. The idea of being my humble slave. You know the old expression: He worships the ground she walks on? Well, that's nothing. He worships the pot I piss in. He simply can't do without me, as long as I kick him, insult him, and humiliate him. And he is not the only one in my stable. But the most important one, yes, and by far the richest." She winked. "A big point in his favor. But listen"—she glanced at her diamond wrist watch—"I have someone coming soon. How long will you be in Amsterdam?"

' "I have to be back Tuesday evening."

' "Then come back here Monday afternoon at three sharp and I'll show you something. It's not much use talking about it, you must see for yourself how these things work." She stretched out a slender arm and put her hand on my shoulder. Not the way Marina would have done it; this was more a friendly gesture, a touch of comradely understanding. "You know why I am doing this for you? All my instincts say you're a natural."

' "A natural? Natural what?"

'She gave me a deep, mysterious smile: "A natural-born Mistress. I think you have it. Now run along, dear child; I expect you Monday at three."

'She had not even asked where I was staying, or with whom.'

'I had hardly hung up my coat when Marina came bursting in, loaded with parcels and a bunch of tulips. She jumped at me with a hug and a kiss and a rapid feel.

' "Look at all the things I brought for us. We'll have a little party tonight. How was your day? Did you miss me?"

'I told her about some of the things I had done that day. About some of my impressions of the wonderful city. But I didn't let out a peep about Gonda. And not because Gonda had told me not to. I kept my mouth shut intuitively, in the same way that a woman does not tell her husband about having met a man who will later become her lover. It's a sort of instinct and I've always done a great many things by instinct.

'The party that evening turned out to be a hen party—women only. I was officially presented as Marina's new girl friend, which position I took no trouble to deny. I smiled, nodded, and was nice to everybody. Which wasn't hard, for I got compliments fired at me from all sides. Fundamentally, I did not much care what they thought of me, or what Marina intended to do to me in bed that night. I was just biding my time . . . until Monday at three.

'Next day I sat around the apartment reading, and let Marina wait on me, which she seemed happy to do. She cooked, brought me cups of coffee, and when she talked too much I picked up a newspaper or a book.

'On Sunday we went to the beach at Zandvoort and I remember being shocked that Marina put on a pair of men's bathing shorts. At that time the beaches of Holland were not the tourist paradise they are today; army engineers were busy blowing up the concrete bunkers and barbed wire entanglements that the Germans had left everywhere. So there were not many people around, and no one seemed to notice anything out of the ordinary. And why should they? Marina had no breasts to speak of; just a pair of rather prominent, dark brown nipples. And in those trunks, her luxurious bush of pubic hair could very well pass for a man's bunched-up apparatus. We horsed around, lay in the sun, and had a glorious day.

'The moment Marina left to go to work on Monday morning, I began to glance at the clock. So much time to kill until three!

'That afternoon Gonda was wearing a black velvet negligee with wide sleeves, trimmed with white fur. When her coat fell open in front, I saw black silk stockings and black, shiny, high-heeled shoes. I felt like a poor relation in my so-called Scottish skirt and white blouse with frills. I had been secretly proud of my not-so-low heels, but compared to me, Gonda was walking on stilts. Nevertheless, she looked me up and down in an approving way.

' "You should always wear your hair like that, sweetie, loose around your shoulders. It makes the contrast in you stand out. What will you drink? Sherry or port?"

' "Can I have sherry?" I said, wondering what she could mean, this remarkable woman, by "the contrast in me".

'All the curtains were tightly closed. Did she never open them? Outside the sun was shining brightly, but perhaps she didn't like daylight.

'As if she could read my thoughts, she said nonchalantly: "Lamp-. light has so much more atmosphere, I think. Here's your sherry Do you appreciate lovely things? Do you ever go to art auctions?"

' "God, no", I said. "I've never been to one. What would I do there? Look at expensive things that I don't have the money to buy?"

'That made her laugh. "Yes, I already knew that you were a

sensible girl. And if you play your cards right, some day you can be a queen with scores of slaves who pay you for the privilege of kneeling for you and feeling your angry spiked heel in their necks. Shall I show you what I bought at auction the other day? I've always wanted a statue, you know. But marble is so cold, so bare and chaste. What do you think of this, as a corner decoration?"

'She took me by the hand and led me to a dimly lit corner, where she pulled aside a Chinese curtain. She had a low, round table there, on top of which was a life-size statue of a man. A completely nude man, with his arms in the sort of mad posture you generally see in shop window mannequins. I was no expert in statuary or sculpture, but to me it looked like amateur work. I found nothing better to say than: "Why is it painted light blue?"

'She stood looking at the thing with her head sideways, considering it critically. "Yes. Perhaps it wasn't such a good buy, after all. Shall I give it to you as a present?"

'Again I didn't know what to say. "To me? But where shall I put it?"

' "There's that, of course", she said pensively, and let her hand slide along one light blue hip. "Still . . . it has something, you know. Just feel it."

'Well, why not? I put out my hand and stroked the contour of the thing at the same place where Gonda had. Then pulled my hand back as if I had burned it. The statue was warm, live-warm.

' "Gonda . . .!"

'That amused her very much. When she had stopped laughing, she took me by the hand and began to walk back to the sherry, calling over her shoulder: "Get down now, Freak. Take a shower and get that stuff off and come back in your work clothes."

'I turned around just in time to see the light blue specimen tiptoe out of the room. I downed my sherry and lit a cigarette. Asked no questions. Gonda poured us two more sherries, talking about antique furniture as if nothing had happened. And then, apropos of nothing, said: "Would you mind taking your stockings off and putting your shoes back on?"

'In that atmosphere I considered this an unusually normal request, I put my shoes back on and listened to more conversation about Chippendale chairs and Louis Seize tables until I heard a scratching noise to my left. I looked and saw Mr. Freak advancing across the carpet on his hands and knees, his lower part dressed in green ballet tights. Having reached a position between us, he stopped, motionless, his head lowered in a hang-dog fashion.

' "Ah, there you are", Gonda said, in a not-unfriendly tone. "Now prostrate yourself and clean my girl friend's shoes." He flattened himself completely on the floor, crawled nearer, and began to lick my right shoe. He licked most conscientiously: sides, soles, even the difficult space in front of the heel. He had to force his neck around to do it. Gonda put her high-heeled shoes against his rump and went on talking about antiques, using him as a footstool. Without interrupting the flow of her chatter she suddenly ordered him to take my shoes off and lick my toes one by one and then my soles.

'To my surprise I soon began to like the ticklish feeling of a warm, human tongue slithering in and out between my toes. An exciting glow began to creep up my legs. Until Gonda lifted her foot, kicked him in the ribs and snarled: "That's enough. Up! Up on your knees!"

'He shot upright and sat back on his heels, his hands hanging limply in front of him like a dog's paws, his eyes downcast. By this time I had stopped seeing this creature as a man and regarded it as a curious sort of animal.

' "Jesus, Gonda! I never saw such nipples!"

' "All a matter of training", she said, a cigarette in the corner of her mouth. She took two large safety pins from the table, opened them, pushed their sharp ends right through those elongated nipples and clicked them shut. It gave me the shivers, but the kneeling creature didn't bat an eyelid. He got another kick in the ribs. "Now go get my instruments."

'He crawled out of the room, and came back with an old leather hold-all on his back. Gonda got up, opened the bag, and handed me some steel eyebolts, hasps, clamps, leather thongs, and whips.

' "Beautiful workmanship, eh?"

'I let the braided whips slip through my fingers, smelled them, and felt delicious. Yet, frightening shivers ran up and down my belly and legs. Would she really . . . ?

'Gonda had rolled back one end of the persian carpet and was screwing the eyebolts into holes in the floor. She muttered something, straightened, and suddenly shouted: "Get going, you lousy slave! Are you stalling again?" She gave him a vicious kick in the rump with one high heel. He hobbled into position between the four bolts, then turned around, and now stood completely bent over, with legs straight, hands and feet touching the floor near the bolts. Gonda now took the leather thongs and fastened his ankles and wrists in place; while he remained motionless, his ass a good deal higher than his head and shoulders.

' "Hand me the cat-o'-nine-tails, Monique", Gonda said. I handed her the whip, and the next second she pulled it lovingly through her fingers, spread her legs, and slashed it down over his tensed buttocks. Until that moment I had not really believed she would actually do it . . . and certainly not in full earnest. I saw the buttock-flesh shiver like a horse's hide when the flies pester it. He let out a low, deep moan, and Gonda said, between her teeth: "That's it, my brave slave—let's hear how you like it!" Up and down went the whip, and I felt a hot tingling excitement coursing through my body. Glancing up at Gonda's face, I saw a flush in her cheeks and a sparkle in her eyes. She was more beautiful than I had ever seen her. Now I understood what being a Mistress with slaves really meant, and I began to wonder if she would give me a chance to try it. I realized I was up out of my chair and was watching from close up, licking my lips, my breath coming in quick gasps. She must have seen me from the corner of her eye, for she suddenly stopped, straightened up, pushed her hair out of her eyes and said: "Strip down his tights. We'll work on his bare ass. I want to see some blood."

'With two quick movements I tore those stiff green tights down over his calves, and when I straightened up, Gonda handed me the other whip, the one with hooks and bent nails at the ends of the thongs. She nodded at the quivering posterior offering itself to me: "Go ahead".

'A sort of excited fury got hold of me. I took a small step back, lifted my arm, and slashed down with all my might, pulling a bit when I hit. I saw a row of criss-crossing welts and bloody slashes. I stood staring at them in hypnotized fascination.

' "Go on!" Gonda urged me, and ordered sharply, "Count to twenty, slave!"

'I heard him begin to count, "One . . . two . . ." and after each count I raised my mean whip and let him have one—from the right—from the left—across the buttocks—across the thighs. The meeker he became and the more obediently he counted, the more furious I got. I felt a madness welling in me. My body began to glow in the most intimate places: my vagina, my breasts began to prickle and tingle, and finally, after the count of twenty, Gonda had to take my upraised wrist and steady my arm. Slowly my hand descended and I stood looking at my handiwork. Freak's thighs and buttocks were a pattern of red and bluish welts and punctures with blood slowly welling out and dribbling down.

'Gonda bent over and loosened the four straps. "Now get out of here and ring me Wednesday morning between ten and eleven. Got that?"

' "Thank you, Mistress", he whispered, and crawled out of the room, blood trickling down his thighs and those ridiculous tights still hobbling his calves. I sank into an overstuffed chair, still all confused and hot inside. Gonda placed herself in front of me, put her fingers under my chin, raised my face, and said teasingly: "That was really something, huh, kid? The moment I saw you I just knew you were this way. Now at least we know what we're talking about in the future. Tomorrow is your last day, isn't it? We'll have coffee at the Leidseplein at eleven. Okay?"

'I walked all the way to Marina's flat in a sort of dream, floating along, whispering in realization: "I had a slave today. I had my first real slave today. This is how I want to live too."

'Marina was waiting for me at home and I felt her inquisitive glance.

' "You look very well. There's a sort of glow all over you. Did you do anything special?"

'I told her exciting stories about antique shops and furniture. I told her all sorts of things, but not one word about Gonda. That night, when she began to fondle me and kiss my pussy, I closed my eyes, relived the whipping scene in Gonda's apartment, and let myself go. I had two climaxes, one right after the other . . . wild ones. Proudly and contentedly, Marina said: "You're really thawing out, darling. Didn't I tell you this would happen? You have to let yourself go, that's all . . . oh, darling Monique, you can learn a lot from me." Yeah, yeah.

'Next morning, alone in bed, I began to realize that there are different kinds of orgasms. The ones with Marina, when she was licking and sucking me, had been explosive and violent. But I was quite sure that I had had one while I was whipping Gonda's slave, and it was completely different, coming over me gradually . . . creeping up on me from deep inside, and then gushing over and out of me in a flushing ecstasy.

'I got up to get dressed for my appointment with Gonda. There was a book on the table, with a note in Marina's handwriting:

"This book, *The Well of Loneliness*, is my greatest favorite. I present it to you, my darling Monique. It truly is the Bible for girls like us. Please, please write to me often and remain true to me, my love."

'With a feeling of irritation I tore up her note. I didn't much mind a lesbian experiment. I didn't mind her kissing and sucking me. After all, she had put me up and had been very nice to me. But mash notes full of sentimental drivel were something else again.'

'In July, 1949, I passed my final examinations and became a qualified nurse. The same afternoon I got a message to report to the director of female personnel. I had been fairly continuously in hot water and my immediate reaction was: What NOW? But I didn't worry much, for there was an enormous shortage of nurses everywhere and with my official certificate I could get a job wherever I wanted.

'I was admitted to her office. The old gray cat was sitting behind her desk wearing a sort of synthetic grin. When she offered me a chair it began to dawn on me that she was trying to look friendly.

' "Well, Von Cleef. How do you feel, now that you have your certificate?"

' "Oh, very well, Director. I feel wonderful. Yes."

'She glanced down at a typed list. "Yes. You could be a very good nurse, although you have the longest disciplinary record in this hospital's history. Ahem. What are your intentions now? I could put you at the top of the list for obstetrical specialization."

' "Uhhh . . . yes', I said.

' "You don't want to go in for that?"

' "No, Director. I, uh . . . I would prefer to give notice, for"—I desperately cast around for a likely story—"I am going to get married."

'She sat staring at me. "Are you by any chance pregnant?"

' "Oh, no. Lord, no!"

' "You just want to leave here?"

' "Yes, that's it."

'I saw her getting red, then pale. She jumped up from behind her desk, banged her fists down, and began to call me more bad names than I had ever heard before. No sense of responsibility, undisciplined, oversexed, arrogant, pagan. Predestined to come to a bad end. The longer she screamed at me, the fiercer she became. By that time, six other nurses who also had recently qualified, were waiting outside and heard it all, word for word. Which gave five of the six the courage to give their final notice too.

'After number five resigned, the director suffered a breakdown and was put to bed under sedation. Two days later I got a message saying that under the circumstances I need not serve out my last month but could pack my suitcase and leave at once.

'I went straight to the nearest cafe and rang up Marina.

' "I'm through here once and for all. Is it possible to get a room in Amsterdam?"

' "Only for people with a lot of money. But why don't you come and live with me for a start?"

'Yes. I could always do that to start with. The wear and tear on my pussy would only be part of the bargain, I supposed. Oh, well . . .'

'I paid a visit to my parents and watched my mother's face and mouth set when she heard that I was going to live in Marina's apartment.

' "Are you throwing in your lot with that . . . that . . . ? I'd rather see you unhappily married."

'I shrugged. She had been unhappily married for thirty years, and I felt she was hardly in a position to play counselor to me. So on the first of August, 1941, I entrained for Amsterdam and the real start of my career.'

'The fantastic began to happen almost at once. Marina met me at the central station, took me home, and on the stairs we met her landlady who was coming down with two heavy suitcases. She said that she was going to stay with her married sister for a couple of days, and asked us to look after the house.

' "That's funny", Marina said with a slight frown. "She never trusts anyone. And why was she so nervous?"

' "Perhaps there's illness in her family?"

' "Pah! She wouldn't bat an eye if her whole damned family perished in an earthquake. Look, darling, I emptied out this cupboard for you, you can stay as long as you want. I bought some good things to eat and a bottle of wine. Let's celebrate your arrival."

'We celebrated it, all right. She could cook, I'll say that for her. The wine was all right too. I suppose she wanted to create a romantic atmosphere, for against soft background music she began to read one poem after another written in my honor and extolling the virtues and beauties of my breasts, hair, etc. To put a stop to that I suggested going to bed, which the poetry reading was intended to lead up to in any case, I suppose.

There was suddenly a colossal banging of doors, stamping feet on the stairs, weeping, shouting, and a loud German shout of "Heil Hitler!"

'Marina and I sat bolt upright in bed, listening to that truly frightening ruckus, and unable to imagine what it could be.

'I slipped out of bed to check if the door was locked. The pounding, weeping, and stumbling continued, and then there was a heart-rending cry.

' "This isn't funny any more", I said. "I feel really frightened. Shall I slip out and get the police?"

' "No, no! Don't leave me alone!"

'Huddled against one another, we lit cigarettes and sat there, listening and shivering, until gradually the last footsteps went down the stairs and the noise subsided.

'The next day Marina accosted one of the other tenants on the stairs about the upheaval. She came back into our room and stood looking at me with a chalk-white face.

' "What's the matter? Have you seen a ghost?"

'Marina went to the little sideboard and poured herself a large glass of straight Dutch geneva.

' "I just talked to that teacher who lives at the end of the corridor."

' "About last night? What was it?"

'Marina downed the glass of gin in one swallow and gave me a frightened look.

' "She maintains she heard absolutely nothing. And she says she was up correcting exercise books until two in the morning."

'We sat staring at each other for a long time. Then decided to get dressed, go to a bar, and get good and drunk.

'Three days later the landlady was back. She knocked on our door to announce that the rent would be raised if both of us were going to live in the room. We came to an agreement on that, paid her the money, and then Marina broached the subject of the mysterious goings-on during my first night there. Our landlady fidgeted a bit and then said: "These seem to be the only two rooms that have trouble on that date. This one and mine upstairs."

' "What trouble? What date?"

' "Well, you see, Miss . . . there were Jews living here during the Occupation, and on the night of August first, as I heard it, the

Germans raided those rooms. And . . . when the first of August comes I go to visit my family. You haven't been here a full year, Miss, and I thought that perhaps this year . . ."

' "Only on the night of August first?"

' "Yes."

' "And only these two rooms? This one and the one upstairs?"

' "Yes, Miss. No one else in the house ever hears a thing."

'We split a bottle of sherry and spent the rest of the evening at Marina's homo-club.'

'I had registered with an agency and the first job they got me was in a rest home for aged widowers run by a pair of overaged homosexuals. The conditions there were so incredible that it could have come straight out of Edgar Allen Poe. The third day I reported back to the agency and the director listened to me, sighed, and nodded: "I know all about it", she said. "But they do pay you, don't they?"

' "Yes, but . . ."

' "The rest is up to the authorities. Do me a favor and stick it out for two weeks, I promise you if you do that, if you help me out for fourteen days, I'll give you a first-class job right away."

'I looked her straight in the eye: "Is that a straight deal?"

' "A straight deal."

'She kept her word, and I got some fairly cushy first-class nursing jobs in South Amsterdam. Generally the night shift, from ten at night until eight in the morning, which gave my pussy a chance to escape Marina's nocturnal nuzzlings. There were a lot of wealthy people in South Amsterdam, but rich people are capable of the damnedest meanness.

'They were supposed to provide me with at least one meal, or pay me the equivalent in cash. One night I am suddenly sent to take care of a frail little lady who has just been brought home from a hospital. The day nurse has left a note: "This patient has to have her injection at eleven o'clock without fail or she won't shut an eye all night."

'This patient has a face like a frustrated bat, and she attacks on sight. "Another nurse. Another one of those amateurs, I suppose."

'Her husband, a tired-looking man, says: "I won't mind if you make yourself a cup of coffee tonight, nurse."

' "Fine", I say, "as long as you pay me the cash instead of a meal."

‘ “Impertinent and insolent, too”, says a voice from the bed. But her husband takes me into the kitchen: “A sandwich, then?”

‘ “I always have three.”

‘He opens the icebox. “Ham or cheese?”

‘ “Two with cheese and one with ham.”

‘The shrill voice from the sick room: “HENRY! Don’t forget to lock the icebox!”

‘I’ll be damned if they don’t have an icebox with a Yale lock in the handle.

‘The husband vanishes and I go back to the sickroom. “And now, Mrs. De Vries, we’ll bed you down for the night and give you your injection and then you’ll have a nice night’s sleep.”

‘She immediately begins to whine: “No consideration, none at all. I need another air cushion. In that cupboard over there.”

‘There must have been a dozen of them inside: round, square, oval.

‘ “And which one would you prefer, ma’am?”

‘ “How can I tell? I have to try them.”

‘ “Oh, no, ma’am, You must choose one.”

‘ “I’ll tell my son. He’s a doctor.”

‘ “Really?” I say. “Have you decided yet?”

‘I rub her back with camphor oil, powder her down, arrange her pillows, and pick up the hypodermic needle.

‘ “Oh, not tonight”, she says. “My son says . . .”

‘ “What I say goes just now”, I reply, and give her a shot.

‘She makes a noise of disgust: “Everything calls itself a nurse nowadays.”

‘I put out the light, go into the adjoining room, and curl up in an easy chair with an interesting-looking book.

‘ “Nurse . . . I’m uncomfortable.”

‘I ask, without getting up: “What’s the matter?”

‘ “I think I need another air cushion, after all.”

‘ “That’s just your imagination, ma’am.”

‘ “Nurse! I’m going to scream!”

‘ “Go ahead, if that will make you feel better.”

‘When I tiptoe into her bedroom half an hour later she is gently sleeping. I don’t hear a peep out of her all night, give her a nice wash in the morning, change her bed linen and nightgown, and she’s as sweet as pie.

‘ “Will you be back tonight?” asks her husband meekly.

‘ “Allah willing, yes”, I say. “Why do you ask?”

'He gives a deep sigh: "Nurse—she's been home for ten days now and we have had nine different night nurses".

'The next night the icebox stays open, and I have no trouble whatever with my patient.

'Army and naval officers, I have read somewhere, have to have the habit of command. I seemed to have a natural-born habit of authority.

'Was that what Gonda had spotted in me when she said, with that mysterious smile: "You finish your nurse's training. It may come in handy later?" '

'Not long after that I was assigned to another rest home, situated on a picturesque canal. But this one was completely different from the first. Gay and healthy sept- and octogenarians of both sexes. The youngest woman there was sixty-eight and had the time of her fading life flirting with the doddering gentlemen. One of them had a speciality of slipping her folded pieces of paper, which she received with hot flushes and high giggles, and then sneaked out into the corridor to read them. When she came back some minutes later, she coyly took up her embroidery and set to work again, now and then exchanging naughty glances with the old sport of the *billets doux*. She had a private sport of her own: collecting teaspoons, as many as she could get hold of, and hoarding them in her handbag. Every second or third day we had to lure her away somehow to recover the loot. She never missed any of her spoons, she simply started over again. Of course, we got hold of the *billets doux* as well. One of them read: "Dear Janet—three kisses on your little cunt. Herman."

'A gay old dog, that Herman.

'All in all it was not such a bad life, I thought then. Hard work, lots of variety, and lots of laughs. Occasionally I took two or three days off for a rest and a bit of sightseeing around Amsterdam.

'There are hundreds of centuries-old curiosities in that city that an ordinary tourist never sees or even hears about. That you wouldn't believe exist until you see for yourself. Because the entire ancient inner city is built on moor and mud, every building there is set on a foundation of wooden piles driven into the deeper layer of solid glacier sand. During the religious wars between the Catholics and Protestants, people managed to build tunnels through the mud under several of the canals, lined them with bricks, and used them to get to clandestine places of worship. I walked into one of them that runs under the Prince's Canal, starting from the cellar of an old coffee house. At another place there is an entire false brick wall built behind a warehouse, hiding a church behind it. And there still exists a church called Our Lady in the Garret. And it's in a garret, too!'

'And then, quite suddenly, I had a small fortune thrown into my lap. My life has always been like that: everything in leaps and bounds and surprises out of the blue.

'The agency asked me to help out with a piece of dirty work. Their message read: "Patient awaiting hospitalization dying with last stage lung cancer and no help available so please oblige."

'You can't always pick and choose, so I sped to the address, where the neighbors let me in with shaking heads.

' "It's an inhuman situation", they said.

'When I entered those stinking rooms I did not get the impression that the neighbors had done much to humanize the situation. An old man lay flat on his back in a rusty bedstead, rotting in his own excrement. I rushed into the kitchen and put some buckets of water. on the gas, then began to search for clean underwear and bed linen. There simply wasn't any. I never found out what happened to it. Stolen, probably. In that kind of situation I could consider myself lucky that the gas had not been cut off. When the water in the first bucket was hot I tore down the kitchen window curtain to use as a towel, found a dried-up cake of soap, and went back to the bed.

' "How long have you been lying like this?"

'The old man just shook his head. He had lost count of the days.

' "Don't you have any family?"

' "My wife has been dead for years. No family at all. Neither of us."

' "Then how have you lived? What did you eat?"

' "Social security . . . small pension."

'He could hardly breathe or speak, and I asked no further questions. I wasn't much in the mood for talk, either, for by that time I was beating off the fleas, which were attacking me from all sides. There was nothing in the kitchen but a heel of dried-up bread and half a bottle of milk, curdled solid.

' "Do you have any money? For milk and food, I mean?"

'He began to scratch around under his pillow, and when I burrowed there I came up with a worn leather purse containing thirty-eight cents.

‘ “Now don’t get worried”, I said. “I have to go and buy some food and soap for you. I’ll be right back.” He nodded weakly.

‘I had only five guilders with me. I bought some milk, oranges, and disinfectant; and rang up Marina.

‘ “I cannot leave here. This is a real emergency: Do me a favor, bring me some money and buy some towels and sheets.”

‘ “Right away”, she promised.

‘I must say this for her: she didn’t bat an eye when she entered that stinking hellhole. She helped me clean up the old fellow as well as we could, sprinkled some disinfectant around, and went out for more food. Then she managed to put her hands on her hips looked around, and grinned: “When you get fed up with me you can always move in here.”

‘ “Bloody funny”, I snapped. (I had had a row with her the day before, and I was more or less getting fed up with her.) “Just stick around for five minutes while I ring up the agency.”

‘In a phone booth around the corner I stood stamping and scratching the flea bites, waiting for someone to answer the phone.

‘ “Look”, I said, “this is really impossible. I’m not talking about myself, but if this poor bastard isn’t admitted to a hospital at once I’ll have to use the curtains for sheets. Or do you want me to use my own hope chest?”

‘ “Monique”, I was told, “we have been telephoning the hospitals for two days about this case. There’s a flu epidemic, as you know, and there’s not one available bed.”

‘ “Well, there’s a flea epidemic here”, I snarled. “For God’s sake, keep trying, will you? I’ll stay around for the time being.”

‘It was twelve degrees below zero outside and the only stove he had was a rusty kerosene burner and no fuel. I stomped back through the snow, relieved Marina (who had been discovered by the fleas, and was insisting that they could give you bubonic plague), heated some milk, and fed my patient what he could manage to swallow. Which wasn’t anything to speak of.

‘I covered him up with curtains and old clothes to keep him as warm as possible, and sat, huddled up in my coat, waiting for help to arrive. At ten o’clock in the evening he began to make strange noises. I went over to his bed, and a few minutes later he simply died under my hand. Just like that. Perhaps it was the best thing that could have happened to that sad bunch of human misery. In death his ravaged old face had a far more peaceful look than on the last day of life. I was sincerely sorry for him, which surprised me a little about myself, for nurses soon unlearn the luxury of sentiment and I had never been a sob sister, in any case.

'But . . . a sense of duty is a pest forever. (Keats?) Shivering with cold, I went to work tidying up the body, for now there was only the problem of a cold, dead body. I did not expect any delay in having it picked up.

'While pulling the old clothes and curtains and dirty blankets off the bed I couldn't help thinking about the universality of human hypocrisy. This poor old man had been mortally ill and dying in utter loneliness. Why? Just because he didn't have any family or children? Utter shit. Time and again I have heard the nearest and dearest say: "Nurse . . . ah . . . if Father (or Mother) should expire tonight, don't ring us up before nine in the morning. We are very tired already and the telephone also tends to frighten the children when it rings in the night."

'Now that the man was dead, he could not object to my stripping off his filthy clothes. And while getting the urine-wetted sheet out from under him, I realized that the mattress was also hopelessly soaked and stinking. There was nothing to do but lift the naked, still warm, emaciated body, put it gently in an armchair, and then go to work on the empty bed.

'I took one side of the wet, stinking mattress and lifted it. The rusty springs were covered with an old board. On the board lay something that looked suspiciously like a wallet.

'It was. And it contained 8,700 guilders in banknotes. Smelly but nonetheless legal tender. Sitting on the edge of the empty bed I sat gazing at the naked, dead man, We've all read this kind of story in the newspapers. For less than half this amount, the old crank could have died in luxury, and still have had enough left over for a nice stone on his grave.

'As I trudged home through the snow on that bitterly cold morning I resolved one thing for sure: I would keep the money for myself, and would not be so stupid as to tell anyone about it.

'When I entered our room, Marina woke up at once.

' "Darling . . . you must be exhausted. Shall I make coffee for you?"

' "Go back to sleep, I can make it for myself."

'But no, she had to rush around, making coffee and frying eggs. I just sat at the table in a sort of inner money-daze. As prices were then, I had enough to buy a three-storey house. When the eggs and the coffee were in front of me, Marina stood behind me and began to stroke and nuzzle my neck.

' "For God's sake!" I shouted, pulling away. "Stop messing me up all the time. Besides, I stink to high heaven."

' "Oh, I don't mind that, darling."

'I said wearily: "Why don't you just go to hell? You bore me. I wasn't cut out to be a lesbian, anyway."

'An explosion of weeping and hysteria. I got up, left her with the damned coffee and eggs, and walked through the snow to an early morning cafe near the harbor. There were some straightforward, honest drunks there who were always good for a talk and a laugh.'

'I took a train to Brussels, where absolutely no one knew my face, and went to a bank. I showed my passport plus my nurse's papers and said I was planning to open a small private nursing home. Then I deposited the old man's money in my own name, giving my parents' address in Limburg. That covered my tracks for the time being. I knew the danger of suddenly spending too much money. The only luxury I afforded myself was a very expensive pair of Norwegian sealskin boots. Warm and watertight.'

'Back in Amsterdam, Marina was really in a state. I tried to reason with her. I told her I had absolutely nothing against her, that I was grateful for her hospitality, and would always enjoy talking to her, but was simply fed up with having my cunt roughed up every hour on the hour all night long.

' "Look", I said, "let's buy a couch or a second bed so I can sleep by myself. And you find another girl friend. What you need is a nymphomaniac lesbian, there must be such a thing."

'Bursts of weeping, but I refused to give in, and ordered a second bed, which I paid for myself. She was in turns mad and moody for a couple of days, then went dramatic on me and wrote drippy poems, but finally seemed to accept the new terms of our relationship. I think I am fairly truthful when I say that the sheer fact of having that wad of money in the bank changed my whole point of view. It gave me a sort of inner certainty that I had lacked before. It may even have been the decisive factor that precipitated my breaking off my sexual relationship with Marina. And from that moment on a strange interlude in my life began . . . a sort of treading water, interspersed with ludicrous, or crazy, or illogical incidents. Subconsciously I was waiting for something, that's obvious in retrospect. But I did not realize it at the time. Something had to happen to trigger my move in the direction that my life was predestined—as I am convinced—to take.'

'Got a part-time job in a children's hospital. I don't mind being rough with an adult, but with a child it's something else. They are so alone and helpless. I wasn't really tough enough to remain objective when still another one was brought in for a tonsillectomy. The surgeon had ruled that no child under four be allowed to have anaesthetic, but the head nurse had other ideas. We hid a bottle of French brandy in a cupboard, made a sort of lollipop from a wad of cotton with sterile gauze around it, filled a cup with brandy and sugar, soaked the lollipop in it, and let the poor mites suck on that. They loved it and we noticed the funniest effects. Some of them became quite jolly, others a little belligerent. Just like an adult's reaction to alcohol, but in miniature. But it kept them happy, and it worked better than anaesthetic.'

'Met a nice, frail Chinese doctor in a coffee bar. He took me to a movie and invited me to his rooms . . . for coffee.

'He undressed me very politely and very gently, then said: "Now you lie on you little belly and I'll stloke you velly nicely."

'The stroking and tickling was very soothing, but that's all. I finally tumbled to it that something else was expected of me, so I began to move and groan and then heaved myself onto my back—sunnyside up. He looked down at me radiantly and asked: "How many times you come?"

' "Five times", I said. He very carefully put a condom on his penis, showed it to me proudly, put his machinery in me and oh so nicely and gently and had an orgasm in a very refined and polite way. He then got up, made a little bow, and said: "Velly nice. Thank you", and gave me ten florins, "to buy flowels with."

'I began to see him regularly. It was mainly his gentleness and politeness that got to me.'

'Switched to a part-time job as night nurse, men's surgical ward. There was a male nurse in charge of penicillin injections, which he had to bring up from downstairs. When he used the service elevator he never took the trouble to close the door, which forced the rest of us to use the stairs.

'One morning at six o'clock, after a beastly night when everything had gone wrong, I had to go down in a hurry and again found the elevator blocked. I dropped everything in my hands, ran down those stone flights in a state of total fury, and looked around. There he was! I sprinted after him with outstretched hands, got hold of his throat, and began to shake and choke him, hissing: "You goddamned son-of-a-bitch—I'll kill you, I swear, if you leave that door open one more time!"

'I suddenly realized that something was wrong. I let go . . . and looked into the deathly frightened face of the Roman Catholic priest who always sneaked along the corridors at that time of morning, carrying the Holy Communion.'

'Marina had got it into her head that she too wanted to be a nurse, which wasn't really a bad idea, and not long after that we moved into a larger room in one of those colossal old mansions in the Koninginneweg. Our landlord—Marina had met him through her homo-club—was an old and deaf homosexual who wrote music, thought he was a descendant of Beethoven, and used an enormous funnel that he held to his ear when he wanted to listen. There were more than thirty people living in the house and they all did their cooking on a gas ring. There was always something brewing, night and day, and in more senses than one. Our landlord was fond of hiring "normal" boys for twenty-five guilders a night. He would drape a red velvet curtain around his shoulders, put a gilt cardboard crown on his head, and march up and down the stairs, singing all the way, with his hired boy carrying the red velvet train. In those pantomimes he was the queen, and if we should meet him on the stairs during one of these parades we curtsied humbly. That pleased him very much.

'One of the tenants—or should I say inmates—of the house was a sort of priest who wore a long black cassock, a funny mitre, and a cross on his chest. They called him André.

' "What sort of church does André belong to?" I asked one day. The question caused hilarity and I was given to understand that André had at one time been a parson in The Hague, but could not keep his ordained hands off minors of the same sex, and was defrocked. He then designed his own frock and began to canvass private houses for contributions. People assumed that he had something to do with a white Russian sect, for he always spoke in an undecipherable language that he had made up himself. This avoided difficulties, should he run into someone who spoke real Russian, red or white. He seemed to do quite well at his game; for two out of three nights he came home drunk.

'One night, at Marina's homo-club, we met a fellow in his late thirties, who was living with his mother on the third floor of a house on the Overtoom. In a moment of weak idiocy, Kobus had confessed to his mother that he only liked boys. From that moment on she threw whole sequences of fits and scenes whenever he wanted to go out alone at night. She always ended by threatening that one day she would jump out of the window.

' "Ha, ha!" we laughed. "Never heard of bluff? Never heard of blackmail? You let yourself be taken by that kind of hysterics? We're professional nurses. She'll never jump out the window. She just wants you to keep on being Mother's little helper. Next time she throws a fit like that and threatens, you just open the window and say, 'All right, go ahead and jump!' "

'His face was a visible mixture of doubt and hope. "You really think so?"

' "We're nurses, aren't we? Teach us something about hysterical patients!"

'A couple of weeks later I was called to the telephone: "It's someone called Kobus . . ."

' "Hello, Kobe, boy, what—?"

'Now he was the one having hysterics. "Now cool down!" I shouted through the horn. "What's the matter with you?"

'Sobbing and stuttering, he explained that he had been thinking about our advice. About his mother's fits and threats.

' "Yes, yes?" I asked.

'He related how he had finally screwed up the courage to do as we advised him, and had opened the window.

' "Yes?"

'He wailed. "And she jumped, Monique! She went and did it!"

'By this time Marina had come up and was listening in, her ear glued to the horn. We looked at each other, and she took the telephone while I raced back to our room, plopped down on the bed, and went into howls of laughter. A little while later Marina came in and joined me. Now it was her turn to have hysterics.

' "And she . . . ha ha ha . . . did it!"

' "She . . . she's in the Wilhelmina Hospital . . . ho ho ho . . . with a concussion. . . ."

' "Ha ha ha . . ."

' ". . . and a double fracture of the . . ."

' "Ho ho ho . . ."

' ". . . p— . . . p— . . . pelvis."

'By that time we were lying in each other's arms, tears streaming from our eyes. We ran into Kobus several times after that. He refused to talk to us.'

'If I give you the impression that during this time I was doing more horsing around than nursing around, that is pretty accurate. I felt that I wasn't cut out to be a nurse. But I certainly didn't visualize myself as a staid, happily married housewife either. By this time I was also sure that I would never and could never be a confirmed lesbian . . . so what else was there?

'I think it was Stephen Spender who wrote about (and I quote from memory): ". . . a working sea of indecision like the soul of a woman, making up her mind." And that, roughly, was the matter with me. One of the most lucidly intelligent men I have ever met later became a permanent client of mine, and I had several long, fascinating talks with him. I have never forgotten how he cleared up something that had me confused for a long time. I asked him to write it down for me and I still have it:

' "All human beings are subject to a desire for *construction*. Nearly everybody likes to construct, improve, or assemble things, whether this is a rail new fence, a toy house, a rock garden or just confines itself to the repainting of the garage doors. People simply derive a fairly uncomplicated satisfaction out of the construction or embellishment of something, however simply. Hence the use and usefulness of work therapy with unbalanced or mentally sick people. There is no tension or stress involved and either it keeps you 'normal' or it helps you to become 'normal' again.

' "But a *creative* urge is something completely different. It defines a capacity for construction to which a mad element of originality is *added*—is, so to say, superimposed on it. This may well be a constructive drive to find an entirely novel method of DESTRUC-

TION, as long as this operative element of originality is added. The creatively gifted person is always, somewhere in his psyche, essentially different from his merely constructive neighbor. He breaks away, sooner or later, from the existing order, habit, or trend and therefore has to be, to a smaller or larger extent, an originator, reformer, or revolutionary and will always be slightly mad, with a personal slant."

'Please do not get the impression that I am suggesting that I suffer from megalomania or feel myself a frustrated female Einstein. No, no, no. For me the whole meaning and sense lie in the sentence: "This may well be a constructive drive to find an entirely novel method of DESTRUCTION, as long as this operative element of originality is added."

'You see, at that time I did everything by instinct. I had no book, no religion, no teacher. I played life straight off my nurse's cuff. I had no cut-and-dried conscience, and was basically both immoral and amoral. The only thing I felt certain of was that I was suited to do something better than it had ever been done before. But I didn't know then what that thing was! And . . . Gonda wasn't there to help me. Several times I had rung her number, but had gotten no reply. That did not surprise or worry me. In some way, I felt, that was as it should be. I admired her so much; I looked up to her so much, that I did not expect her to be available when I wanted her. At that stage she was, to me, perhaps, something like a shooting star. So I had to figure it all out entirely on my own.

'Because I had lost my belief in my vocation, and at the same time was gradually being sucked into the human millrace of Amsterdam's mezzanine world, I began to take part-time jobs in hospitals more or less as my fancy moved me. I worked for two months in Marina's hospital and there I met two middle-aged nurses, X and Y, who began to fascinate me with their exalted stories of a new religious sect founded by an ex-shrimp fisherman who preached that he was the one and only true reincarnation of Jesus Christ on earth. He had a following, a very select following, they stressed, of exactly one hundred disciples, of whom ninety percent were women. When I asked them whether they belonged to the Chosen, I got evasive answers and dirty looks. But when they managed to get their hooks into Marina and managed to get her half converted, I thought it time that I took a good, hard look myself.

'One balmy evening in spring, Marina and I climbed the steep, bare stairs of a ramshackle house near the Haarlemmerdyk. We were received by two forty-ish women, one fat and one scrawny, who served us weak, undrinkable coffee. Normal small talk was discouraged, but I felt I was being scrutinized from head to foot. I was wearing my nurse's uniform, and perhaps it was because of that that I passed muster, for in about ten minutes we rose, left that house, and walked to an old house on the Singel, where there were more stairs to climb. And when we were admitted into a large, rather bare garret with about thirty people, mostly middle-aged women, sitting around on wooden benches sipping tea and lemonade.

'Under breath I began to hum: "Rum and Coca-Cola", which was a big hit right then, but Marina gave me a vicious kick in the ankle and snarled: "If you don't intend to behave, you'd better get out of here right now."

' "Jeez", I muttered. "You've certainly got it bad." And I grew even more curious. At that moment there was an excited stir—like in a chicken coop—and a woman burst into the room. "It's Brother! Brother is coming!"

'A man appeared in the open doorway and paused there, gazing around the assembled believers as Moses might have done, looking down from his mountain. He was a big, rough type, in dirty corduroy pants and a dark blue sweater. An ex-shrimp fisherman. After all . . . wasn't Saint Peter originally a fisherman? His eyes roamed from face to face and stopped on mine. I held his eyes for a little while and I knew he did not regard me as the holy Virgin Mary. Mary Madgalen, perhaps—before she got herself converted. But had not Saint Paul been a great sinner before he suddenly saw The Light?

'The man tore his reincarnated gaze away from me, advanced into the room, and lowered himself into a carved oak seat, the only decent piece of furniture in the place. In a stern voice he said: "Has the Bible reading taken place?"

'In some confusion the congregation explained they had taken the liberty to take time for tea and lemonade. His gaze came back to me.

' "Who are you? A new believer?"

' "No, no," I said, "just an interested guest."

'Jesus Christ reincarnate was served lemonade and surrounded by a flock of fawning, chattering women. The few men who were present just sat around with a helpless, hen-pecked look. They didn't look virile enough to wear a decent pair of horns. I nudged Marina: "Can I find a toilet somewhere?"

'I got a disapproving look. Evidently that kind of bodily activity was too profane for this exalted atmosphere.

' "Corridor. Last door on your right."

'The cubicle was as expected: a rickety wooden door, secured on the inside with a nail and a piece of string. A toilet bowl with yellow-brown sediment and no toilet paper. I always carried Kleenex, so I sat down contentedly, pulled down my red panties, and lit a cigarette.

'A floorboard in the corridor squeaked. Before I had time to take another puff, the door was torn open, breaking the string, and Jesus Christ stepped swiftly into the WC, pulling the door shut behind him. I just sat there gaping up at him, my mouth half open.

' "You want it, sister!" he growled, "I know your type."

'I hurriedly got up from my own humble throne, but he grabbed me by the shoulders, swung me around, raised my skirt as high as it would go, and I felt him fumbling with his trousers. I began to struggle, but now he had his fly open, one arm around my throat.

'I tore out of that smelly hole, rushed back to the holy congregation, and stopped just inside the door, waving my red panties and shouting: "Your holy Jesus Christ just pushed his prophetic prick into me in the toilet!" And with that I threw my panties at their faces. They fluttered down between the teacups and lay there. For a couple of seconds there was utter, frozen silence. Then the scrawny women who had brought us slowly rose and stuttered: "You . . . you whore of Babylon! Get out of here!"

'With a mad hoot of laughter I did precisely that, stomped down the flights of splintery wooden steps and straight into the nearest café where I had two double gin-and-oranges.

'When I came home, sometime after midnight, Marina was waiting for me with a stiff face. "If you suppose that I'm ever going to introduce you anywhere—ever again!"

'I snapped back: "Your Christ Almighty did all the introducing I'll ever need of that sort," and went to bed. Next day I went to look for work in another hospital. I did not want to be confronted with the religio-manic faces of Nurse X and Nurse Y.'

'I had heard about a place that was always desperately short of nurses. It was hidden away on the outskirts of the city, stashed alongside a dike, among rusty cranes and discarded machinery. It consisted of some wooden barracks heated with old-fashioned coal stoves and its function was to let poor and lonely people die under a roof instead of in the streets—or in a city hospital, where they would take up space that could be used for other purposes. Who decided what purposes, I never found out. Not to be too unfair, I must say that most of the people there were hopeless cases anyway, and they died off like flies. In eight hours, three out of a ward of seventy was nothing. Most of them were kept quiet with weak solutions of morphine or other sedatives. All that hopeless suffering, in the poverty, misery, and squalor of those unpainted barracks and their Siberian surroundings produced a marked reaction among the nursing personnel. The very worst cases were handled by professional male attendants, most of whom had seen worse during the war, with bombardments and the later cleaning out of concentration camps. In that kind of work you can keep your spirits only through religious fanaticism or its opposite: resorting to your basic animal nature. We were familiar with the usual run of doctor and undertaker jokes, but they were Winnie the Pooh stuff compared to what we thought up there.

'There was one patient who had outlived all the others. He shouldn't have been there in the first place; an administrative error. He had chronic asthma, but I guess that's nothing to laugh at. There were days when he couldn't do anything but sit in his bed, using all his strength to try to pump air into his lungs. He had an oxygen apparatus by his bed marked FOR ACUTE EMERGENCY ONLY, but how define "acute emergency"? When one of us took pity on him we gave him the nozzle and turned on the cylinder, but the head nurse—I'll never forget her name: Van Voorden—was a pious Roman Catholic with mean pig eyes. When she saw the oxygen turned on, she closed the tap, hung up the nozzle, and explained, in a soothing, unctuous voice that made me want to throttle her and stamp my heels in her face: "Come, come, Mister Jansen. Are we acting up again? We must show some spirit, mustn't we? We cannot be weaklings and cost the community too much money." As if she had to pay for it out of her own pocket, dammit. Sometimes Jansen flew into a terrific rage, when the oxygen had given him enough breath to scream at her. "You lousy, dried-up cunt! You parson-fucker! See those sea gulls flying outside? When I'm dead I'll come back as a sea gull, follow you everywhere, and shit on your hateful face!"

'By then he had used up all his breath, and subsided, whooping and keening. He always found new insults. I suppose he thought them up during those miserable hours when he sat pumping for air. But his final threat to come back as a sea gull after his death . . . he never varied that; it was like the fate motif in a symphony of retribution.

'I wouldn't have stuck it long there except that I had become very thick with a certain Frieda, a healthy, straightforward, Frisian nurse, full of life and fun. She used that rare combination of primitive strength and health coupled with a mad and morbid sense of humor. When she was in the right mood she could come up with sick jokes and perverse puns that left even the tough male attendants behind.

'She had found out that the operator of the only crane still in operation in Amsterdam was a confirmed homosexual, and she knew no peace until she had made a date with his young boy friend, Appie. She took me along to meet him in a coffee shop. Just for curiosity's sake. She simply had to know what the two of them did together up there in the cabin of that crane. Appie supplied us with all the details. "Oh, darlings", he gushed, "it's really out of this world, sitting up there in that crane and making it swoop around and looking down on everything and everyone and me sitting on his lap and then feeling him coming into me, with me at the controls. . . . There's nothing that can beat that."

'Frieda and I soon teamed up. She didn't like straightforward fucking much, but occasionally the two of us masturbated one of the male attendants. "Blowing Off Steam", we called it, and we did it in the damnedest places—for kicks.

'But my nursing time was running out, though I didn't know it. One stormy, wet afternoon we found a dead sea gull that was only slightly smelly and that gave us a brilliant idea. We knew that head nurse Van Voorden always left at a certain time and bicycled home along the dike. We hid behind a deserted warehouse, Frieda holding the sea gull by one leg, and waited there until we saw Van Voorden coming, pedaling hard against the wind and rain. When she was very close, I cupped my hands around my mouth and produced some very spooky and eerie screeches. At the same time, Frieda, wearing a white cloth with little holes in it over her head, jumped out of hiding and threw our sea gull into Van Voorden's detestable face.

' "You lousy witch! Here I am! Jansen's come to get you?"

'We were more successful than we had bargained for. As the gull smashed into her face, Van Voorden threw up her hands, lost control of the bike, and the gusty wind blew her off the top of the dike wall. The last thing we saw of her that day was a confused tumble of wheels, arms, and legs disappearing down the steep slope on the other side. We raced away around the back of the warehouse and made our way into town where we celebrated with hot toddies and a movie.

'When we came back at midnight everything was in an uproar. Van Voorden had broken an ankle and lay there, in the rain and the wind, for more than two hours before she was found. Mad Frieda had told several people what she intended to do, and of course she didn't even bother to deny it; in fact, said that she would do it again, and then sailed out in the middle of the night with one suitcase and her coat billowing. No one mentioned me. Frieda, of course, kept mum.

'The next day, Marina came by in weeping hysterics. Her mother had been admitted to the Leeuwenhoek Hospital with terminal cancer.

'And that did it. I just couldn't take it anymore. I didn't even bother to give notice or think about the salary due me, I just packed my suitcase and walked out of there.

'I had been living on my earnings, so there was still all that money in the bank in Brussels. When I got home, Marina was gone. I stripped off my uniform, put on my nicest dress, made up my face, and went straight to the homo-club in the Rozenstraat. At least I was sure to meet some amusing and gay people there. And that's exactly what I needed, for I had all of a sudden remembered that I had never asked for Frieda's home address. I knew she lived somewhere in Amsterdam West, but that was all. With Frieda around I could have stuck it out. All by myself . . . no.'

'A couple of days later when I again dropped by the Rozenstraat homo-club for a drink and a chat, a tall, slightly drunk but nonetheless elegant woman—slightly older than I—sat down at my table. She planted her elbows, put her chin in the palms of her hands, and sat looking at me.

' "You are Monique, aren't you?"

'I took a sip of sherry. "That's what I'm called, yes."

' "I've been watching you for weeks. You are the person I've been looking for. I'll make you a straight proposition. I want to keep you."

'I didn't get it right away, and the only answer I could find was: "But you haven't got me yet."

' "Funny", she said, her chin still in her hands. "I detest stupid women. We are made for one another, I think. What I mean is: I am fairly wealthy, so I can afford to be choosy. You are a nurse, aren't you?"

'I replied, a bit absent-mindedly: "I think I was a nurse."

' "Fed up?"

' "To the gills."

'She nodded slightly, as if that confirmed what she had been thinking. "I have a three-storey house in Haarlem. It's my own property. You can have your own car plus a regular allowance per month. To buy clothes with."

' "And I am to sleep with you?"

'She had lovely, gray-green cat's eyes, and I saw them narrowing slightly. "Yes, you sleep with me. And with no one else."

'I let out a sad sigh: "Ah . . . I knew there was a catch in it somewhere."

'I felt her wavering between fury and amusement. She decided she had better be amused. So she laughed, straightened up, and ordered more drinks. "Listen, darling, I just wanted to see how you would react. Why don't you meet me in town tomorrow and we'll have lunch? No strings attached. My name is Sonja, by the way."

' "All right", I said. "Where and when?"

' "Eleven o'clock. In the bar at Dikker and Thys. We can have lunch there or upstairs. Have you ever been there?"

' "Never." It was one of the oldest and most stylish bar-restaurants in Holland.

'She nodded and said, in a sort of aside: "I dislike people who make a habit of being late."

' "I am never late, dear Sonja."

'She raised her hand and a waiter came running. She paid, nodded to me, and walked out of there. I watched her go. Quite an operator. She reminded me of Gonda. WHAT THE HELL HAD HAPPENED TO GONDA? I went to the phone and rang her number. No reply. She hadn't answered for God knows how long. But someone had to be paying the telephone bill, or it would have been cut off long ago. I shrugged and went home.'

'My lesbian-on-the-make had clearly made up her mind to be charming. Well, she was. Amusing, too. We had a fantastic lunch, with glorious white wine and over the coffee and Armagnac she said:

"Darling, will you let me do something for you? With no strings attached?"

'What with the wine, the liqueur, and her charm, I felt ready for anything. "What are you plotting now?"

' "Just . . . Would you mind if I bought you some clothes? I would really love it, you know. I saw a hat that would be absolutely perfect on you. With a half veil all around. Please, Monique!"

'Well, why not? I was quite prepared to concede that her taste in clothes was a sight better than mine. I still had a lot to learn.

' "I'm game", I said.

'She banged her glass down and caught the waiter's eye. "Fine. But let's have some more Armagnac first."

'I was beginning to realize that she was quite a boozer. Lots of them are, you know. And at that time, drugs were something you had only heard about. If you had a psychological problem you drowned it in alcohol or sexed it away.

'She rapidly downed three more glasses of that wonderful liqueur, paid the bill, and walked out as straight and upright as a guardsman, with me in her wake, feeling dowdy and frumpy. Yes, I could do with some proper clothes.

'Well, I almost got them. She worked from the head down. We bought the hat first, went to a nearby bar, had some whiskey sours, ordered a taxi, and were whisked to an exclusive shop. Everyone seemed to know her, and she ordered people around as if she was born to be obeyed. But then, maybe because of all that liqueur, she began to . . . not actually throw her weight around, but to behave pretty high-handedly. Now, I'll occasionally take that from an honest-to-god straightforward man, but never from a woman. So when she finally made up her mind and decided that I must have a truly magnificent, very simple, powder blue ensemble which normally I would have done anything to get, I suddenly got a perverse streak and refused to accept it.

' "Now, don't be so stubborn and self-willed", Sonja said curtly. "That ensemble was made for you. And it will make you, too."

'I snapped back: "I am perfectly happy the way I am."

'We stood with our eyes locked, and to everybody around us it was clear that this was a battle of wills. If Sonja had been sober, or had a bit less to drink, she would have tactfully eased out of the situation, backed down temporarily, and then renewed her attack later. But she was getting impatient and irritated because she wanted to get out of there and have another drink. So she snapped: "For God's sake, make up your mind or I'll have to do it for you."

'I sat down on one of those fragile gilt chairs with a great show of cool: "That will not be necessary. I don't want it and I won't wear it. Shall we go?"

'As my uncertainty began to wear thin, my real toughness began to show. I had called her bluff and now there was not a damned thing she could do, and she knew it. To offer me something else was put of the question. We stared at each other in complete silence, then she turned and stalked out of the shop.

'In my nicest voice I said: "Good afternoon, and thank you for all your trouble." I was prepared to lay ten to one that I wasn't the first daisy she had tried to buy clothes for.

'She was waiting outside, looking in a show window. The moment I came out she turned on her heel and said, from one corner of her mouth: "Let's go and have a quiet drink and talk this over."

'To this day I can recall the exultation that ran through my entire being. It had nothing at all to do with sex . . . I think. It was a sense of sheer power, of having won a battle. Of having imposed my own will on someone else. And the ecstasy was all the greater because Sonja was herself a real power. As I walked beside her, I was thinking: I've got you by the balls now, sister.

'Those seemingly minor episodes are like the tops of psychological icebergs. Now I realized that I could use my will, the pure power of my will to defeat and dominate. I was learning that these significant incidents always happened at critical stages in my life. A year earlier I couldn't have done it. I would have been too awed by Sonja, too unsure of myself. A year later I had already progressed to a stage where no woman, wealthy or not, would have dared attempt that kind of proposition. But in that period of transition I was still in an intermediate stage of development. The number of guns I carried didn't show yet. Years later I made the mistake of flaunting the guns I carried. Until I found out how silly that was, for it enables your enemies to size you up at once. Women have taught me a lot, but so have men, too.

'A naval officer I knew had a lucid thing to say about this: "Every naval officer dreams of making his battleship look like a minesweeper and then having his enemy come into close range. And then letting go with one perfect broadside."

'By that time it was about five in the afternoon, and Sonja led me into another expensive-looking bar, where I had never been before. But where, obviously, everybody knew her. She plunked her tight, aristocratic ass down on a bar stool and peremptorily ordered two whiskey sours. Not bothering to ask me what I wanted.

'I changed the order, and took some money out of my bag: "These are on me. I'll have a sherry instead of a whiskey sour."

'Sonja got up and said, again out of the corner of her mouth: "I have to go to the loo. And make a telephone call."

'There was a tall man sitting next to me, a highball in front of him. He half turned to look after Sonja, then turned to me and said in an amused voice: "How did you get mixed up with that dyed-in-the-wool dyke? She's probably masturbating over the telephone with some girl friend. That's one of her games. I like your face. And that hat. Why don't we get out of here and go dancing at Zandvoort? They just reopened the beach hotel there."

'Nothing could have suited me better. The man, Eric, plunked down some money, winked at the bartender, took my elbow, and steered me outside.'

'He had a brand new diesel Mercedes parked on the Leidseplein. In those years that was really impressive. In my new hat and with my newly realized sense of power I felt I was really impressive, too. I began to cotton onto an idea that had been nudging away at the edge of my consciousness; when you begin to move in circles where people have money, you can get much more with no extra effort.

'I relaxed in the front seat and he began to chat. Nonchalantly, pleasantly, with a sense of ironic humor that I understood perfectly. He told me he was a lawyer with an office on the Heerengracht. Recently divorced, ex-Catholic. We danced, had some drinks, had a bite to eat and it was all nice, gay, unmessy fun. Then he said:

' "This may sound crazy to you, but I have an appointment at midnight. With a businessman who arrives at Schiphol airport in a couple of hours. Do you mind if I take you home?"

' "Good Lord, of course not."

'We zoomed back in the Mercedes, Eric chatting away. When we entered Amsterdam he asked—throwing it away: "May I have a cup of coffee or something at your place?"

'That was the last thing in the world I wanted. I already had enough trouble with Marina, who had gotten herself involved with two detestable lezzies, and the damnedest people were dropping in at the most inopportune moments.

'I laughed gaily: "That's not such a good idea. The girl I room with is a confirmed lesbian, too."

'He answered rather gruffly: "How the bloody hell did you get mixed up with that bunch?"

' "Oh, that's a long story. But no one forced me into it." After a pregnant pause—isn't that the expression?—I added: "But there's one thing you spotted right . . . right from the start: I am not a les myself."

'He kept his eyes straight ahead: "But you tried it?"

' "Oh, yes. I'm naturally inquisitive, I guess."

'That seemed to satisfy him. At the next intersection he tapped the steering wheel as if a bright idea had suddenly struck him: "Why . . . we can have a nightcap at my office! Perhaps you would like to see it, anyway."

'Yes. One of those stately ex-mansions on the Heerengracht. Hardstone steps outside, marble hall inside. Carved oak bannisters.

'That may not sound so impressive to you, in the States, but a large part of the unique architecture of those merchant mansions derives from the fact that Holland has no natural stone, except for some soft sandstone in the extreme south. The Dutch had to work with brick. Everything else had to be imported by sailing ship or cart. But in order to manufacture the kind of hard-baked brick that lasts for centuries you need a lot of fuel, and Holland has no oil or coal, either. How they did it is still a source of wonder.

'He waved his arm: "Sorry, my dear. Inherited, not earned. I think there's some wine here somewhere."

'He thought. He had a complete wine cellar in a colossal antique cabinet. I dropped into a genuine old leather chair—the kind that get that lovely color from a century of oiling and waxing. He came back with a tray with an assortment of foreign cheeses. What did I feel right then? This is life, Monique . . . you were never cut out to be a housewife with a flock of sniveling brats.

'While he poured the wine and peeled the foil off the cheese, he began, very adroitly, to ask me questions. He hadn't done that before. Until I kicked my shoes off and said:

' "It must be something in the atmosphere here. Stop behaving like a *juge d'instruction*, and sit down and tell me funny stories."

'For a moment a look of surprise flitted across his face. Then he grinned, put down his glass, went to a wall cupboard, opened it, and pulled down a folding bed. Two minutes later we were fucking away like foxes. That is, I panted, grunted, said some dirty words, and moved my hips in time with his rhythm. He roared when he reached his climax, and I gave a few rutty cries that I had picked up from the cats who owned all the roofs of Amsterdam.

'It's so ridiculously easy to fool a man. Even a clever man like him. I had certainly learned a lot since I left the parental nest. I paid myself a special compliment. What other girl would have the inventiveness to borrow her so-called orgasmic cries from alley cats? They had certainly convinced him! If that was all it took to be a wonderful fuck, then what was all the shouting about? With a faint tinge of regret I came to the conclusion that men in general are colossal fools where women are concerned.

'Why the regret? Because in some faraway corner of my psyche I still had a lingering, old fashioned idea of someday, somewhere running into a man I could look up to, who would cherish and protect me . . . who would bring me flowers at odd moments and . . . who could make me come in bed in a normal way. A man to whom I could surrender. With body and soul.

'Eric took me home in the Mercedes.

' "You are a nice child, Monique. If ever you need me, or need some legal advice, just ring my office."

'In later years I often needed legal advice. When I rang him up then he invariably said: "A good lawyer never gives advice over the telephone. Why don't you drop by?"

'And just as invariably we followed up with the traditional routine: a bottle of wine, the foreign cheese, the folding bed, the wild fuck, and my caterwauling cries deftly synchronized with his ejaculation. When his secretary was in the next office, I caterwauled into his coat. It smothered the sound very effectively and it gave him an extra kick.'

'There's an inescapable, fateful logic to life. From that week on I really started to move.

'One day I was in the Leidestraat, doing some light shopping when I saw Frieda in a taxi waiting at a traffic light. I gave a colossal yell and jumped between two cars, just as the light turned green. But she had seen me and directed her taxi to turn into the next side street.

' "Frieda, how are you! What happened to you? I didn't have your address. . . . What a lovely coat!" I rattled away, and she just sat grinning at me through the open window.

'When I paused for breath, she said: "Get in, you crazy girl. We'll have coffee and pastry in Formosa. With all those old, sour, rich bitches. I have a lot to tell you."

'Over the best coffee in Amsterdam and delicious French pastry, she looked at me with a new twinkle in her eyes. I was dead sure she was up to some fresh deviltry, but much as I wanted to know all about it, I kept mum. Till she asked: "Von Cleef, what does a qualified nurse earn?"

'I stared at her: "Dammit, you should know."

' "No, I want to hear you say it. With my own Frisian ears."

' "Well, in private practice, about a hundred every two weeks."

'She blossomed into a devilish grin, got up and made a pirouette, her skirt swirling and arms spread. Right in the middle of that room full of expensive fur-coated bitches.

' "I make that in a day. Look at me."

'She certainly looked it. A hundred a day. How did a girl like Frieda, who was certainly no beauty, make a hundred a day?

'She leaned forward and said, under her breath: "I work in a massage parlor."

'I tried to digest that. "You have to have a diploma?"

'She got a piece of pastry down the wrong way. Leaned forward again: "The house is run by two male homosexuals. One is a masseur and the other runs the place.

' "Frieda, you think they would have a job for me?"

'She signalled to the waitress. "Give me your address. I'll ask about it tonight. In any case, you'll hear from me, I promise you that." '

'One good thing about those northern girls: when they promise to do something, they do it. I was at home, reading and listening to the radio, when the bell rang.

' "It's me. Frieda!"

'She was in a hurry, and panting. "I have a taxi waiting with a customer. I told them about you and gave my personal guarantee that you are the real McCoy. You start Monday at nine. Here's the address. Haarlemmerstraat. See you Monday. . . ." and she was gone.'

'I was still in a daze when the door opened again and there was Marina, carrying two suitcases. Behind her loomed a big carthorse of a girl, wearing soiled jeans and a dirty white transparent blouse that showed a pair of enormous udders that she must have been proud of, for she wore no bra.

' "My new friend", Marina announced proudly. Dumped one suitcase on my bed, opened it, and took out some bottles of dark Belgian beer. They sat down at the table across from each other, drinking and talking in mysterious allusions. It was obvious that I was being deliberately ignored and excluded. Well, that suited me. I took my coat, went out, and saw a movie. Then I went to a bar and had a couple of beers. When I neared home I saw that the light was out. Excellent. I listened outside our door. Heavy panting and groaning, even yelping. If I had picked up my rut sounds from cats, there was no doubt where The Fat One had learned hers: wolf bitches. I stood in silence for a moment, undecided what to do. Then I turned away and made a beeline for the Park Hotel.

' "A room with bath, please. I'll pay in advance."

' "Certainly, Miss."

' "And breakfast when I ring for it."

' "Quite, Miss."

'The times that other people could push me around were fast disappearing.'

'It didn't take us long to reach a showdown. When I came home about one o'clock the next day they were lying on Marina's bed without a stitch on and all the lights still burning. I stood and looked around me.

' "What are you two playing at? The Black Hole of Calcutta? This whole room reeks of cunt and stale beer." I started emptying ashtrays, opening curtains and windows.

' "The lady does not like our ways", Marina said with that needling laugh that can really get under your skin.

' "This lady is NOT a tramp", I cracked back. "And there's a lot of tramp in here. About two hundredweight, I'd say. You better have the springs of that bed reinforced."

'The Fat One reared up like an angry sea elephant, udders swinging. "If you don't like it here, why don't you get out and go live somewhere else?"

'Ah, I felt that hot ecstasy spreading through me. She wanted a fight, did she? In any fight I was out to win, I had the WILL to win. Attack! I sat calmly on the edge of the table, leaned slightly forward and looked straight into her bulgy eyes. I spoke softly but clearly: "Listen good, you unwashed cow. You are too lazy to work, too stupid for blackmail, and too ridiculous to earn dry bread in an honest cathouse. You may think you took that neurotic piece away from me, but let me tell you: no one takes anything away from me. You can have my discards, and you should be damned pleased to get them. Lick each other all day and night, maybe it'll clean you up. But remember this: I pay rent, four-fifths of everything here was paid for by me. That weepy bag went to pieces months ago. She doesn't earn enough to buy sanitary napkins for two. I'll stop our credit with the baker, the grocer, and in the café on the corner. When you get really hungry, we'll talk."

'There was complete silence. I took my suitcase and began to pack what I needed for a week. Then Marina began to wail: "Oh, darling . . . what did I ever do to you to deserve this?" That continued for quite some time. When I had the door open, my suitcase in my fist, I said, over my shoulder: "What you'd better do, Marina, is pull yourself together. You're going to pieces. But fast." '

'I did it too. Stopped all our credit. Told them I wasn't going to pay for anything that I hadn't bought myself. Then I went straight back to the Park Hotel. I didn't care what it cost. I had money in the bank, and my new life would start on Monday. There is a very strange thing about power: when you have it, there always comes a time when you MUST use it. If you don't, it becomes rusty, wastes away. You lose the ability to make it work, to handle it. This appears to be one of the laws of nature. Not long ago I was reading Churchill's war speeches. There's one line I will never forget. When he took over from that doddering umbrella-fool Chamberlain, he said in a speech to the Houses of Parliament: "In nineteen-eighteen we had victory in our hands . . . and like the fools we were, we threw it all away." If you don't use your power people will think you a fool, a coward, or a softie. And to rectify that misunderstanding will cost you ten times more trouble and nastiness than if you had shown your teeth in the first place. Yes, Mistress.'

'On Monday morning at five to nine I ring the bell of a quite ordinary-looking house in the Haarlemmerstraat. A tall, bony man in his forties opens up: "Ah, you must be Monique. Come in, dearie. Frieda is waiting for you."

'He leads me down a long hall and throws open a door. I look into the happy, grinning face of Frisian Frieda.

' "I have coffee ready. Today I'll teach you the ropes. Tomorrow you can go to work on your own in the next room."

'I look around. Everything spotlessly clean. A white enameled operating table with a sheet over it, stacks of white towels, a brand-new washbasin, and some steel chairs. A hospital couldn't have looked better.

' "I forgot to tell you to bring a long-sleeved apron. Borrow one of mine."

'While I'm getting into it, there's a knock on the door. First customer? No—an old man carrying a tray with two steaming cups of coffee and two cream buns. He nods and goes away. Frieda explains: "She—he—is the female partner. Cooks, cleans the house, and takes better care of me than my mother ever did. Another thing I forgot to tell you: he likes cooking, so the food is free here, and damned good, too. Listen now, our fee is ten a spout. Six go to the house, and four into our pockets. We can keep all tips and extras and the tips often are more than our fee. There's the bell—first customer."

'She ushers in a hefty man with flaming red hair.

' "Fred", Frieda introduces me, "this is the new masseuse. I'm teaching her. All right?"

'He nods amicably, and undresses while Frieda spreads a towel across the work table. He lies down, buttocks up. I see red hair sprouting between them.

' "Monique, you stand on the other side of the table and do exactly as I do. We'll give our Freddy double value for his money."

'He laughs in happy anticipation. Frieda sprinkles talcum powder on his back and begins kneading him, with me following her lead: shoulders, back, the muscles along his spine, his buttocks. And hardly in solemn silence. Oh, no. Frieda chats away happily and makes jokes, for all the world like the conversation in a men's barbershop. All at once she winks at me, spreads the man's legs apart, and lets the tips of her fingers walk up his anus valley to where his spine begins, then back to his scrotum; tickling and wiggling. All the while chatting and laughing. For the life of me I can't understand how any man could be expected to get really excited with two girls giggling and chattering above his bare ass, but Frieda seems to know what she's doing, so I follow suit.

' "Now you do it all by yourself", Frieda says, and stands watching with an impish look on her face while I begin to experiment. I soon get the hang of it: every time I do something especially stimulating, the man's body reacts. It doesn't take me long to excite him to a state of groaning unrest.

' "Okay, Fred", says Frieda, "now turn around."

'He flops onto his back and lies there with a penis like a totem pole.

' "You have a really good one on this morning", Frieda says approvingly. "Two girls are better than a pound of starch, huh?" She reaches behind her, grabs a bottle of olive oil, and gently lubricates the length of his penis, then gently begins to shove the loose skin up and down. I am leaning way over, watching intently. I have always been conscientious that way—eager to learn to do everything right. After he had come, he got dressed, whistling gaily.

' "You two are a pair of real dolls. Here—share this." He hands Frieda three tens.

'She sees him to the door and when she comes back I am laughing hysterically, the tears running down my face.

' "F . . . Frieda—that's not the kind of massage they taught us in nursing school."

' "Here's twelve for you. Today we share everything fifty-fifty. The boss says anything goes except straight fucking."

'The bell rings. "Here's our number two."

'She comes back with a boy hardly out of his teens, who looks shyly around.

' "I, uh . . . can I have a . . . massage here? I mean . . ."

' "The fee is ten guilders", says Frieda. "The size of the tip is left to the customer's discretion. Take your clothes off, will you? . . . You see"—she winks at me—"our slogan is: We aim to satisfy."

'I clap my hand over my mouth, swallow my rising laughter, and move my hand up and down in a well-known gesture. Say: "Ask the man who owns one."

'Frieda spins around and begins to blow her nose. By now our boy has stripped and now he turns around, showing a nice-looking prick, in a healthy state of ascendancy. He looks down at it, then back at us, and actually blushes.

' "My, my", says Frieda, stroking it admiringly. "That's one of the finest I've seen in a long time. Don't you agree, Monique?"

'I bend over and go tut tut, as if I were approving a new baby.

'The boy looks down again, prouder now. "You girls really think so?"

' "Oh, yes!" we breathe. "So stiff."

' "And what a nice color. And big, too. Now you lie down here. Nono . . . on your belly first. It works better that way, you'll see. Just leave everything to us."

' "Not everything", I say.

'Frieda and I go to work. The boy asks her: "Are you from Friesland?"

' "From Leeuwarden. I was born there."

'They soon discover that they were born practically around the corner from each other. He tells us that he got this address from an ad in the paper. I glance at Frieda.

' "Yes", she says, "anyone is allowed to run a massage parlor, a turkish bath, or anything like that. Look in the paper tonight."

'This gives me something to think about while giving the boy his warm-up. All at once Frieda stops, taps him: "Turn over. . . ."

'He does, and we see a large wet place on the towel.

' "Couldn't you hold it any longer?"

'The boy grins: "I didn't know how it was supposed to work. I'll be back this afternoon." He gives us each a two-and-a-half tip. For the next three days, he comes twice a day and tips us the same each time.

'At seven o'clock we close down for the day, count the kitty, and find we each have ninety-four guilders. Then we clean up a bit, go downstairs, and find a lovely meal waiting for us.

'At eight o'clock we are standing on the sidewalk under the stars.

' "Shall we get some coffee somewhere?"

' "The very thing." She puts her arm through mine.

'Walking along in step with her, I say, reflecting: "Ninety-four clear profit. I used to work myself to death for two weeks to earn that much."

'She is serious for a change: "In that last hell-hole they died like rats, and here they go away full of life. . . ."

' "Ha ha! And lighter than when they came in."

' "Buy some smocks tomorrow as soon as the shops open, and be there at half-past nine. You'll work by yourself tomorrow. See you." '

'That next day we each worked in our own room and chatted when our slack periods coincided. The old queen spoiled us with tea, coffee, and a gorgeous hot supper.

' "Are you tired?" Frieda asked over the veal cutlets.

'I stared at her: "Tired? From what? Stroking ass?"

'In the next six days I made about five hundred guilders. When I sauntered home to my hotel I found Marina waiting for me with a chastened and woebegone air. To this day I don't know how she found out where I was staying.

' "What now?"

' "Oh, Monique! I am so desperately sorry. You were right and I was a complete fool. I kicked her out two days ago and ever since then. . . ." She began to weep right there in the street. I quickly glanced around.

' "Come on, we'll have a drink somewhere. But for Mike's sake get hold of yourself."

'She calmed down soon enough when she found out I was prepared to talk. I took her to one of the hundreds of Amsterdam cafés called brown cafés, because of the centuries-old patina of smoke and alcohol fumes that thrive on quiet drunks and snivelling women.

'Oh, those wonderful Amsterdam cafés! They come in all shapes and sizes. You can spend your whole life in them and never get bored. Many of them refuse to serve even coffee—or sausage or cheese. Too much trouble. The old, tired, flat-footed owner will serve you anything that's drunk from a glass. Those cafés are strictly for professional boozers, diet boozers. There was one I particularly loved, near the old jail on the Amstelveense Weg. Just-released convicts and con-men made it their first stop. And for a girl on her own it was probably the safest place in the whole town, a lot safer than those lousy, expensive, imitation nightclubs.

' "I promise to behave, Monique. I really will. I know that you don't love me, but please come back. I can't bear being alone." And the poor girl burst out weeping all over again. I patted her hair. With Frieda I would probably have stroked it, but I was afraid Marina would make the wrong interpretation of that. She was a neurotic and a lesbian and a fool and all that, but . . . she hadn't exactly had a happy childhood, and she had never played me any dirty tricks.

' "All right", I said, "we'll go home and get the place cleaned up. Get the smell out."

'She looked up radiantly: "I've done that already. All by myself."

'I noticed that she looked a bit pinched. "Listen, have you had any hot food today?"

'Tears again. "I've hardly eaten anything for two days. I got my last money from empty bottles."

'I began to laugh and cuffed her lightly around the ears: "Run along home. I'll get my suitcase and be there in an hour. Here's some money. Buy what you need."

' "But the shops are closed."

' "The delicatessen, you idiot. You can spend it all." '

'Tuesday morning I bought an icebox, a luxury I had been pining for as long as I could remember. I paid cash. The week after that I rented a deposit box and began to stash cash away. Marina behaved like a good girl. She even began to look around for a job. Hopeful signs of returning normalcy.

'One evening she asked: "You're very happy in your new job, huh?"

' "Oh, yes."

' "What do you do exactly?"

'Like a fool I told her. She nearly screamed the house down. "They're making a filthy whore out of you!"

' "Pipe down or I'll throw a bucket of water in your hysterical face. Copulation isn't even allowed." I explained the technicalities. "Aren't you happy with the icebox and the new phonograph? Besides, I am saving up for a second-hand car."

'She gaped at me as if I had promised her paradise with bells on. "You really mean that?"

' "Don't you know me by now? A couple more weeks and I can pay cash. I hate debts."

'She brooded for a bit, then said: "As long as you don't let yourself. . . . Don't let a man do it to you. I couldn't bear that. Not sleeping with you is bad enough, but that would be too much to take. I mean that." '

'Completely out of the blue there was a tremendous row between Frieda and one of the homos. It started over nothing, but within ten minutes had mushroomed into a brawl and wound up with Frieda yelling: "I'll never set foot in this lousy hole again!" You know how Frisians are: once they've said a thing like that, even in anger, there's not a power in the world that can make them change their stubborn minds. And out of sheer solidarity I walked out with her.

We got good and drunk together. Then I took three weeks off and did something that had been on my mind from the very first: I took a couple of courses, showed my nurse's certificate, and finally pocketed my official diploma as graduate face- and body-masseuse. A certificate is a certificate, and in our over-administrated Europe they set a lot of store by those official papers.

'Between one thing and another I was more out of the house than in, and had been seeing very little of Marina, only vaguely noticing that she was getting moodier and moodier.

'One evening as I walked home, I saw her parading up and down the sidewalk in front of our house. The moment she saw me she rushed up to me.

' "Monique, can I talk to you? Let's go to the café around the corner."

'God, the talks that café must have witnessed. . . . We had hardly sat down at the rickety table, our sherries in front of us, when she took a deep breath and came out with it:

' "Monique, I can't take this any more. I've been thinking about it for weeks. You can have your choice: either you buy the Volkswagen you promised me, this week, and register it in my name, or you'll have to leave and go live somewhere else."

'I sipped my sherry and lit a cigarette. Then blew the smoke into her ridiculous face, and asked: "Who's behind this?"

' "W . . . what do you mean?"

' "You don't have the guts or the brains to think up a thing like this on your own. I never told you, but I accidentally found out a couple of things about your heroic role in the—haha—underground. And why here? Why were you walking up and down in front of the house like a sentry? Who's in there?"

'She sat looking at me with a white, stricken face. A horrible suspicion welled up in me.

' "Oh, no. Not The Fat One?"

' "Y . . . yes. It's Ina."

'I emptied my glass and ordered a second drink. Then said: "This is the end of the road, you know."

'She gave a gulp and brought out her pre-rehearsed line: "I have a list here of what everything is worth. You say how you want to divide it."

'I said nothing for some time. I had roomed with her for years, we had had our laughs together, our financial troubles, had helped each other out. I felt great pity, some anger, and a lot of contempt. And under all that, a tremendous emptiness. I remember wondering vaguely if this is how a mother feels when she loses a child. But then, even children can blackmail you. . . .

' "Marina, you are a piker. You were born to be small fry and you'll never get any bigger. Remember the saying: Who's born to be a dime will never be a dollar. You can keep the whole caboodle. Get that lump of blubber out of there for a couple of hours and I'll pack my clothes. But I want my records. And now get out fast, before I change my mind. And come back and tell me when you've got her out of there. I don't want to come face to face with that fat vampire." '

'Where did I go with my suitcases? Right: the Park Hotel. It would have been easy to find a less expensive hotel, but in a certain respect it was good training. You see, wherever I went, even when I came down early to eat breakfast in the dining room, men tried to pick me up. Not because I dressed sexily or anything like that, but simply because I had what it takes. And a young woman on her own, in a hotel. . . . But by that time I had sense enough to know that I had only to make one wrong move and I would be politely asked to leave. I mean: professionally you should never even try to make a hotel your base of opertion, or every hotel in the world would be a whorehouse before you could say "cock". So I took great care to behave like a nun on vacation. During meals there I kept my eyes on my plate or on a newspaper, and I never entered the bar. As a result I was treated with polite respect. Hotel personnel know a hell of a lot, and I would have been surprised if they hadn't had their suspicions about me, but as long as I stuck rigidly to the unwritten rules, I think they actually liked me the more for that. Now and then I caught a faint glance of amused understanding from the head receptionist. . . .

'With my new massage diploma in my bag I rang up Blond Henny's massage parlor on the Sloterkade, and was immediately hired.

'The proprietress, a middle-aged but still juicy ex-whore who had had the sense to get out of the rat race, lined her four girls up in a row the morning I arrived. I was the fourth in her stable. Then she distributed ten condoms per head. Excuse me, per cunt.

'I stood there with the things in my open hand and said: "I never fuck. This is a massage parlor, isn't it?"

'She looked me up and down and the other girls gave me pitying looks. Then she shrugged: "I'll be interested to see how many customers you're going to keep."

'When I closed shop at ten o'clock that evening I paused for some deep breaths of wet, fresh air, and glanced across the rippling canal . . . straight at the faded door of the house where I had once worked for a mere pittance—the house where I had found those 8,000 guilders under that urine-soaked mattress.'

'The only girl there that I could get along with was nicknamed Fat Flossie. She was tops in popularity, but very soon I had built up my own following, and rated a close second. But I was never really accepted. According to their standards, I "held out", and they suspected me of being a lesbian, working with my hands to keep a private girl friend. They were straightforward fuckers, and in their way they honestly delivered the goods. Which I did not. I did not seriously attempt to wise them up.

'Came the day when the whole house was in an uproar, for not one toilet, not one washbasin would work. The entire ground floor was two inches deep in stinking water. A platoon of plumbers went to work and in between free fucking (to stimulate their zeal) they found that the root of the trouble lay outside in the drainpipe beneath the sidewalk that led to the main sewer. But no private plumber was allowed to touch that. That job falls under the authority and capriciousness of the community of Amsterdam. When, after days of delay, the pavement was finally broken up and the drains inspected, they found thousands of condoms clotted together. I don't really know why that disgusted me so much, but it did. So I walked out, took a couple of days off, then went to work as a masseuse on a houseboat lying at a marvelously picturesque spot on the river Amstel, after which Amsterdam is named.

Almost a thousand years ago the Dutch constructed a dam either across or along the Amstel, no one knows where, or why. The first houses were built by the Amsteldam. Same thing with Rotterdam, where they built a dike or dam on or along the river Rotte.

Yes, by that time I was getting culture. I could afford to. I wasn't making as much as I had at the house with Frieda, but pickings weren't bad. That boat had an atmosphere all its own. That kind of atmosphere is unique to Amsterdam, because of the way the city grew.

Our catboat was run by a fine-looking blonde who lived with an Indonesian boy who regularly beat her up. On deck, preferably. People hung out of the open windows of nearby houses to watch our traffic. What can you do? It's for real, free, and better than television. And you never know when you'll spot someone you know. . . .'

'I got my driver's license and bought a second-hand Volkswagen. The dealer who sold it to me kept looking me up and down, front and back, hungrily. I maintained my Park Hotel manner, paid cash, and took care to do everything exactly right. That was in Hilversum, where he had his business. I drove to Amsterdam and that evening at nine the desk rang my room. A visitor for me. That was exactly the kind of thing I emphatically did not encourage. Once your entourage begins to drop by, you'd best drop out.

I said in my coldest voice: "Is it a man or a woman?"

' "A man, Miss."

' "May I speak to him on the phone?"

' "Of course, Miss."

'It must have been quite an ordeal for my visitor. He had to make his play right there at the desk with everybody looking the other way and discreetly not listening. With a good deal of heeing, hawing, and stuttering I learned that I was speaking to the son of the dealer who had sold me my Volkswagen. He was just dropping by to inquire whether the car was satisfactory. Well, that was all the satisfaction he was going to get that night—I made that abundantly clear. It was also clear that this was the moment to leave the Park Hotel before anything else happened. My reputation there was excellent, and I wanted to keep it that way, in case of future emergency.'

'By that time I knew enough about the business to avoid its most disastrous pitfalls. I took a comfortable room in Old South with bath, telephone, and central heating.

'The difference in atmosphere between Old South and New South is colossal. They are both built of brick, but God! what a difference! New South was built around the turn of the century, during the time that the mass-minded fanatic, Berlage, was preaching his architectural gospel of brick, functional brick, and nothing but brick. The result was a brick desert: rows and rows of sad, cheap-looking houses, uniform, comfortless, and a veritable horror to look at. Everything sober, everything straight. Only a Marx or a Cromwell could have conceived of such housing. But Old South, beginning along the famous Vondelpark, is romantic and charming.'

'I made a deal with two homosexual boys who had been trying to run a perfumery-cum-beauty parlor in the Staalstraat. They were too lazy and lackadaisical to make it a going concern. Behind the shop was a roomy space with washbasins and tiled compartments. I undertook to take over their business for five thousand guilders, with one thousand down and the rest in weekly installments. That suited them perfectly. They took the first thousand, gave me the key, and left for the South of France. I promised to send them the weekly installments.

'My next move was to ring or write all my old customers whose number or address I had. I managed this quite cleverly, for I couldn't very well write to their home addresses. In the shop I found a boxful of glossy picture postcards with the Staalstraat address, obviously intended for advertising purposes. I typed up the cards and left the rest to the grapevine. Within two weeks I had more work than I could handle . . . literally.

'For the time being, I was set. And I had set myself up. With some help from that poor bastard who died in his own shit.'

'Monday was invariably my busiest day, because of the corn and stock exchanges. I never resorted to advertising, for there is a limit to what one girl can do with one pair of hands and one pussy. I stuck to my rule that fucking was out, and there was never any real difficulty about it, for as my business grew I saw it confirmed how many men preferred to kiss a nice-looking pussy as long as they believed that it excited the girl too. I developed a grand technique of wriggling, groaning, and panting, and I had days when I managed more than sixty of these "comes", which I considered a real feat from every point of view. No one seemed seriously to question my capacity in this direction, which occasionally gave me reason to doubt the sanity and sense of many of my clients, for most of them knew each other and I knew (they never made a secret of it) that they exchanged impressions and information about their visits to the Staalstraat. My clientele was widely diversified: artists, advertising executives, lawyers, businessmen, many of whom occasionally stuck around for a glass of sherry or beer before or after the act. On certain days you could hear the shouts of laughter all the way out in the street and in certain circles it was not long before it was not unusual to say: "See you at Monique's place."

'I bought a fine-looking boxer bitch and named her Pierre. I now had the dog I had always wanted. One day, shopping in the Kalverstraat, I ran into a middle-aged madam who had been in the business since she was fourteen and was one of the rare hookers who had managed to hook an ex-client with two cars, a fat bank account and a newly built dream house in the exclusive resort of Bloemendaal, on the North Sea beach.

' "Darling!" I said. "You look simply fabulous! How does marriage agree with you?"

' "Soso", she said with a long face. "Let's go get some coffee."

'Over coffee, our heads together, she told me about her troubles and woes. "Monique, I have everything I could possibly want: a personal maid, a chauffeur, and look at these diamonds . . . but God, my girl, I get so horribly, damnably bored with the same man and the same stupid routine. I sometimes wish a maniac would break into the house and try to strangle me." She looked quickly around, leaned still farther forward, and whispered: "You know—when he wants something I let him put a one-hundred bill on the night table. If he doesn't, I freeze up completely and can't come myself!"

'That was the damnedest thing I had heard yet, and I sat howling with laughter into my handkerchief. I finally managed to bring out: "Leonore, you are completely nuts! Do you need the money? He gives you enough, doesn't he?"

' "Oh, yes. I guess it's just a habit. Or maybe it's principle. Or—who knows? If he doesn't pay, I don't believe he loves me. Or I just hate to give it away for free. I dunno."

'She stuck it out for three more months and one fine day simply ran out on him. Come to think of it, it wasn't even a fine day. It was raining like hell.'

'I knew a lot of advertising and public relations men who all knew from each other that they were clients of mine. One of them, Karel, had dropped in one afternoon for a quickie, and left his monogrammed undershirt in his hurry to get to a business appointment. That evening two of his friends came by for a toss-off and a chat. One of them said: "Oh, by the way, Karel left his undershirt here and asked me to pick it up."

'I looked at them with suspicion: "No funny business, boys."

' "Now, Monique, you know we wouldn't do that. And how could we know he had left his shirt here if he hadn't told us himself?"

' "Yes, but giving it to you two jokers is something else again. Not all of us have your sense of humour, you know."

' "Nono, don't worry. You can give it to us."

'The next afternoon Karel rang up: "You know what those stinkers did? We had a meeting this morning, there were about a dozen of us in the conference room. The porter came in with a large box tied with a ribbon and bow, and marked 'Personal and Urgent'. I open the thing and out comes my goddam shirt, smelling up the whole place with your perfume. It still reeks of it. They must have gotten a whole bottle of it. They all laughed like hyenas."

' "Well", I said, "better that than putting it in your mailbox at home."

'That taught me a lesson. After that I locked everything anyone left behind in a heavy oak chest in my private bedroom.'

'My second-hand Volkswagen was acting up. I called the dealer and found myself speaking to that same son who tried to visit me at the Park Hotel. He made a big spiel and told me they had a really fine Kharmann Ghia for sale, less than a year old, and with a small extra payment and the trade-in I could have it. He personally would drop by with the car. That evening we went for a trial drive and closed the deal over a glass of sherry. And from that day on he kept buzzing around like a fly. He was tall, with dark hair and always well dressed, but he had a stupid face. As if all his life he had been fed baby food into a baby face. His name was Ted and what's more, he was four years younger than me. And not my type at all, really. But he brought me flowers, perfume, and every time I was absolutely sure that he had run out of all possible excuses and pretexts, he managed to come up with a new one. Perhaps that was what finally wore me down; at last I said that he could take me out for dinner at the Lido and dancing at the Casino. But it took him another six weeks to get to first base.

'Then one day, quite out of the blue, his father dropped by . . . to ask whether the Kharmann Ghia was satisfactory. He soon became one of my best customers, but during one of the first massages I gave him, he warned me: "For God's sake, if my son ever drops by, don't let on what I'm coming here for."

' "Goes without saying. I never talk."

'That made me think. His son had a habit of dropping in at the most unpredictable times and sooner or later they were bound to bump into one another. I decided to leave it to fate, for the father invariably paid fifty guilders cash and never stayed long. And to be honest about it, I really preferred the father to the son. Although I went to bed with young Ted fairly regularly, and admirably dressed as he always was, he was never quite clean. He had a body smell, and he didn't wash his penis. So I always had to push him under the shower.

' "You're dirtier than any of my other clients", I told him. Came a weekend when I let him stay overnight, and while he was taking a shower the next morning (with me listening for the taps, for he would do his damnedest to avoid getting wet), I picked up his filthy shorts. While I was still gazing at them in amazed horror he came popping out of the shower, grabbed them out of my hand, and pulled them on.

' "How often do you change your underwear?"

' "Why? Once a week", he told me proudly.

' "No wonder you always smell! If you want to keep coming around, you'd better buy some underwear and change more often."

'He was not at all insulted, just looked at me in amused surprise, shrugged, combed his hair, and actually bought some extra underwear. But his mother did his washing, and some weeks later, when we had been for a drive in the country, we dropped by his home in Hilversum and I met his mother. She looked me up and down and asked me to stay for dinner. Later on she suddenly said: "Are you by chance that girl who's trying to make a queer out of my son?"

'I must have been gaping at her, for she explained: "I never yet heard of a normal man who put on clean underwear every single day." '

'Isidore is one of my regulars, the owner of a prosperous jewelry store. Quite suddenly I do not see him any more, and I begin to wonder what can have happened. Accident? Illness? I think of dropping by his shop, but on second thought discard the idea. He has often told me about his suspicious wife.

'Then, one afternoon, he pops up again.

' "Izzy! I thought you were dead!"

'He wails: "Monique, I'm in real trouble. I have to talk to you." I give him a glass of sherry. He sits biting his knuckles.

' "Oh, Monique. . . . Oh, my God! What if my wife finds out and begins to scream it all over the house? What must my children think?" He clasps his hands over his eyes and sits shaking and moaning.

' "Izzy, calm down and tell me all about it. Start at the beginning."

'He shivers as if he had a fever. Then begins in a rush: "I've gotten a young girl with child. You know how crazy I am about virgins. Hardly seventeen and now she's threatening me. I have to marry her, she says, or she'll break up my marriage and you know my wife—I'll never see any of my children again. Oh, my God, how could I have been such a fool!" He pulls out an expensive, perfumed handkerchief and sits weeping and snottering into it.

' "Where did you meet her?"

' "In a bar."

' "Was she really a virgin?"

' "Well, she did bleed. But . . . you know the way I'm shaped."

'Yes. I knew. Like a prize steer.

' "But haven't you talked about an abortion? And about giving her some nice jewelry? A diamond watch or something?"

' "What do you think? I've been trying and asking everywhere, but there are three Amsterdam doctors behind bars right now, and everybody has his wind up."

'I go to make myself some coffee. I have always liked the silly idiot and I try to do some practical thinking. I finally say: "Stop whining and snivelling, get out of here now and be back tomorrow at eleven. I'll think of something in the meantime."

' "Monique, do you really mean that?"

'That evening I ring up a doctor I've done some business with. (There was very little wire tapping in those days, or if there was, we didn't know about it.) At first the doctor wants no part of my story. He knows what happened to his colleagues. But after much begging and pleading he finally says: "In the Jordaan there is a female abortionist. At least that's what she calls herself. If she can get your client to bleed, you can send her to me at three o'clock, and I'll do the rest for the fee you mentioned. But she must bleed, or I'll send her away." Then he hangs up.

'That gives me something to think about. Of course it isn't me, but these self-styled, so-called abortionists are too often sheer murder. I have seen and heard too much about those cases during my hospital years. I don't want it on my conscience.

'But something is prodding my conscious: "She has to bleed. . . ." And then something clicked, *Der Groschen fiel*, as the Germans say.

'One of the best-known men about town is known as The Kaiser. This emperor owns a string of fabric shops, and his private aberration is an obsessive preference for copulating with menstruating women. He will gladly pay a hundred for the right to go to bed with you when you're having that time of the month. When he finishes he pulls out his penis all covered with blood, beats his hairy chest gorilla-fashion, and shouts: "I am Caesar the Emperor back from the bloody battlefield and still alive and kicking!" The conviction and triumph in his voice when he shouts is unbelievable.

'He has a red leather book with the names of almost all Amsterdam's professional girls together with their menstruation dates. The girls who go in for his game (a lot of them refused to) generally receive a phone call the day before M-day. To check that they are on time, I suppose. He calls them "the regulars from his battle troops". The whole town knows him.

'I call him at his office: "Bernie—Monique here. How's business?"

' "Soso. What's up?"

' "Which one of your regulars is having it right now?"

'Some moments of silence: "Why should you want to know a thing like that?"

' "Just for a gag", I say. "Tell you about it later."

'He doesn't even have to consult his little red book.

' "Mia the Dish", he says.

'I ring up Mia the Dish: "Listen, it's Monique. Nothing personal, but are you having Eve right now?"

' "Oh, lord yes. Practically gushing. Say . . . how do you know?"

' "The Kaiser, of course", I laugh. "Will you sell me a couple of your soaked sanitary napkins?"

'Silence. Then: "That's the damnedest question I ever heard."

' "I'll pay you a tenner apiece."

' "A tenner apiece? At that price you can have them gift wrapped. Wait . . . I have some extra-special Christmas paper left. When d'you want your gift?"

' "I'll pick them up in an hour."

'Izzy arrives at eleven on the dot, looking nervous but hopeful.

' "Have that piece of jail bait of yours here at half-past two on the dot with five hundred guilders in an envelope."

' "Anything, Monique. Anything if you'll get me off this hook."

' "Off this hooker, you mean", I say, and push him out. At Mia's place I pick up a neatly gift-wrapped parcel, complete with a blue ribbon and a pink bow. I pay her and she says: "If you need any more, just call, dear. Even if it's five times a day."

'At half-past two sharp a measly, thin, ratty-faced kid rings the bell and comes in shyly.

' "My God, Izzy", I think, "couldn't you have found something better than this?"

'I lock the front door, disconnect the bell, and take her into the back room.

' "Take off your panties", I order her.

'She begins to whine. I have no time or patience to waste on this third-rate bag, so I snap at her: "I'm not doing this to admire your silly cunt, but to get you and Isidore out of trouble. Now drop your pants at once or I'll throw you into my car and drive you straight to the police station and charge you with attempted blackmail!" She looks at me, then strips off her cheap cotton panties. I hitch up her skirt and outfit her with the two wettest of Mia the Dish's napkins, plus a clean folded kitchen towel to make it look like a real emergency. Get her panties up and skirt down, and put her in the car. With the envelope, of course. I ring the bell, watch her go in, and get out of there.

'At eleven that night Isidore drops by. "Monique, here—this is for you." He drops something in my hand, wrapped in thin tissue paper. A platinum ring with a medium-sized pearl. "You've saved my life."

' "Everything went well?"

' "Oh, yes. I let her choose between a present and cash. She preferred the money."

'And I, of course, had a good customer back.'

'My relationship with Big Boy Baby Face dragged on and on, but I was getting terribly fed up with it and with him. He was good in bed, but his mind never rose above the level of driving a car or reading Donald Duck, so we seldom had anything to talk about. His income consisted of pocket money plus a commission whenever he sold a second-hand car.

'I had been trying to get rid of him gently—easing him out, but he stuck like a leech and kept coming back. And he seemed to earn less and less, so every time we went somewhere I had to pay an increasingly larger share and that, my dear people, is the way pimps are made (they are never born!) by girls who are lonely or think they are lonely and want to show that they can get a man of their own—for keeps. And then they begin to believe that the man really loves them for themselves, and he can't help it that he isn't making enough money—yet.

'Then one day I heard from three different sources that my Baby Face was fucking not just me, but half the girls in Amsterdam. When I asked him straight out whether there was any truth in this, he just grinned at me and cracked: "And what do you think YOU are doing?"

'I yelled at him: "At least I ask them for money and I earn it honestly. All you do is lie and loaf and pimp and sponge on me. Now get out of here!"

'He laughed in my face: "Try getting me out, You run a nice, quiet place here. Think of what the neighbors will say."

' "The hell with the neighbors!" I screeched.

'He was a big boy and over six feet tall, but I attacked him like a mad lynx, climbed into his clothes, tore off the lapels, bit his ear, kicked him in the balls. I got beaten up myself, but he was not really a dirty fighter and had obviously never expected me to get that desperate. At some point we were both rolling on the floor, me trying to kick him in the balls. I sprang up, jumped him, opened the front door, and began to kick and push until I got him out into the street. He was a sight all right, but so was I. I yelled at him:

' "And don't show your pimp face here again or I'll call the police!"

'I slammed the door and staggered back to the back room. About half an hour later the bell rang. I had put on other clothes and was more or less myself again. I picked up the poker, went to the front door and asked: "Who is there?"

'A surprised and slightly hurt voice replied: "It's me, Monique, Harry."

'I recognized the voice. One of my publicity boys. I opened the door and quickly looked up and down the street.

'He asked in a slightly worried voice: "What's the matter? Had a police raid?"

'I grinned at him: "I just threw out my lousy pimp."

' "But . . . I never knew you had one."

' "No, neither did I. But it began to look too much that way for my liking. Are you in a hurry?"

' "Not particularly."

' "Then let's keep the door locked and I'll close up shop. We'll celebrate with champagne."

'I put my feet up, kicked off my shoes, and relaxed. Harry was a very understanding boy. He got the glasses and out the cheese. Finally he asked, off-handedly: "Want to talk about it?"

' "Not much. It isn't all that important, you know."

' "Is it that big fellow who . . .?"

' "Yes, him."

' "Yeah. We occasionally saw you with him. Lido and other places. The general consensus was more or less . . ."

' "What does she see in him?"

'He began to laugh: "That's what it boiled down to, yes."

'We emptied two bottle of champagne, but did not get too drunk, and had all kinds of sex. Lying beside me with his hands under his head he let out a big sigh: "If I had a wife like you . . ."

' "You would still be looking around for fresh nooky."

'Next day he rang up: "Jeez, Monique. I completely forgot to pay you."

' "Then go on forgetting. This time it was on the house."

' "Hahaha. On the house. That's a good one." '

'Fat Sam was another regular customer whose only need was for a nice, very gentle massage until he got a hard-on. When he had reached that stage, he rushed out of the house and got into his car to go fuck his wife, he said. Well, why not?

'But one day he says to me: "Monique—I know a good-looking Indonesian woman in Amsterdam South who massages women, too. Here are fifty guilders and I want you to go there, and when I come here tomorrow evening you tell me exactly what she does and how." Well, why not?

'The moment Fat Sam is gone I ring the number and a soft, smooth voice with a vague accent tells me: "No, Ma'am. I do massage to men only." But I keep talking and finally, after a promise I'll pay her double, she agrees and we make a date for nine o'clock that evening.

'She opens the door herself, dressed in a beautiful sarong. She is good-looking, too: delicate face with big, slightly slanting eyes. She shows me into her massage room, then hesitates, and with a slight gesture at her sarong, says:

' "Generally I do not dress this way, but . . . is this just a visit, or do you really wish a massage?"

'All at once I do not want to go on with the game, and so I tell her who I really am.

'She smiles: "Would you like a cup of coffee?"

' "I would love one."

'While she's gone I look around the room. The usual: clean, small room, stacks of towels, wash-basin, and massage table, plus some steel chairs. What more does a woman need in this line of business? Her main tools she carries with her; in principle we could ply our trade anywhere.

'The door opens and she comes back with two cups of coffee and some cake.

' "May I call you Monique? I am Anita."

' "Of course you can. And may I pay you fifteen guilders for taking up your time?"

' "Oh, no. I'd really rather not. I have heard a lot about you and I'm glad to have met you. You know how some men run from address to address, just to have seen and tried them all? One thing that puzzles me though, is why did you insist on coming here to be massaged by me?"

'Of course I had seen that question coming, and had already decided to play it straight. I began to laugh.

' "You see, I have a customer whom we call Fat Sam; a smallish, red-haired type with freckles and a Citröen. Know him?"

'She shakes her head and stirs her coffee: "What about him?"

' "That's what I don't understand. He told me that you sometimes massage women and gave me a fifty to come here and get one. Perhaps he hopes you'll lick my cunt and that he can get his kicks when I tell him about it tomorrow. That's what I figure, for otherwise I can see no sense to it."

'She gets up, stands thinking for a moment, then rushes to a paneled side door, pulls it open and shoots inside. There's a lot of noise and then our slender little Anita comes backing into the room, dragging Fat Sam along by his ears. And I witness one of the loveliest fights I've ever seen. That small Anita bashes him around the ears, pulls out his red hair in handfuls, kicks him in the balls, and all but cuts him to pieces with a meat cleaver. He does not fight back, just runs around the room bent almost double, hiding his head in his hands with her screaming at him in that Indonesian accent:

' "You not well in ze head, you, to inzult me to ze face of zat Hollands mevrouw!"

'While she is still pummeling his head with her little brown fists, I get out, into my car, and home. Soon there is a violent ringing of the doorbell. In comes Fat Sam with band-aids over his nose and ears, groaning: "Why did you do that, Monique? Why did you do that to me?"

' "Me do it to you? You fat, stupid double-crosser. What were you doing in that house?"

'He wails: "I live there. She's my wife."

'I stand staring at him: "The one you always fuck after I . . .?"

' "Yes, yes."

'I still don't get it. "But what were you doing behind that door?"

'He waves his arms. "She thought I was out. And I crept silently back and sat behind the door, listening."

' "To . . . to her and me?"

' "Yes."

' "But why, goddammit?"

'Still those waving arms and hands. "I suspected her of secretly doing it with women. And the bloody blasted hell of it is, that after all this I'm still not sure!"

'Then he runs out into the street, furiously banging the door behind him. French bedroom comedy. And what a cast!'

'I always rose fairly early in the morning, switched on my telephone answering machine with a message at what time I would be back, and went to play tennis or have a swim, taking the dog along. The rest of the day was mostly fun and games. By now I was really set. I had what I had always wanted: clothes, dog, sports car, lots of customer-friends, and money in several banks.

'Then, one day, between customers, I was leafing through some weeklies. One of them, *Elsevier*, had by far the best section of marriage advertisements. You know how women are, they always read that kind of stuff. Advice to the Lovelorn, etc. Ever since I had booted out my amateur pimp I had been thinking of getting myself someone permanent. Not necessarily a husband, but what better way of making contact with a man who has honorable intentions than through a marriage ad—if it's placed by the man? And this one was:

> Gentleman of excellent family, middle-aged, living abroad, Dutch nationality, seeks serious contact with elegant young woman, who can get along in foreign languages.

I may not have quoted it verbatim, but that was the gist of it. Well, why not? I wrote a short, rather nonchalant reply. I didn't even take the trouble to mail it myself, but later than night gave it to Izzy (the virgin-violator) to mail.'

'It was May 1959 and along the canals the trees were getting their leaves back. The bridges were getting their organ grinders back and I felt I was getting my own back on a life that had given me so little for the first twenty-one years. I had taken the dog for an early morning run in the Vondelpark, returned home and opened the mail. I always got lots of postcards with the damnedest pictures and messages from all over the world. Customers who were funny or thought they were. But letters? Hardly ever.

'This time there was an elegant envelope with a return address from Nice, France. French stamp. Now who could be writing me a formally addressed letter from Nice?

> Dear Miss Von Cleef,
> Apologizing for some delay, caused by business commitments, I hereby reply to your pleasant letter of—On the 2nd of June I shall be in Holland again (Hotel Des Deux Villes) and shall not omit attempting to contact you by telephone. I add that the tone of your letter struck me as very pleasant and spontaneous, and I express a hope that our future relationship can continue in the same atmosphere. Could you, in the meanwhile, oblige me with a photograph?
>
> Yours very sincerely,
> Edward B. Van S.

'I sat down and only then began to realize that this was a reply to my letter to the *Elsevier* advertisement. Businessman who stays in one of the most exclusive hotels in The Hague. Beautiful notepaper. Staid, old-fashioned writing. And an aristocratic-sounding, double-barreled family name. Jeez, Monique, aren't you getting into water that's a bit too deep for you?

'Walking up and down, making myself some coffee. I felt myself getting nervous and immediately the well-known reaction set in. Me getting nervous? Who did this geezer in Nice think he was, getting me nervous?

'I told myself: "You've always been a lucky piece of ass, Monique, so what can happen to you? As far as you know he's an important old bastard who's bloody lucky to get the chance to marry a technically perfect . . . uh . . . wife. To warm and cherish his old cockles before he croaks. There are no perfect men, you should know that by now. If they behave, they are bores, and if they are real men they can't leave other women alone, because they are natural pirates. Think of this as a lottery and send the guy a photograph, any photograph. If he doesn't like your snoot or your tits, it's no sense meeting him, anyway".

'So I rummaged in a drawer and found a snapshot with me in the middle with Gonda on one side and Mia the Dish on the other. We had been to the horse races that day. I was wearing a simple corduroy dress that someone had sent me from Italy.

'I wrote a quick note (what had he said about my writing? Oh, yes: pleasant and spontaneous), pointing out in a pleasant and spontaneous way that I was the girl in the middle. Then I sat looking at the snapshot again. Girl. She was thirty-three years old now, that girl. Oh, what the hell! What did he expect? Lolita? I wrote the address and and mailed the thing.

'Six days later another one of those distinguished envelopes. This time from Rome:

> . . . and I am looking forward to a personal contact, which I shall attempt to arrange as soon as I arrive back in Holland. I confess that I have been feeling progressively lonesome for years, this in spite of the fact that I am most of the time surrounded by people, most of whom I have known for a long time, but none of whom I can truly feel as belonging to me personally. On the small snapshot you strike me as an elegant young woman of a type that has always appealed to me. I hope, however, you will not feel insulted when I say rather the opposite is the case when I regard your female companions . . .

'That was good for a laugh. He struck me as more honest than tactful. His handwriting was extremely regular and old-fashioned. How old could this geezer be? He had not said a word about that. I put the whole damn thing out of my head, and went on enjoying life and spring in Amsterdam.'

'One of my colleagues rings up: "How's business in the Staalstraat?"

‘ “Getting out of hand.” That was a standard joke.

‘She giggled: “You know those complaints you get in certain professions?”

‘ “You mean—?”

‘ “Nono. Like tennis elbow, and housemaid’s knee?”

‘ “Oh, those? What of them?”

‘ “Doctors here in Amsterdam have spotted a new one: massage wrist.”

‘ “That’s nothing. My customers like licking pussy so much I have to oil their tongues if I want to stay in business.”

‘ “Haha. You know what that same doctor told me?”

‘ “He’s quite a talker, isn’t he?”

‘ “He can talk you into anything. He had a woman who wanted a check-up. Married for three years and not pregnant yet. He checked everything, sat down behind the desk, and said there was nothing at all the matter with her. With her husband, perhaps? But her husband had been married before, and had two children. The doctor became impatient and said perhaps it was something psychological and why didn’t she consult a sexual or marriage counselor. Then she said: ‘No, doctor—I think the real trouble is . . . I can’t get it down my throat.’ ”

‘ “Veeery funny.” ’

‘I came home with the dog early one sunny morning and heard the telephone ringing and ringing. Didn’t I leave my answering machine on? Oh—the machine had said I would be back at eleven and it was five past. Must be a customer with a hot-headed penis. I grabbed the horn: “Yeah?”

‘A distinguished, calm voice asked: “Is this Miss Von Cleef’s number?”

‘I became impatient, for the dog was trying to devour my beef-steak. “Yes, of course it is. Who are you?”

‘ “Am I speaking to Miss Von Cleef in person?”

‘I was just about to tell the joker to stop being funny, when I caught myself. In my politest voice I said: “Could you hold on for a moment, please? I’ve just come in, and the dog is trying to get at the meat I just bought”.

‘ “By all means, by all means . . .”

‘I saved the beefsteak and went back to the phone. “Everything under control now.”

'Nothing in that measured, cool voice had changed: "Miss Von Cleef, I presume?"

' "Yes, this is she . . ."

' "Miss Von Cleef, this is Edward B. Van S. speaking from The Hague. I have the impression that you are very occupied right now. Shall I call you later?"

' "No no. It's just . . . I'd just come in from playing tennis when I heard the telephone."

' "Ah, you play tennis. That is most interesting. Ah—would it be convenient for you to have dinner with me at my hotel in The Hague this evening?"

'My reactions have always been quick. Of course I could have made it, and I was excited and curious to meet this fish. But I did not want to seem too eager. I put polite regret in my voice: "I would love to, but I have a business appointment. I can make it tomorrow, though."

' "Shall I send my car for you?"

' "Thank you, but I have my own car and I love driving."
(Jesus . . . not his private chauffeur picking me up in the Staalstraat!)

' "In that case I shall expect to meet you at seven in the Hotel Des Deux Villes. You know how to find it?"

'I said boldly: "I know where it is. Good morning."

'In the past weeks I had done some thinking and had also had a little talk with Gonda about this marriage game. We had decided that the most sensible thing for me to do would be to tell him that I was a business woman, trained as a nurse, with some inherited capital—not much—and I was looking around for a location to start my own rest home. That would explain a lot and explain away a lot.

'Gonda talked real sense. She said: "Take it from me, darling: always lie as little as possible. Stick as close to the truth as you can. And if you cannot do that, then think up such an impossibly colossal lie that no one in his senses would even dare think of it. And I'll back you up if I can."

'I rang up Gonda and told her I was meeting my expatriate the next morning. She said: "I cannot see you before then. I have to leave in an hour or so, for a couple of days, at least. The main thing is for you to think of a role for yourself. The ex-nurse with a little money who is always a bit afraid that men would marry her for that capital. Warm-hearted, etc. but with her head screwed on right. And whatever you do—stick to it. All your reactions have to be consistent with that role. Get me?"

' "I get you. Ring me when you're back." '

'Next day at five I tossed my last customer off and out. Disconnected the bell and telephone. Took a shower and selected a simple black flannel dress studded with tiny pink flowers.

'It was beautiful weather and I drove calm and collectedly, mentally preparing myself while humming something melodious and romantic. On my right the sun was sinking down over the North Sea, and my heart was full of hope and expectancy. Which did not lessen any when I found a parking space between a Chrysler and a Cadillac, for I could not help but see all those little things as happy portents.

'I stalked into the lobby high on my legs (the quality of snootiness is not strained), inquired after Mr. B. Van S., and two bellboys escorted me through a thickly carpeted corridor—on the ground floor, no less!—and while one of them made a deep and respectful bow, the other one knocked on a carved oak door.

'The moment the door swung open a tall and distinguished-looking gentleman rose from behind an antique desk and came forward to greet me with both arms outstretched:

' "My dearest little women . . . how I have been looking forward to this happy moment! Ah, your face is even lovelier than your photograph led me to imagine. Place yourself comfortably on this sofa . . . I have had the champagne prepared for us."

'I sank about half a yard into the cushions in a state of immediate confusion, for I had to get rid of my bag and gloves and at the same time try to pull my skirt chastely down. Whatever I had expected, it was never this exuberant and at the same time over-stylish reception. Was this kind of greeting standard procedure in his circles, or was he slightly mad?

'I had hardly gotten myself organized when he sank down in the other corner of the sofa, handed me a cut crystal glass, looked me in the eye, and proposed:

' "Shall we drink this—to our love?"

'Recalling my position as a warm-hearted but nonetheless level-headed business woman, I managed to reciprocate with a level look and a warm-hearted tremor in my voice:

' ". . . to our love."

' "My dearest darling", Edward B. Van S. went on, "by and by we shall have some caviar. Now let me have a good look at you. Yes, yes. Very lovely hair . . . excellent figure, superb legs. Yes, yes. Just what I have had in mind for years."

'By this time I was so damned nervous that I was afraid of coming back with a giggle or some idiotic crack, so I kept my eyes sedately downcast. Which proved to be the right thing to do, for my new-found love reacted at once with an enchanted exclamation:

' "Ah . . . look at her, the shy little darling. I believe she actually blushes!"

'Whether I did or not, one of us at least rated an Oscar. This throwback to the French Revolution now proceeded to show me his pad: sitting room, bedroom, and bathroom, furnished with antiques and vases full of flowers. The bathroom was fit for a royal concubine.

'While I stood still in the open bathroom door in admiration and amazement, he gently pushed me inside, saying: "You adorably shy little darling. You have to make wee wee, but do not know how to say it? You just go ahead." And he softly closed the door of the waterworks.

'I stood staring at the door in a half daze until I came sufficiently to my senses to make wee wee, biting my knuckles to stifle an up-surging spasm of nervous laughter. I felt sure that he was listening outside the door, so I neatly washed my hands, checked my face and hairdo, straightened my stockings, and gently but suddenly opened the door. But no. He was sitting behind his desk, busy with some papers.

' "Shall we have dinner? That will give us time to get used to one another."

'By the time we had finished dinner, I was becoming sure that Edward B. Van S. was the real goods, as far as his social and financial position were concerned. I had enough experience to spot the difference between the manners and speech (not to mention the behaviour of the old-fashioned waiters) of the newly wealthy and the scions of the old and established European families. An address in Nice fitted with the well-known habit of many of the latter to avoid paying inordinate taxes.

'At the end of our dinner my new-found love ordered coffee and brandy in his suite, and once there he pulled me close to him in his corner of the sofa, sat stroking my hair and murmuring into my ear, ranging from "his sweetest little woman" to "my elegant dreamgirl".

'I let myself rest against his shoulder, floating around in rosy dreams, and I admit he had me completely off balance. This may make you grin, but you must consider that the rough-and-tumble life I had led had done everything for me except equip my defenses against this kind of courtship. And the overwhelming atmosphere of old-world romance and wealth had a powerful allure. Ah, yes . . . and the flattery.

'He said: "May I meet you again tomorrow?"

'I dreamily nodded and saw my Life and Times in the Staalstraat as infinitely unreal and remote. I felt sure that this was the life I was born for—that everything in my past had been only training for this . . . for being Mrs. Monique B. Van S.

'He kissed me on the tip of my nose, got up, pulled me up gently by my hands, went to his desk, and gave me an envelope. "Take this, my sweet, to buy a nice frock with."

'In a slight daze and singing with the music of my car radio I drove back to Amsterdam, letting fragments of the film of my impressions float in front of my eyes. What an incredibly polished and charming man! What could his age be? About sixty? Precisely the type I had always wanted and dreamed of—but never imagined I could possibly get. Just in time, I realized I was running out of gas. Stopped at a service station, opened my bag and saw that envelope. Opened it and sat staring down at a one-thousand guilder note. Well, well. I handed the attendant a guilder tip and drove slowly on. The situation, I felt, was getting more and more improbable by the hour.

'Next morning, half-past ten. I was handling an early customer and the phone kept ringing, stopped, and began again . . . and again. Which was unusual, for all my customers knew that I either picked up the phone at once, or was busy with you-know-what. With a hearty curse I went over to the damned thing and snarled: "HELLO?"

'"How is my sweet little woman this morning?"

I cooed back: "Oh, Edward—it's you".

' "Does my sweet darling have any jewelry?"

'With truly fantastic presence of mind I said in that warm-hearted yet level-headed voice: "I . . . I love jewelry. But, you see, Edward—I have to save my capital and I simply hate junk."

' "Excellent, excellent, my little one. Shall we meet at four tomorrow afternoon? Then we'll buy some real jewelry and have dinner afterward. All right?"

' "All right."

'I was level-headed enough to go straight back to work, but

avoided making appointments for the next afternoon and evening, which turned out to be profitable enough as it was, for I was presented with a two-carat canary diamond, a long jade necklace, and on top of that we selected sufficient lump jade to make two jade earrings with a circle of small sapphires. The jeweler and his assistant bowed us out into the Palace Street, me telling myself that this kind of thing simply did not happen to a poor, hard-working girl.

'During dinner I glanced at my left hand again and again, which did not escape Edward's attention. With a tender smile he patted my hand: "This is nothing, my sweetest. Wait until I begin to really take care of you in earnest." '

'A period now started in which we had dinner in The Hague every night and some of my clients became irritated, some curious.

' "Monique, for God's sake, where are you every evening?"

'I smiled mysteriously: "That's my little secret. For the time being you have to come between nine and five."

'Which all of them did, and they preferred to shorten their sessions rather than go to the competition. I regarded it as a real compliment when one of them begged me to help him at eight in the morning.

' "You see", he explained. "I can then go to work with an empty bag of balls, don't miss you so much, and do my work a lot better." '

'Edward rang up with a new idea. The day before we had picked up my jade earrings and while we were there bought a real beauty of a red coral brooch: a bunch of grapes fitted in an antique gold setting.

' "How would you like to spend a weekend at the seaside, in the Huis ter Duin Hotel?"

' "Oh, I would love that: I've never been there."

' "And listen—if you have an amusing girl friend, bring her along and we'll have some fun. I'll have my chauffeur pick you both up. Saturday afternoon at one."

'Before I could protest or think up an excuse he had hung up.

'My fairy-tale romance had been going for some weeks now and I had become more confident about its happy ending. I was less happy with the idea of being picked up at my business address, for the Staalstraat was not in an exactly solid district, to make an understatement. I considered ringing Edward back and asking him to have me picked up somewhere else: a hotel or restaurant. But I did not do it. It might make him suspicious, and that kind of shenanigans have a nasty tendency to get uncovered. I rang Gonda, and to my joy she answered at once. I told her my predicament.

' "No", she said, without hesitation. "You have your car in front of your door. I'll be there well before one o'clock, with my overnight bag and an extra coat. You'll be rummaging around in the glove compartment while I stand talking to you through the window. As if we had just arrived at your place after picking me up. Before the bastard has time to really look around or ring your bell we'll be in his car and out of there."

'That went off like clockwork. The moment the sleek Chrysler stopped we had slammed the door of my car and were being whisked away toward Noordwyk-by-the-Sea.

'Two stately suites had been reserved for us there: one for dear Edward and one for Gonda and me. Edward explained: "Looks better that way, from any point of view."

'We hung up our evening clothes and arranged our toilet articles. I impatiently asked Gonda: "What do you think of him, now that you've met him?"

'She was non-committal. "Hm. Too early to say yet."

'Our phone rang. "Champagne and caviar in my suite, ladies."

'We sat by the open balcony windows, looking out at beach and sea, laughing and chatting, when suddenly Edward got up without warning and beckoned us into the room. He said to Gonda: "You strike me as a girl with some experience. Take the clothes off my little princess."

'Gonda didn't hesitate for a second. Put her long cigarette holder in one corner of her mouth and laughingly and teasingly began to take my clothes off. Edward sat down on a fragile gilt Louis Seize chair, and looked on with an admiring expression.

' "Excellent!" he nodded. "She is even more beautiful than I had hoped." Then he reached out and pulled down the long zipper of Gonda's summer dress. A minute later the three of us had jumped into the large canopy bed and were licking, sucking, kissing and fucking at, on, or in every available place, slit, and hole. I automatically fell into well-known routines, and part of my mind remained removed enough to let me realize that I had never before seen Gonda completely naked, and certainly never in bed. Everything had happened so spontaneously that everything we did that afternoon was just clean, dirty fun.

'Later we sat out on the terrace, drinking cocktails, with dinner following. We then drove back to The Hague where we dropped Edward off and the chauffeur brought Gonda and me back to Amsterdam. A shorter weekend than we had expected.

'That Chrysler had glass sliding panels between the passengers and the driver's seat, so that Gonda and I could have a quiet, private talk.

' "What do you think of him now?"

'She turned slightly toward me, looked at me pensively, and slowly said in that lisping voice: "Yes. For his age he is sexually quite something. But very vicious. Real nastily vicious. You won't have an easy life with him."

'I looked at her in amazement and just shrugged my shoulders. I couldn't for the life of me see where she had gotten that crazy idea.

'Three days later Edward was on the phone: "Dearest little woman, my chauffeur tells me that you appear to live in a neighborhood of poverty and squalor. And that is hardly—"

' "Absolute total nonsense", I replied at once. "It is an old district, certainly. Not everything here is painted every six months. But squalor? Definitely not."

' "Well, let's leave it for the moment. I am leaving for my place in Nice tonight. I would very much like you to see it. Will you be my guest for a day or two? I have reserved a seat for you at Sabena, Leidseplein. The Belgian Air Line."

'When I checked with them, I heard: "By all means, Miss Von Cleef. We have a first-class ticket here for you. For tomorrow afternoon at three."

'At the Nice airport I found Edward waiting for me in a Bentley, his French valet-driver Pierre at the wheel. This was getting madder and madder. I began to feel caught up in the production of an international super-movie.

'We zoomed along the sunlit highway, with Edward kissing my fingers one by one.

' "Darling, you cannot imagine how I have missed you."

'I smiled at him most tenderly: "But my dearest—you phone me practically every day."

' "That is hardly the same as having you here. I want you entirely and permanently for myself."

'I nestled into the crook of his arm, thinking: "My dear boy, don't you know by now that you can have me and keep me forever?"

'His villa was built on top of a not-too-steep hill, surrounded by a high stone wall with olive and oleander trees everywhere. His housekeeper Thérèse was waiting to welcome us on the porch. Inside, Thérèse showed me up a marble, double-winged staircase to my room. "Can I unpack for you, Madame?"

'I changed into something more airy, and found Edward downstairs mixing singapore slings. (He was an absolute past master in the art of mixing drinks, far better than most bartenders.) Later he took me around the house: a library with tons of leatherbound books, enormous carved stone open hearth, wine cellars, enormous bathrooms . . . the works. He opened a door to a private wing on the first floor.

' "This room I have intended as your private bedroom. Let's hope you won't sleep here too often. . . . And this smaller room you must furnish yourself as a private sitting room. A boudoir, as we call it here." He let out a long, sad sigh: "It has all been waiting for its mistress too long."

'That evening we dined on the terrace of the Carlton in Cannes, and for the first time we slept together in one bed—no sex.

'I woke up the next morning to hear Edward telephoning his valet, Pierre, who entered immediately afterward with tea and biscuits. I glanced at the clock. Seven in the morning. I yawned and Edward got up.

' "Use your own bathroom, will you?"

'I took a luxurious bath, dressed with care, and met Thérèse in the downstairs hall.

' "Good morning, Madame. I have served breakfast in the morning room."

'Edward sat waiting for me with newspapers. In the afternoon we went for a drive along the coast and had lunch at Eden Roc (Juan Les Pins).

'We had our siesta during the hot part of the afternoon and later met for cocktails on the side terrace. I decided we would have to cut down on our drinking, but I would take care of that later.

'Things seemed to move faster and faster. That same evening we had dinner at La Bonne Auberge in Antibes and afterward went to visit Madame Zodiac, the famous astrologist. She asked me my birth date, consulted the illuminated astrological signs on her table, took my left hand, studied its lines, and finally said: "You will lead an unusual and turbulent life."

'In Edward's case she became very pensive after a while and merely said: "You will never be happy."

'Back in the car, when Pierre had swing us back onto the main road, Edward suddenly burst out:

' "That gipsy witch is completely mad. She is an impostor!"

'Later that night we danced on the terrace with champagne and moonlight. Edward seemed to be moody, but covered it with a sort of forced gaiety.

'The next morning at breakfast: "Darling, I want you to stop working. I'll buy you a nice apartment in a renovated mansion. Look around in Amsterdam. And in any case ring me up tonight the very moment you get home."

'I shook my head: "Oh, no, my sweet. I am far too independent to let myself become a kept woman. I run my own business and I do not need to be kept by any man."

'He then said curtly: "You don't understand me, as usual. I want to marry you."

' "Later, darling. I'm in no hurry." '

'He rang up every day, with more and even longer tirades and endearments.

' "My business manager in The Hague tells me that it is possible to get a quite decent flat for fifty thousand guilders."

'Meanwhile I had been doing some sensible thinking myself, and had been looking around, had found a nice flat near the Beethovenstraat. For very near the amount Edward had mentioned.

'I rang him up in Nice: "Darling—the agent says fifty thousand, with some small improvements included. It's in a co-operative building and in really excellent state. If you say so I'll go talk to his brother this afternoon. He handles the financial side of the business."

' "That will be perfectly all right, my sweet. Just tell him that your fiancé in France will pay through his business office in The Hague."

'At precisely three that afternoon I presented myself at the agent's office, and the secretary showed me into the office of the financial partner. I nearly had heart failure, for I was looking straight into the face of a man who had come to my place in the Staalstraat for a massage. He had stretched himself out on my work table with a smelly cock full of lice and nits. When I refused to touch him under those circumstances, he jumped off the table, red with fury, calling me all the most insulting names he could think of. I came right back at him.

' "Before you start calling me names, you bugger, better go and get yourself deloused. What you need is a massage with DDT."

'In one lightning flashback that entire scene full of mutual invective passed through my mind. And through his, judging by his face. My God, what a pickle!

'At that moment his brother came hurrying in. "Ah, Miss Von Cleef! Excuse me for being late." He began to explain to his brother: "Miss Von Cleef's fiancé in Nice will pay cash through his bank in The Hague."

'The brother, no longer red but now chalk white, took some papers from his desk and said, in a thick voice: "Further discussion is superfluous. We do not want kept women in our co-ops."

'Instead of slamming him in the mug and inquiring whether he still had his private crab plantation, I turned on my heel and got out of there.

'Looked around some more and found a far better apartment in the Henry Zagwynstraat. Edward rings up again: "What's holding things up?"

' "Oh—I ran into something better. But this one is fifty-five thousand. And it's not available until the first of August."

' "It makes no difference to me, my love. Why don't you come here for the weekend, and bring that tall, lisping willow; what's her name?"

'You mean Gonda?

' "There'll be two tickets waiting at the Sabena office."

'The two of us flew to Nice and everything was lovely in the plane. Gonda and I had a lot of fun. In Nice Edward was waiting for us with the Bentley, but from the moment Gonda entered that colossal house she began to behave unpredictably. When I showed her around and asked her what she thought of it, she made a funny face and said: "Could be worse."

'She began to tease Edward, and showed a tendency for too-loud laughter—at the wrong moments. That first evening the three of us had dinner at La Bonne Auberge, went home early, and had sex. So far, so good.

'Sunday morning we got up late and she screeched with laughter when Pierre served us, wearing white gloves. And from that moment on it got worse and worse. We decided to have dinner at Eden Roc, and as usual were served by at least three bowing and scraping waiters. We concluded our meal with coffee and Courvoisier served in those monstrous snifters. Edward moved one hand and ordered: "Serve it in smaller glasses."

'The snifters were taken away and put aside on the serving table standing next to ours. But Gonda got it into her head to have a large glass, got up, took one, and poured her brandy back. I saw Edward's face get as dark as thunder, the veins swelling on his forehead. He hissed at her: "Don't ever do that again. You're no better than a kitchen maid."

'She laughed at him mockingly, straight in his face, got up, took the brandy bottle, and poured herself an extra shot. He refused to speak to her after that, asked for the bill, ordered his car, and drove us home. There he went straight to his room and when I looked in he got up, left, and went down to the library. I heard him lock it from the inside.

'Next morning, as we were flying back to Amsterdam, I said to her: "Now listen, Gonda, why did you do all those provoking things yesterday?"

'This time she laughed at me: "Don't burst your bra, my pet. It's nothing to get up on your hind legs about. That man is just a dirty old pervert, and far sicker than you have any conception of."

'In the evening Edward rang me up again, and he was very nice and sweet, then suddenly added: "That so-called friend of yours, that Gonda, is a low-class oversexed slut. Her influence on you is simply disastrous. I forbid you ever to speak to her again."

'That gave me something to think about. I made myself some tea, then rang up Gonda and told her what Edward had said, adding very calmly:

' "This may sound bloody funny to you, but you rubbed Edward the wrong way, and it's not all that funny to me. I want that man and you know it. Now let things cool off and when I've got him I'll straighten everything out; leave it to me. I'll give you a ring now and then for the time being. All right?"

'She coos and lisps: "All right, pet. Let's play it that way, then. I'll miss you." '

'The agents handling the other apartment are a completely different type. I size them up and decide to tell them the story of the man with the crab complex. They roar with laughter, slapped me on the back, and promised me:

' "Monique, we know all about you. You're a regular girl and the hell with all those lousy hypocrites. You arrange to have the money paid and you get in there on the first of August." This is a real load off my mind. I ring up Edward and he promises to have the cash transferred first thing in the morning. Then he adds: "There's a ticket waiting for you at Sabena. I want to see you Friday evening."

'But some instinct makes me feel increasingly nervous. The closer Friday comes, the jumpier I get. I write it off as nerves resulting from the tribulations of the purchase of a flat, but when the plane lands at Nice I am met by the Bentley with Pierre but no Edward.

' "Bonsoir, Madame."

'I look around with thumping heart. "Where is Monsieur, Pierre?"

'He mumbles: "Monsieur did not feel very well", and opens the car door. I sink down in the back seat and think: "Here is where all hell bursts loose. My intuition was right, after all."

'I see Edward standing in the hall, his hands behind his back. He gives me a peck on the cheek and says coldly: "Had a good trip? You'll find me on the terrace."

'I go upstairs, unpack, freshen up a bit, take a very deep breath, and slowly go down that monumental staircase. I find him outside, preparing singapore slings. He hands me one, picks up a letter, and hands it over.

' "This is an anonymous letter and not a very nice one."

'I recognize the handwriting at once. Gonda's. I cannot possibly be wrong. I had always wondered how anyone who dressed, spoke, and walked so stylishly could have such impossible handwriting. With large, irregular, completely characterless letters, for all the world as if a drunken chicken had wandered into a pool of ink and then across the pages:

> DEAR MISTER B. VAN S.:
>
> May the good lord have mercy on you and open your too trustful eyes. Prepare yourself for a colossal scandal when the Staalstraat business is transferred to Amsterdam South. The Jews, peanut vendors, and ice-cream magnates will pay ten bucks more a toss-off at that superior address. That's the whole game. May God give you the strength you will sorely need in the days and weeks that will follow.

'Edward sits watching me, empties his glass, and says:

' "I wanted to personally show this to you. That's why I sent you a plane ticket. We had better finish the whole thing right here and now, hadn't we?"

'I pick up my handbag and say, as cool as you please: "Very well. Can I catch a plane back tonight?"

'He sits staring at me, begins to shake all over, then quakes: "My dear woman, is that all you have to say? Are you going to leave me so flat and cruelly?"

'What do I have to lose? My back is against the wall. I feel a cold wave of anger, and say, with voice shaking but still calmly:

'Edward, you must know that my life is not strictly virginal. But I earn my daily bread in a completely honest way. You have been married twice yourself and have had whole strings of adventures. I was prepared to begin completely afresh with you, and forget all about my past. I simply love you. That's all there is to it. But if this kind of dirt keeps cropping up . . .'

He pops up from his chair, kneels down and puts his arms around me. "My dearest darling, that's all I wanted to hear. I ask you to forgive me. I have a confession to make myself. I was so terribly upset when I received this letter . . . I rang up a private detective agency in The Hague and asked them for an urgent and complete report on you."

'Well, that did it. I shrugged him off and got up. "I couldn't care less what they come up with. I have a solid business in Amsterdam, and I am going back to it as soon as I can catch a plane. I don't need anybody but my own . . . but myself. If people get fun out of sticking knives into my back, let them go ahead."

' "But my darling, can't you understand how upset and dismayed I feel by all this . . . this calumny?"

'There was no plane that evening, and after hours and hours of talking I was so tired and disgusted that I went straight upstairs and fell into bed. I woke up in the middle of the night and discovered him on his knees by the side of my bed, his hands folded on the blankets, wailing and beseeching: "How can you sleep so cruelly and heartlessly while I lie here, praying for our happiness! Oh Lord who art in Heaven, I pray for Monique's soul and forgive her her trespasses."

' "Go straight to hell and stay there!" I thought to myself, and tried to go to sleep again. But before I dropped off for what remained of the night a vague idea began to grow in the back of my mind.

'It was full grown when I woke up in the morning. Edward was gone. I had a lonely breakfast and saw Edward writing furiously in the library. Just what I needed. I went for a walk in the garden and managed to intercept the mailman. Nothing from any detective agency, but some business letters, and . . . a letter *plus* a postcard in Gonda's handwriting! I hastily pushed them into my skirt pocket, slunk into the house, put the rest of the mail on the hall table, and disappeared into the toilet under the stairway. The postcard read:

> Poor misguided man, may the merciful Lord have pity on thee, for your money is all she is after.

'And the letter was just as short and in the same spirit. She apparently intended to make quite a campaign of it.

'I soft-shoed upstairs, hid both messages between the lingerie in my suitcase, and resolved to go straight to the best graphologist in Amsterdam. I simply had to be certain they were written by Gonda.

'I wandered downstairs again and out into the garden, snipped some roses, and on an impulse put them in a small vase on Edward's desk.

'He leaned back and sat staring at them for a few moments, then pulled me tight to him: "Oh, my darling! I really love you. No woman has ever put roses on my desk before." While he was still fondling me, Thérèse looked in at the open door.

' "Excuse me, Monsieur, here is a special delivery letter for you. From The Hague."

' "Ha!" said Edward. "The report!"

'While he hurriedly opened the envelope I sat on a corner of his desk and listened as he reads it to me. Three typed pages about where I was born, never been married before, trained nurse and now proprietress of a beauty parlor in the Staalstraat . . .

> According to information from several reliable sources Miss Von Cleef is rumored to be a woman of remarkable charm. Some say she had a biologizing influence on men and some of our informants go so far as to state that every man who comes in contact with her is sooner or later ensnared by her in such a way that he remains permanently subjugated and under her fatal influence . . . As a consequence of the fact that she dresses very well, owns her own car . . . she appears to have envious enemies.

> In this connection we have contacted a Miss Gonda Van Buren who is apparently a friend of Miss Von Cleef of years' standing. According to this lady, Miss Von Cleef's reputation is far from favorable in a moral sense . . . Miss Van Buren further reported that Miss Von Cleef recently managed to ensnare a 'sweet old gentleman' who presented her with an apartment in the Herni Zagwynstraat number 4. Our personal impression is that Miss Van Buren is personally influenced and certainly prejudiced against Miss Von Cleef and . . .

'Edward shot upright from his chair and banged his fist down on the desk: "That dirty slut . . . filthy tramp! How dare she say those things about my little woman!" He pressed the bell to summon Pierre, and ordered champagne and caviar on the terrace. Then he took me in his arms. "My dearest little girl . . . how can I ever have doubted you!"

'While he was still caressing me, my mind was cool and clear. So it had been Gonda, after all. Well, live and learn. Who was it said "Protect me from my friends . . . my enemies I can handle myself"?'

'When I went back to Amsterdam on Monday morning I had Edward's birth certificate in my bag to arrange for our wedding in Holland. I closed up shop and rushed around arranging for our happy future. The fifty-five thousand guilders for my flat arrived by telegraph, and the next day ten thousand more came to buy furniture.

'This had just been arranged when Edward rang up with a new idea: "By the way, darling, I noticed in that famous report that you were educated at a Roman Catholic School. Perhaps you know I am a Roman Catholic myself, and it might be a good idea if you took instruction so we can be married in church later, if you want to."

'After I hung up I sat looking at my dog, Pierre, stroking his head. My cup overfloweth . . . All my life I had wanted a dog . . . and to be a Roman Catholic. It looked as if I was going to get everything I had ever wanted. And how!

'I inquired about, and learned about a holy order whose priests specialized in instruction for converts. My priest turned out to be a nice young man who would be glad to give me the necessary schooling, twice weekly to start with. We made an appointment for the next evening. Meanwhile Edward arrived in The Hague, rang me up, and wanted me to have lunch with him there the next day. Asked me to pick him up at his office at half-past twelve. He said: "Have you had those photographs taken?"

' "Yes. I have them here."

' "Do not forget them, I want to see them."

'One of the many things I had done at Edward's request (or command?) was to visit a (homosexual) photographer-friend of mine for a set of large photographs.

'In view of the fact that I was to be married we strove for utmost decorum and decency (and laughed a lot while doing so). As a consequence if there was anything I felt sure about it was the undefiled modesty of those photographic images. But I didn't know my dear Edward—yet.

'Now that the Big Decision had been made I was deemed fit to meet the director of Mr. B. Van S's office. I had seen him at a distance and taken a violent dislike to him at first sight. Now he came bowing and scraping: a small, ratty little man, and my initial reaction was intensified. There was absolutely nothing about him that did not irritate or disgust me, from his weak, clammy handshake to his shuffling gait and mumbling way of talking. Fortunately he did not stay long, muttered some excuse, and left the office. Edward glanced at me sharply: "You do not like him much, do you?"

' "No", I said. "But I'll try not to let it show too much."

' "Three years ago he had a third-rate job as an economist, and now he is already dreaming of owning a house of his own. He happens to have the ideal talents (Edward smiled faintly) for my transactions here. What have you got in that envelope? Ah, the photographs." He eagerly opened the flap and studied the top one, then nodded in approval.

' "You had the sense to pick one of the very best men in the field. Hmmmm, yes. Sensitive and distinguished. Yes, that's the way I prefer you. . . ." He kept humming and nodding until he reached the last one. That one had been taken as a sort of afterthought, in half profile, with a cashmere shawl draped over my breasts and shoulders. The photographer and I had been extremely circumspect in view of all that had recently happened, and I felt quite sure that any one of those photos could have been used as images of the Holy Virgin Mary. But my dear Edward shot straight up in the air, banged his fist on his desk, and shouted:

' "Look at this! Just look at this filth! The same thing all over again! Must I show this to people as my official wife! That dirty queer must have been coming in his pants while you were exhibiting yourself like . . . like . . ." He was speechless with rage, tore the photograph into small pieces and threw them around the room. The whole scene was so ridiculous, and his accusation so unfounded, that I sat in stony silence and finally replied:

' "My dear Edward, you know that this man is an out-and-out homosexual. And that type doesn't 'come', as you call it, at the sight of a woman's breasts. We both thought that you would like to have a more or less old-fashioned one. With a draped shawl. A very decently draped shawl, I may add. That's all."

'He reacted at once with one of his typical about-faces. He took both my hands, kissed them, behaved as if nothing had happened.

' "Come, let's have lunch together. By the way, what were you thinking of for a wedding present?"

'I had been thinking about that. "A sports car?"

' "My foolish little woman. Why not jewelry? But all right, We'll see the Jaguar dealer right after lunch."

' "But, uh . . ."

' "But what, my sweet? Out with it. No secrets for my little girl."

' "I've always dreamed about having a sports Mercedes 190 SL."

'He patted my hand: "We'll get you the finest one in Europe. Can you wait another five minutes?"

'He left the room and came right back with an envelope.

' "Here's three thousand to buy something to get married in. A simple something, I detest all those frills and fiddle-de-dees of brides in white."

'It was another busy afternoon. But no one could say I had nothing to show for it.

'Over cocktails he suddenly asked: "How are your Roman Catholic lessons going?"

'I told him about my priest and even managed to name the order he belonged to. Then added: "One thing I wanted to ask you: do I have to pay them?"

'Edward smiled and shook his head, then took out a small card case: "Next time just give him my personal card. We own one of the largest printing firms in Holland. Tell him that anything he wants to have printed goes on my bill. He'll understand. I have to be in London tomorrow and want to go to bed early. Do you mind going back to Amsterdam now? As soon as we are married you will never be alone any more, my darling."

'The next days were one continuous whirl of a chaos. I was suddenly presented with a fat envelope with forty-thousand guilders worth of stock. We went to still another jewelers to buy rings, and also a string of pink-glowing pearls. A platinum wristwatch with sapphires. We spent one entire afternoon at the office of a notary public to change Edward's last will and testament. By this time I was in such a daze from so much champagne, so much driving around, so much telephoning and making decisions, that my mind could not register much more. I knew that there were people who were very wealthy, but Edward's coffers seemed literally inexhaustible. Something on the Aga Khan level, it seemed to me. He would just pick up a telephone and mention his name, and jewelers, lawyers, hotel owners would bow and scrape. And not only in Holland—the same thing happened in France.

'It did occur to me, though, that he never operated in Amsterdam. At the beginning I had entertained lurking suspicions—You read the damnedest things in the papers. But it soon became apparent that my Edward was what is called the real goods. The honest-to-God heavy-ingot, certified and warranted Real Stuff. Allah's gift to the poor working girl. We were making plans for a safari and a cruise around the world.

'Back in Amsterdam I went to see my padré. I handed him Edward's card, plus the message about the printing plant. I had my religious instruction, did some talking, and came home at half-past ten. The telephone rang. A customer who didn't yet know that I'm out of that business? No—Edward.

' "And where has my little woman been?"

' "Having religious lessons."

'He laughed gaily: "I cannot complain about that, can I? What did the padré say?"

' "Nothing in particular. I gave him your card and message. He seemed pleased."

' "Yes, yes. I know them. They can always use the money. Shall we have dinner tomorrow in The Hague?"

' "I'll be there at six." '

'I want a bath before going to sleep. I am really exhausted. The bloody telephone begins to ring. Stops and begins again. It could be Edward, of course. What has he thought up now?

' "Miss Von Cleef here."

'I recognize the voice at once. It is the padré, speaking in a slow, measured, and hesitant voice.

' "Miss Von Cleef? Uh . . . that card you gave me"—I recall Edward's remark and expect him to ask how much credit they have at the printing plant—"is your future husband the owner of that firm?"

' "Yes, that's what he gave me to understand."

' "Is his name, uh . . . B. Van S.?"

' "Yes, padré."

' "Does he now live in Nice, France?"

' "Yes, he does."

'He begins to talk very fast and in a nervous voice: "Then I am very sorry, but I am not allowed to give you instruction any longer. Will you please be so kind to come here tomorrow morning at ten o'clock and ask for Father Superior . . . I'll give you his name. He'll tell you what you need to know. Do you know his name?"

'I hurriedly write it down and start to ask some more questions, but he has already broken the connection.

'I spend a bad night. Jesus priest, what NOW?

'Next morning I ring the bell of the monastery at ten on the dot. A stocky priest with black curly hair opens the heavy door and nods when I mention my name.

' "Will you follow me?"

'The door bangs shut and is fastened with a chain. Mad ideas rush through my head. Our footsteps echo in the deserted stone corridors. Then we climb a broad stone staircase and enter a large room. Oak everywhere. Books. A large desk, behind which my curly-headed priest sits down. Gestures toward a sober, straight-backed chair. He is wearing a simple black cassock. I know too little about the Roman Catholic church to know or even guess to what order he belongs. To me he looks just like an ordinary priest. Of peasant descent, judging from his face and build. I cannot avoid trying to guess the size and potency of his penis, and ban that sacrilegious thought at once.

' "I understand that you wish to become a Roman Catholic?"

'I laugh nervously: "That's right. It's something I have wanted all my life, as a matter of fact."

' "How long have you known this man you propose to marry?"

' "About, uh . . . four months."

'He opens a drawer and gets out two fat files. They make a stack about half a yard high. Taps them with a finger.

' "You see this dossier, Miss Von Cleef?"

' "Yes."

' "It's all about your, uh . . . fiancé." He seems to avoid mentioning Edward's name.

'There is a long silence. Then I say: "A dossier? About what? Not a criminal file?"

' "Not in the sense that you mean. But sufficiently damning to make it impossible for you ever to marry him in the Roman Catholic Church. This man is so evil, through and through, that even if you yourself were the most evil woman in all Amsterdam . . . even in that improbable case, you still would never be permitted to marry this man in any of our churches. And tell him not to attempt it in France, for even if I have to apply directly to the Vatican—you will never be permitted to marry him before a Roman Catholic priest."

'I am trembling and shivering now. "For Heaven's sake, Reverend —what's the matter with him?"

' "Miss Von Cleef—within three months you would come back here a weeping mental and moral wreck. It is completely out of the question. I cannot tell you any more than that."

'I try to plead with him, but he rises silently and precedes me out to the street. The door bangs shut and I hear the chain rattling and echoing inside.

'By this time I know enough not to go rushing around in a panic, stirring up all sorts of things, talking to everyone and getting everything in an uproar. And my common sense tells me that the only recourse is . . . a civil wedding.

'Which was duly signed and witnessed on September 10, 1959.'

'The next day Edward fell subject to a violent urge to show me Düsseldorf. His chauffeur drove us to Schiphol, and there we took the plane for West Germany. In Düsseldorf a limousine was waiting to take us straight to the Park Hotel, where Edward had a corner suite reserved, filled with champagne and flowers.

'I would not be at all surprised if, at this stage in my story, there are some eyebrows raised. I mean, after all this preliminary to-do and hoo-hah, only one short paragraph about my wedding ceremony? Don't worry, dear reader—you'll get your money's worth.

'We had dinner that evening—where? Right on the terrace. With me wearing my pearls and an adequate air of happiness.

'My Edward let his eyes roam around the room, over the newly prosperous West German industrialists and their prize women, then said grumblingly: "My sweet little wife, you are the only one here who is not wearing mink. Tomorrow I'll buy you the finest mink stole in the whole Rhine valley."

' "But tomorrow is Sunday, dear Edward."

' "Tomorrow, I said."

' "Yes, dear Edward."

'When morning came rolling around I woke up first and asked: "Shall I ring for breakfast?"

' "No. I am going to Mass and take Holy Communion."

'I was terribly hungry, but I dutifully said: "Yes, Edward dear. But please do not drink so much today."

'There was absolutely no reaction at all. After church we went for a walk and passed a window display of absolutely wonderful furs. Edward stopped to memorize the address.

' "I'll have the hotel desk find out where the owner lives."

' "But on Sunday . . ."

'My husband sighed patiently: "You have to learn, my dear child, that any German businessman who thinks he can make a ten-thousand mark sale will get into his car if he has to come all the way from Wiesbaden."

' "Yes, dear Edward."

'Walking back to our hotel, he suddenly said, "Did you notice that young boy who passed us just now?"

'I produced some girlish laughter: "You should know by now that I don't like young boys."

'Edward stopped and turned around. When I did the same I saw a young boy coming after us, sauntering up to Edward: "*Haben Sie vielleicht ein Streichholz?*" he asked. Edward gave him a light from his gold lighter, then glanced at me. "Shall we invite him for lunch, dear?"

' "If you want to, dear Edward."

'I had hardly gotten over my amazement when I found myself sitting on the hotel terrace, having cocktails with my husband and this, this . . . my God—I should have known the type! I let them do all the talking that was reasonably possible, until I heard Edward saying: "I'm going to do something about that mink stole now."

'He disappeared inside and I was left alone with that eighteen-year-old juvenile delinquent. He looked me insolently up and down, and asked: "*Und was machen wir später?*"

'I said, in English: "I don't speak German."

'That proved a slight miscalculation. for he began spouting fake American at me at a terrific rate. I just shrugged my shoulders and made a hopeless gesture: he could make of that whatever he wanted. Just then Edward came back in a gay mood.

' "Everything is arranged. We'll have lunch together and in an hour the mink man will meet us there. My darling wife will pick out something really stunning. A bellboy will come to carry the stuff and the hotel desk will pay."

'Was this merry money-go-round never going to stop? I drank a lot of white wine at lunch, then was driven to the fur shop by its owner, and in a state of high excitement picked out a blue-gray mink cape and a brown broadtail coat with a mink collar. I signed for it: eighteen thousand German marks, if you please. Then we went back to the hotel with the uniformed bellboy two steps behind me all the way. If I still had any doubts left, they vanished completely when the desk, after one swift glance at the bill, just nodded.

'At the door of our suite I knocked, for Edward had the key. No answer. I looked at my watch. I had been away one hour in all. Edward must still be out drinking somewhere.

'Then the door swung open, and Edward stood there in a silk dressing gown, looking angry. He took the boxes from the boy and said to me: "You did that at record speed. Why?"

'I was still excited, slightly drunk, and I had to piss like a fire horse.

' "I made the most fantastic buy . . . Excuse me, but I have to go to the toilet."

'I began to push past him and he said, in a strange voice: "Don't go into the bedroom."

' "Why in the world not?"

' "Because I forbid you to, dammit!"

'I giggled a bit, said "don't be silly", crossed our suite toward our bedroom, then suddenly stopped and turned around. He was following me with a murderous look on his face.

' "Oh", I thought, "he's in one of his sudden moods again," crossed the bedroom, took a fast and hissing piss, and left the toilet. He was standing by the bed still with that mad, dark look. But I saw nothing out of the ordinary—until I glanced up and saw the boy, absolutely naked, hanging from the heavy brass curtain rod—tongue hanging out of his mouth, his face red.

' "Edward!" I yelled. "No, oh, no! You've killed him!"

' "Don't be a fool", he said, opening his dressing gown, and began to masturbate. I dropped limply into an armchair and burst out weeping. Edward climbed up on a chair and helped the boy down from his perch. I now saw that the cord around his neck was not drawn tight—he had been holding himself up with one hand. The boy dressed swiftly, Edward gave him some money, and we were alone together.

' "Well now, my sweet," my dear husband said gaily, "let's have some champagne and you can show me your new furs."

'But I was still sobbing hysterically.

' "Edward, must you do things like that? Even if you want sex ten times a day—I am here, aren't I. And I never refuse you anything—you know that."

' "No comment", he said. He opened the boxes, had me put on the coat and then the mink, and was quite content. We had champagne with the traditional caviar, and lay down to have our afternoon nap. He fell asleep very soon, but I could not sleep. I lay there cold with shock, suddenly realizing that this was absolutely impossible. In a flash I saw what I had let myself in for, and that I had lost all the simple and pleasant things I had always had: lost my business, my friends, lost Gonda, and lost my dream of a happy marriage.

'After Edward woke up, he stood combing his hair, and turned around, looked me swiftly up and down, then said: "My dear little girl, my princess. Promise me one thing: don't ever leave me."

'I bathed my face and wrists in cold water, had some more champagne, and began to feel a little better.'

'Some days later, back in Holland, I was reading when Edward came home full of energy and fun: "Let's have some champagne, my sweet."

' "Yes", I said, "and caviar, I suppose?"

'But that escaped him completely. He pulled me down beside him on a couch, tickled my nose, and went on: "I've been thinking about us, darling, and I still think it would be better if, after all, we were married in the church, too. You see, almost all my business, uh . . .

the people I do business with are almost all Roman Catholics. So you'd better go on with your religious lessons."

'My stomach was suddenly full of butterflies. First that naked, curtain-hanging boy, and now this again.

' "Edward", I said cooly, "we cannot get married in the Roman Catholic church."

'It did not register. Edward, in his mad-gay mood, let loose an optimistic hoot of laughter and poured more champagne.

' "You silly little darling. If one knows the ropes and has the right connections he can make a Roman Catholic out of anyone in no time."

' "Edward, listen to me for God's sake. The monks or Jesuits whoever they are over in Amsterdam have a file on you almost as tall as you are." And I told him the whole story. Before I was halfway through he swept the champagne bucket, glasses, the crystal caviar dish and everything else off the table. He ran around the suite roaring like a drunken Genghis Khan.

' "It's that mealy-mouthed cow-cunted brother-fucking holy-water-pissing altarstrumpet who played me that goddamned trick! I swear she's been fucked by every priest in Amsterdam she ever confessed to. I've kept her and her mastodont of a mother for years and years . . . But I'll teach them! I'll get them!"

'Then he rushed out of the room and I did not hear from him until late the next afternoon. I was called to the telephone and heard dear Edward's voice; it was sweet as pie.

' "Is that you, my little one? In a quarter of an hour the chauffeur will come for you and I'll meet you at my office. We'll get this Roman Catholic business settled once and for all." '

'It was another sort of monastery. I was dropped off at the door, rang the bell as my husband had ordered me to, was admitted, and went through the same kind of routine. But with one tremendous difference. Here I heard that it had all been a disastrous and regrettable mistake. A stupid matter of confusing names. It would take one or two days to get the confusion cleared up, and then we could go ahead with the Catholic ceremony as planned. I was seen to the door just as I had been seen to the door in Amsterdam, and found a taxi waiting for me with instructions to take me back to my hotel—where I found Edward behind champagne and caviar.

' "Ah, my darling . . . How horrible all this must have been for you! If you had only told me before! Aren't you happy now that everything has been settled?"

'I stared at him in stupefaction. "Everything settled? How can it possibly . . .?"

' "Dear, dear, dear. Don't you worry your pretty little head over things that you cannot possibly understand. The Roman Catholic Church has its own internal rivalries and feuds, like any other organization. We can get married in Wassenaar within two or three days."

'I nearly gasped: "But I haven't even been baptized! That's the least that . . ."

'Dear Edward patted my hand. "You just do as I say and everything will be perfect."

'Next day he handed me a letter. "We are to be married tomorrow in Wassenaar. Before we begin the official ceremony you hand over this letter. Better read it first."

> My dearest girl,
> I cannot tell you how happy we are with the news of your recent marriage, unexpected though it is. About this matter of religion I can put your mind at rest. I have never told you, but when you were nine months old you contracted double pneumonia, and since every Roman Catholic mother has the right to have her child baptized in case of mortal danger, that is exactly what I did. But because of the fact that your father was so irreligious and difficult about these things I have never told anyone.
> Your ever-loving
> Mother

'I think I must have read that letter four times. Then I began to tumble to it.

' "Edward! In the first place this is not my mother's handwriting. In the second place she would never write that sort of hypocritical shit. In the third place she was never a Roman Catholic herself, I told you that!"

'We sat staring at each other and I suddenly burst out in wild laughter. Edward said, with a tight face: "If and when anyone asks you for that letter, you will hand it over. First the letter and then this envelope. And you will say: 'This is a little something to embellish your church'. That's all."

'I was married the next day at half-past eight in the evening. With Edward's ratty director and his sleazy wife as witnesses. That's the way they did it. Curtain down on that act.'

'I was informed that we would definitely leave for Nice within two days. My dog (Pierre, remember?) had been staying with good friends for the last two hectic weeks, but the Dutch chauffeur was now ordered to drive there and pick up the dog. My wedding-present-Mercedes had been paid for, but there was a two-month delay in delivery.

'The first night after I had my dog back I woke up in the middle of the night and saw Edward, in a dressing gown, writing furiously at the small desk in our bedroom. I got up for a glass of water and stopped to look at him.

' "Can't you sleep, Edward?"

'He was apparently in a good mood. He looked up laughingly, signed a letter, and said: "That dog of yours snores like a blasted buzzsaw."

' "Yes, sometimes she does." I stood there, drinking sips of water, and then he gestured at a stack of signed letters on his private notepaper.

' "Know what this is?"

' "No idea. And I did not want to ask."

' "I am writing letters to all my ex-girl friends. Look—I have all the envelopes already stamped and addressed."

' "About twenty?"

' "Twenty-three, as a matter of fact. But their contents are all different. Read one of them. Go on."

'I took up one of the sheets and read:

> Dear Miss Van de Bos,
> I have been so fortunate as to finally meet a chaste and generous woman who has consented to become my wife. This means that hereafter I have no more need of your filthy and degrading practices in which I have, as I now realize, always participated with great inner disgust.
>
> Yours truly . . .

'Yes, they were all slightly different, but all highly insulting.

' "But Edward . . . is this really necessary?"

' "Most certainly", he replied resolutely. "I am making a clean break myself, just as you have done, my sweet."

'Next morning I was putting on my underwear when Edward looked in.

' "Before I forget: I want you to buy woolen underwear. The flimsy things you wear now make you look like a woman of easy virtue."

'Before I had time to recover and protest, he added: "And I told the chauffeur to take that dog of yours for its morning walk. If you do it yourself, they'll take you for a street walker. That's an order, don't forget that." And he was gone.

'I did not want any more trouble the last day in that hotel, so I left it at that. The next morning we departed for Nice by chauffeur-driven car.

'Our first overnight stop was Basle, Switzerland.

'Of course Edward had some business to attend to there and I asked him if I could have my hair done in the meanwhile. That was all right.

'I could have had my hair done right there in the hotel, but it was the most beautiful weather imaginable, so I went for a short walk, found a French *établissement*, and spent a most enjoyable hour there; bought some lotions and perfumes and strolled back leisurely. I took the elevator to our floor and found the door of our suite closed. That reminded me of that horrible scene in Düsseldorf, but I also reminded myself that lightning never strikes twice in the same place, so I knocked. The sound had hardly died away when the door was torn open and Edward jumped at me, grabbed the sleeve of my thin summer coat, and slung me halfway across the room, tearing out half the shoulder of my coat. The door slammed shut.

' "You incurable slut! Where have you been?"

' "To the hairdresser. I told you before . . ."

' "There is an excellent shop right here in the hotel. Where have you been?"

'Half weeping, half wailing, I point at my hair: "Can't you see for yourself? And here are the things I bought. At a French *établiss* . . ."

'He tore the packages out of my hands and dumped them into a waste basket.

' "French! Yes, I thought so! Did he have a big cock? Open your mouth, you putain, and let me smell your breath!"

'Instead of doing that, I slammed him one in the middle of his mad face. When I get angry I slam good. That's one thing you learn in a hospital. I don't suppose that had ever happened to him before, for he let me go at once, walked over to the mirror, and began to bathe his face. Lucky for him that I missed his nose and only hit his cheekbone. (I felt my knuckles for days.)

'He poured himself a glass of champagne and paced up and down the room, moaning. "What can I have done to deserve this? Married in church two days ago, and already she is behaving like a rutty bitch."

' "You are completely nuts!" I said. "You better stop drinking." I turned to go into the bedroom.

'He grabbed my wrists. "Where do you think you're going?"

' "To the toilet."

' "Oh, no you're not."

'I said, very reasonably: "Dear Edward—can I go and do wee wee?"

' "No."

' "All right. Then I'll do it here on the floor."

' "If you wish to."

'We stood there with him holding my wrist, and a terrifying fear got hold of me. I tore my arm loose, jumped for the bathroom door, wrenched it open, and looked at the windows. Everything normal. No hanging bodies. The horror was just ebbing out of me when I looked down at the tub, and saw the naked body of a boy in the water, with just his head above the surface. His eyes were open and he looked at me with a mixture of amazement and uncertainty. I was so undone that I automatically went on to the toilet, hitched up my skirt, and sat there, when Edward walked into the bathroom, grabbed the boy by the throat, and pushed him under water, shouting:

' "You dirty whore! I'll kill you, just as I'm going to kill that new wife of mine!"

'I jumped up from my seat of honor, my panties hanging down around my shoes, and began to pull him back by his dressing gown. That seemed to bring him to his senses. He let go of the boy (who had surfaced with mad fear in his eyes), opened the front of his dressing gown, and masturbated.

'I pulled up my panties, staggered into the sitting room, and dropped down into an armchair. The bathroom door was pulled shut. There is another door to the suite, and I suppose he got rid of the boy that way, for a minute later Edward came in, as bouncy as you please.

' "Ah, my dear wife. You must really mind my warnings, darling, but you'll learn, I guess. Yes, you'll learn. Shall we go down for lunch?"

'That afternoon we bought two heavy gold bracelets for me, plus gloves, ties, and shirts for Edward. Then we left for Nice—still in the Chrysler and with the Dutch chauffeur.

'I was beginning to realize that I could not take this for long. I could feel my nerves wearing thin. But what could I do? What was the matter with Edward? Long-term results of too much alcohol? Apart from his homosexual inclinations, of course. During the long hours of driving I recalled Gonda's warnings. I remembered what the padré in Amsterdam had said about the secret contents of that enormous file.

'WHAT HAD I GOTTEN MYSELF INTO???

'The real laugh was on me, of course. Since I thought I knew so much. I had vaguely heard of the Marquis de Sade, and if I had ever taken the trouble to read him, I would have known that his base of operation was located very near to the house to which my dear Edward was taking me now: my first House of Horror and Pain.'

'Arrival of the Master with his Happy Young Bride. Thérèse, the French chauffeur, and two gardeners are lined up, ready with congratulations. The whole house full of flowers, and a basketful of telegrams and letters waits in the hall. The Dutch chauffeur is sent back with the Chrysler. We'll make do with the Bentley and Edward's private Ferrari.

'We have supper on the terrace, and for some unexplainable reason a jingle that I had forgotten for years suddenly pops into my head. One of the Second Tank Division Americans whose name I had forgotten taught me the lines in those faraway and wild months right after the Liberation. To me it was just a silly song then, but the subconscious is a very intricate thing, and now the same lines emerge . . . but loaded with a new and sinister meaning.

'Supper on the terrace and up pops the jingle:

Won't you come into my parlor
said the spider to the fly
I've got the cutest little living room
that you did ever spy.

Oh fly, poor fly
won't you come into my parlor. . . .

Please come in, my pretty maiden,
let me take your dainty hat
We'll have tea out on the terrace
and a cosy little chat
Oh fly, poor fly
won't you come into my parlor. . . .

'Edward is looking through the mail, tossing most of it aside without opening it. He looks up: "You are so quiet. Is anything the matter?"

' "Matter? Oh, no. Just that I am very tired and have a headache to boot." Inwardly I think: "Don't you have any idea how sick and hurt I am inside?"

'He tosses another letter aside and says under his breath: "Tired . . . headache. They always have something the matter with them." He pours himself another double brandy and tosses it down. We sit there silently for two more hours, with Edward drinking steadily. Then we go to bed.

'Upstairs I ask timidly: "Edward . . . can we open one of the windows a little?" I have neither the energy nor the guts to say that his stink and reek of alcohol makes me sick.

' "No. Night air is very unhealthy."

' "Can the dog sleep here?"

' "No. Dogs don't belong in bedrooms. I already gave orders to let the animal sleep in the kitchen in its basket. Ridiculous and sentimental nonsense. Like those whores who have their rooms full of dolls." '

'We go for a drive in the Ferrari, and Edward tears around those perilous curves like a madman. I hold my breath and pull in my stomach, telling myself he is just showing off, or testing my courage. But then I notice that he neither uses the horn nor tries to slow down at intersections, and there are a lot of dangerous ones. I nearly have heart failure. This is no expert driving—only a madman would roar along like this. A madman or a potential suicide. The sweat runs from my armpits, and then I scream at him: "Let me out! If you want to drive this way, let me out!"

'The Ferrari screams through another curve and past the driveway of a white chalet, where a Jaguar is cautiously nosing out.

' "When I am here, everyone else stops", Edward assures me. I realize that my legs are so tightly tensed against the brakeboard that all my muscles hurt. If I survive this, he'll never get me in this murderous car again. Not even at pistol point. That resolution keeps me sane.'

'We generally went to bed at midnight. Generally dined at some restaurant, and Edward never seemed to stop drinking any more. We had to have sex every night, for hours on end. I kissed, fondled, licked, sucked, and massaged him, using all the tricks I knew, but with all that alcohol in him he could not achieve an orgasm. After half an hour of patient hard work I could usually get the thing to stiffen up. Not a real hard-on, but some firmness. When I tried to climb on him to get it in fast, he collapsed at once. Then I was rolled on my back with my legs wide apart, and sucked and bitten. I had enjoyed all those acrobatics before our marriage, he was really expert and knew damned well what he was doing and where and why. But now I was so hurt and disappointed and full of fear that there was not the faintest possibility of my getting an orgasm or even approaching it. I fell back on the old trick of playacting, but that disgusted me so much that I begged him to stop. That made him furious.

' "Cursed frigid lesbian! Just my luck to get stuck with a tribadian trollop!"

'But when I gave in to him and groaned and wriggled and acted as if I had come nine times, he got up, poured himself a double brandy, and stood looking down at me with contempt: "Nine times, and still not satisfied. Could have given lessons to Messalina herself. Hysterical nymphomaniac. Very dangerous type. Can't be left alone for half an hour. Oversexed."

'It became more and more difficult for me to get a healthy night's rest. I dropped off, then woke up and saw the light burning. Opened one eye and saw him on his knees beside the bed, praying with folded hands. Sometimes with a prayerbook that he always held in his left hand. Was he masturbating with his right? Or just playing with his thing? Sometimes he whispered: "Are you awake?"

'But I kept on breathing slowly and evenly, afraid of a new argument. I became an expert at playing possum, and then I soon found out that he actually did masturbate, but with such consummate craftsmanship that I could detect hardly any sound or movement. God knows where he had refined his technique. In church, probably, during Mass.

'Between four and five o'clock he usually came to bed, leaving the light there, and then lay there, tossing and groaning, with the alcohol fumes stinking up the room. An hour later he woke up (usually with a hard penis (took wildly hold of me and tried to penetrate me before the thing collapsed again. Hurting me with his nails if anything went wrong, and growling "Frigid tramp. . . ."

'If I yielded fast enough and he managed to get into me he began to fuck like a madman, ramming and banging, panting and cursing, until at last he managed to fire some sperm with a shuddering spasm. Then he got up at once and went to the bathroom, grumbling:

' "Oversexed witch. She knows how it exhausts me. She wants to kill me . . . that's what she would like."

'But if he did not manage to come in spite of all his banging and pumping, he finally pulled his thing out and lay awake, belching, tossing, and growling until Pierre knocked with the eternal tea and biscuits.'

'I was now practically under house arrest. The standing orders were that I was not allowed off the grounds alone. If I wanted to go for a walk with the dog, the chauffeur had to walk ten paces behind me. Same thing if I wanted to visit the hairdresser. I heard him give the order to Pierre.

' "You will wait in front of the door until Madame comes out, and don't try to go for a quick glass of wine in the meantime!"

'Then, one Saturday, he announced: "We'll go to church tomorrow."

'I replied listlessly: "If you say so."

' "Yes, I say so. I want confession and communion. Better ring up now, find out whether they hear confession on Sunday."

'He came back grumbling: "Lazy dunderheads. I practically support them. Presented them with a stained-glass window. But hear confession on a Sunday? No. All right, then we'll go this afternoon. I want you along."

' "All right. But only if I drive, or Pierre. I won't go in the Bentley or the Ferrari with you at the wheel. Not for all the money in the world."

' "Well, well! The girl from the slums is beginning to throw her weight around. . . . Getting above her station. Must be put down firmly. Kept in her place. Are you coming or not?"

' "No."

'He left the house without saying anything more. Came back later in a mild mood, ordered the Bentley and the chauffeur and took me to lunch in Saint Paul, at a fine, romantic old restaurant. The atmosphere was just as pleasant and relaxed as in the first days of our "courtship". Experience had taught me that these periods of serenity generally heralded the most devastating explosions. But I had now reached such a stage of weariness and nerves that I welcomed them as vital breathing spaces. As someone who is being slowly strangled is glad when the strangle-hold is momentarily relaxed and the victim can gulp some air.

'We returned late in the evening, did some drinking and sitting around on the terrace, and went peacefully to bed. For the first time in weeks I slept like a log. I did not even wake up to check whether Edward was having one of his praying jags.

'Next morning we went to church in the chauffeur-driven Bentley. I had developed a theory that Edward was a religious maniac who could be kept quiet if I encouraged his church-going. I felt a new hope, especially when Edward began to stroke my hair and hands in the back of the car, murmuring how happy he was. It took us more than an hour to get to the modern little church. It was very hot, and a pack of gypsy children were playing in front of the church door. We had not had any breakfast (Catholics are not allowed drink or food before Holy Communion); it was so stifling that I began to feel faint, but every time I sat on the bench Edward angrily pulled me to my knees. It was a High Mass and would last for at least two hours, and I became angrier and angrier, the sicker I felt. All this damned false hypocrisy!

..'After the service the priest stood by the church door, shaking hands. When we came out he made straight for us, a second priest in his wake who turned out to be a Dutch chaplain from somewhere in Gelderland, one of the easternmost provinces.

' "Mr. B. Van S. . . . would you like to see the window that our church owes to your generosity?"

'Edward turned to me: "Yes, my dear. Do you remember that I mentioned the stained-glass window? I told you about it some weeks ago."

'He had only mentioned it the day before, but I nodded, full of understanding and enthusiasm. We walked around the church and stopped in front of a leaded stained-glass window depicting Jesus with his shepherd's staff and some sheep. He was walking on bare feet and wearing a sort of cowl that fell open in front and showed a half a bare leg, the leg that was taking a forward step. Everything quite normal.

' "Magnificently done, don't you think?" the priest said.

'But Edward wheeled around, glared at him, raised his cane, and smashed the whole window to splinters and smithereens, shouting:

' "Profanation! Desecration! Scandalous! Depicting the Lord Jesus with a bare leg! Enough to make anyone an iconoclast!" When the noise of the falling glass had died away there was complete and stunned silence. I sensed both priests looking at me sideways, but kept a straight face, opened my bag and began to look for something. Found my handkerchief and patted my nose. I heard Edward saying, in a perfectly collected voice:

' "I shall pay for a new window. But I want to see the design before its final execution."

' "*Oui, mais oui, monsieur*", said the French priest, and we started toward the car, Edward and the priest chatting in voluble French. The chauffeur was waiting by the car with a completely expressionless face. Edward shook hands with the priest, then turned aside and invited the Dutch chaplain for lunch.

'We started driving back to Nice, and I was immensely grateful for the stream of air through the partly open windows. The Dutch chaplain and Edward talked, but I did not even listen, until Edward said sharply:

' "Dear wife—Chaplain Brouwer asked you something."

'I tried to join a completely meaningless talk, and when we got home there were the inevitable cocktails, and lunch on the terrace.

'Until Edward leaned forward and said to me: "Are you having one of your headaches, my dear? You are so quiet?."

'I hadn't yet gotten over the shock of seeing him smash that window. For the sake of everything that's sane and sensible—what had I married? And me, with my infantile hope that getting him to church would keep him in line!

'Edward said gently: "Why don't you go to your bedroom and lie down for a while?"

'I got up at once, managed a grateful smile, took the dog with me, and for absolutely the first time lay down on my own bed in my own bedroom. Pierre jumped on the bed, nuzzling me, and I said to her: "I wish we were back in the Staalstraat together, Pierre—you and I." The boxer gave me a lick on my cheek and I dropped off to sleep.

'I woke up with a start, glanced at my watch, and saw that it was past four. Oh, Lord. Edward would be furious. I freshened up, put on a nice dress, and met Thérèse in the downstairs hall.

' "Where is monsieur?"

'She evaded my eyes and replied, offhandedly: "I think upstairs, Madame."

'I tripped back upstairs again and opened the door of our communal bedroom. There I froze. Flat on his back on the bed—on our marital bed—lay the Dutch chaplain, his black cassock pulled up to his midriff and his nether parts bare. My dear Edward was on his knees beside the bed, in exactly the place where he always did his nightly praying, with the chaplain's penis in his mouth. He was moving his head up and down while the chaplain moaned and kicked his hairy legs. They were so fanatically absorbed in their corrupt activity that they didn't even hear me open the door. After a short while I stepped silently back, closed the door, and sat myself down in the rocking chair on the terrace. I was cold with shock. You may well ask yourself what I was so shocked about, with my past and experience. I understand now that during those years when I was a little girl, when I so desperately wanted to be a Roman Catholic, I had come to believe that priests were the representatives of God on earth. And you know how converts are—far more fanatic than those who are born to the faith.

'I sat rocking for a while, then called the dog, walked out the gate and strolled aimlessly around.

'When I came back Edward was mixing cocktails on the terrace. Whistling gaily. I expected to be yelled at, and I couldn't have cared less, but he greeted me merrily. Thank Allah, there was no trace of the chaplain. He was not even hanging from a tree somewhere, as far as I could see.

'I was handed the eternal singapore sling, and then Edward remarked: "By the way, my dear—in the future, will you knock on the door before you enter the bedroom?"

'I was absolutely beaten. I just nodded and sipped singapore slings. We had dinner at La Bonne Auberge and went to bed early. Another quiet night.'

'Next morning, after breakfast, Edward locks himself in the library and I wander around a bit in the garden. I am getting inexpressibly bored. Edward always tells Thérèse what he wants to eat. There is no one to talk to, no shopping to do. After a while I drift upstairs and take all my clothes from the enormous walnut wardrobe, with the idea of rearranging them. To give me something to do. It is a truly colossal wardrobe and must be centuries old. As I am reaching to hang up some dresses, I suddenly sense movement, look over my shoulder, and see dear Edward behind me, with one hand on one of the open-swung doors. He gives a slight pull, and the whole wardrobe tilts forward.

'He says, contemplatively: "If this wardrobe should happen to fall over on top of you, everybody would believe it was an accident."

'I drop all my dresses and jump sideways until I am out of range. As I still stand there looking at him in horror, he takes away his hand, looks at it, dusts it off, and adds dreamily: ". . . For who would ever believe that a happily married husband would murder his young and faithful wife?"

'Then his entire demeanor changes, his face takes on a truly demoniac expression. He comes slowly toward me, his open hands clutching, outspread.

' "But I warn you, if I ever find out that you talk about me in any way and to anyone . . . I'll kill you like a bug!"

'God knows where, but I find the courage to scream: "You are mad! You're a madman! They should lock you up! I hope you drop dead, you with your filthy, stinking money!" and rush out of the room.

'That night I sleep in my own room—I have no key for the lock. I have the dog with me and let her shit in the corner, for I am afraid to let her go out. Edward is capable of maiming or poisoning her to revenge himself on me. I dare not go to sleep, and dearly wish I had a pistol. I resolve to sneak into the kitchen in the morning to get one of those pointed, razor-sharp carving knives. I lie with my eyes closed, in a half doze, when the door very slowly opens. I see Edward's face. I fly out of bed and yell: "Go away! Get out of here! Go away or I'll scream the house down!" I take up a chair and stand prepared to sling it right through the plate-glass window. He growls and grumbles, mutters: "Frigid slut. Sleeps with the dog, probably," but backs out, pulling the door softly shut.

'Next morning we do not exchange a single word. Thérèse is in and out of the kitchen all morning. She feels that I am up to something, however. One of those sly French peasant types. When I see that the kitchen is empty I sneak in and look around. But this enormous space is unknown territory, and while I am still standing there, looking at the assortment of hatchets and meat cleavers hanging on the wall, she materializes behind me and I jump with fright.

' "Does Madame wish for anything?"

' "Nono . . . I, uh . . . for a bowl or something for the dog. He gets thirsty at night."

'I get my goddamn bowl. As I cross the hall, Edward approaches me and asks sarcastically, "We will have some English guests for dinner. Is there a possibility that Madame's mood could take a turn for the better by six?"

' "I'll see what I can do," I say.

'A little while later he announces that he is driving into Nice to buy some special caviar. I roam around the house, find the library door open, and see the floor littered with crumpled sheets of paper. I pick up one of them. It is the handwritten draft of a telegram to the notary in The Hague:

> WISH IMMEDIATE CANCELLATION RECENT WILL AND TESTAMENT STOP THIS IMPLIES THAT UNDER NO CIRCUMSTANCES MY WIFE CAN INHERIT ANYTHING STOP DETAILS FOLLOW STOP CONFIRM

'I give a shrug. It leaves me completely cold. I pick up another crumpled paper ball. It is the draft of a sort of ultimatum to me. They all are, and they all say roughly the same:

1. Are you prepared and willing to honor and fulfil your marital commitments and duties one hundred percent?
2. Will you undertake to abandon and exorcise your delusions about personal liberty and penetrate yourself with a sense of obedience to me and your obligation to reside in any house decided on by myself?
3. Are you willing to behave—always and everywhere in accordance with your status as a lawfully and religiously married woman?
4. Are you prepared and willing to lead a subservient and respectful life with and for your lawful husband, you whom

I raised from the gutter and have disengaged from your filthy and disreputable homosexual associations? You, with your twisted and distorted character?

5. That sickly and sentimental gushing over that slavering dog must stop at once, or I will have the creature removed.
6. You will have to . . .

'While I am still comparing the various versions of this stupefying document, I hear the telephone shrilling downstairs, and then Thérèse's agitated voice full of wild alarm:

' "Madame . . . MADAME! *Vite!* . . . *Pour vous*, Madame . . . Come quick!"

'With that wrinkled piece of paper still in my hand I rush into the hall and see Thérèse standing there, her hands clasped together, as white as a human being can be.

" '*Le telephone, Madame . . . Un accident.*"

'I pick up the horn and hear a deep male voice. My French was never very good, but I understand the words "*gendarmerie*" and "*accident grave*".

'Thérèse is right beside me, and the expression on her face leaves no room for doubt. And I am completely calm and collected. I have never been so calm in all my life, go placidly upstairs, and change into something dark and decorous.

'When I come down again I find Thérèse and Pierre in front of the house, standing by a French police car. Pierre has the Bentley ready, and we follow the gendarme's car. I am still perfectly calm. With a heavy inner serenity, not unlike a pool of mercury.

'Then I see a crowd of people up ahead, and more police cars. Silently they make way for us. And then I see the remains of the blue Ferrari, and the black ruins of a second car. A door lies in the middle of the hot road, and . . . a human hand with three fingers. My nurse's training registers that automatically. I am taken gently but firmly by the arm and then I have to look . . . at Edward's head and torso. He no longer has any legs.

' "*C'est lui, madame?*"

'I nod and stand there, motionless, looking down at that rump (yesterday he was still able to kneel). Another gentle pressure on my arm. I am led back to the Bentley, and now we are piloted to a police station, for I have to sign the identification. I sign everything that is put in front of me, and someone brings me a cup of coffee.'

'Thérèse comes running toward me, weeping and sobbing, but I walk straight on, looking for my dog. I find her on the couch, wagging her tail. The couch Edward never allowed her to lie on. I wrap my arms around her neck, kiss her on her wet snout, and keep saying:

' "Pierre . . . my dearest Pierre . . . We are free, FREE, you hear?"

'The next day I take the plane back to Amsterdam, after I have telephoned Director Rat in The Hague, who is shocked, or acts shocked. Now that I am free again I all of a sudden recapture my capacity for making fast decisions.

'Yes, I leave everything to him. No, I do not intend to stay in Nice for the funeral. I wish him to do all the necessary work with the lawyers and the notary.

'I break open Edward's desk and find my passport locked away there. I shake Thérèse's hand and order Pierre to drive me to the airport. I am too highstrung to sit down until departure time. I keep walking up and down until my flight is called. I am still drenched with fear and feel incapable of a sense of real freedom until I have left that place of horror behind me.'

'There was a small mountain of mail behind the door of my flat; I had to push the door open with my shoulder. Nine-tenths of it could be thrown away without a second glance. But someone had taken the trouble to send me a newspaper clipping about the murder of a call girl. The anonymous sender had underlined in red:

> . . . the dog doped and the alarm bell disconnected when the strangling hands closed around her throat from behind . . .

'I shivered, found some whiskey, and took a double shot. Straight.'

# PART II
# THE UNITED STATES

California, here I Come . . .
and back.

New York
October 4, 1963

'All of us, at certain stages of our lives, take time for a look forward, a look around, and a look back. A sort of State of the Union Message to and about ourselves.

'When I decided to try and crack God's Own Country, I think I had, at the back of my mind, two basic ideas:

(a) After the Big Romantic Marriage Dream went bust, to cut myself a fat slice of the Big American Dream.
(b) To get my own back on men in general for what that sadistic bastard had done to louse up my life.

'This was not a process of conscious calculation. I am not a gold-digging, calculating girl. If you don't believe that, then you know where you can shove it. And not up mine.'

'During what I termed my 'period of recuperation"' I had run a hotel. Among other things. And met a gentle, intelligent, generous American boy called Al. Tall, crew-cut, and in business. Nothing sadistic about HIM, oh, no. True blue clean open-minded all-American boy. He moved all over western Europe doing things in the fashion and textile trade. Big spender. Good in bed. Very considerate.

' "Monique", he said, "I want to marry you, Very much."

' "Al", I replied, "I burnt my fingers once. Badly. Let's take it easy, huh?"

'Then he had to go back to the States and I missed him very, very much. One day in October I decided I was fed up with all those old familiar faces, was getting no younger, and if I was not actually running around in circles then I was moving around in spirals. I went to an Amsterdam soothsayer of some repute and asked him what would happen if I should venture the big jump. After consulting stars, crystal balls, and coffee grounds, he came up with this prediction:

' "When you get off the plane in New York", he breathed, "you will be welcomed with a tremendous bunch of red roses."

'What more could a girl want? So I sent off a wire to my clean American Al and was put on the plane in Holland by a good friend of long standing, plus my weepy personal maid.

'The weather was cold and cloudy, and as I crossed the Atlantic it got progressively worse. No matter, there would be roses waiting on the other side.'

'But the only people interested in my arrival were in customs. And they offered me no roses.

'No Al. But I could understand that, he was a businessman and I hadn't given him much notice. The roses would be waiting in my hotel room, of course.

'I took a taxi to the Waldorf Astoria, thinking: "New York, I hope you'll become just as happy with me as I am feeling about seeing you." I must have had hayseeds in my pubic hair.

'I was transported to my room without further ado. No roses, no notes of welcome. I took a bath, ordered sandwiches and coffee, and fell into bed.

'Woke early next morning with the famous Santa Claus feeling. At a reasonable time I rang Al's office. No, his secretary told me, she could not connect me, Mr. Textile was in Washington. No, she knew nothing about any telegram. But I could leave a message with her.

'My timing appeared to be a bit off. But that could happen to anyone who believes in spontaneous arrivals. And Americans are very busy people—aren't they? That's what makes them so rich.

'I consulted my special notebook and rang the number of one of Al's good friends.

' "Monique! What are you doing in New York?"

'My gay and happy laughter filled the empty hotel room: "Nothing in particular. Winter was coming on in Holland and I thought it might be a nice surprise for Al."

' "Well, winter is coming on here", he said. "Just stick around and I'll have coffee with you around eleven."

'We had our coffee and then he took me to the Gaslight Club. Then he began, pensively: "I'm not quite sure what Al will, uh . . . I mean, you didn't pick a very propitious moment. Why didn't you write him first?"

' "I thought it would be more fun this way. But what's the matter? I have my own ticket plus five thousand dollars in cash."

' "The matter? Nothing. It's just that . . ."

'I was still full of merriment: "I guess I'll be able to amuse myself until Al gets back from Washington."

' "Yeah. I guess so."

'Late that evening Al rang up from Washington. No merriment. "Why the hell did you come here, dropping out of thin air without warning me?"

' "But I sent a cable to your office!"

' "God, we get yards of cables every day. No one there knows who you are."

' "Welcome to America. But don't panic, sweetheart. I'll pay for myself."

' "Nonono, that's not the problem at all. Shall we have coffee, tomorrow at eleven?"

' "Let's", I said, and slammed down the phone.

'Promptly at eleven Al picked me up. We went for a drink, then had lunch at the Plaza Hotel. Al was friendly but hardly affectionate. And certainly absent-minded. But you know me: I'm the understanding kind.

'I patted his hand:

' "Al, if you are worried about all those marriage proposals—forget it. I'm not here to chase you. I've worked hard for almost two years and sold my hotel at a very good price. I'll amuse myself here for a couple of weeks and we'll see how it goes. Fair enough?"

'No. Not fair enough. "But, my dear Monique, I don't mean it that way. Don't get me wrong. The thing is that I'm so damned busy right now I'll hardly even have time to phone you. I'm up to my ears."

' "Forget it," I smiled. "I'll be busy myself, so that's all right."

' "Yes, but. . . . Shall we have dinner tomorrow night at the Four Seasons?"

' "Well, if you can find time!"

'He frowned and pursed his clean American lips: "I'll figure out something."

'After this mad ticker-tape reception I was not in the mood for much, not even shopping. I went back to my hotel room and watched television. But early that evening I got a call from Larry, an American homo who had run an antique shop in Amsterdam for a year or so.

' "Monique, are you in New York? That's wonderful! I'll have a welcome party for you next Saturday. Will you be staying there until then? Write down this address just in case. But I'll come and pick you up about eight."

'That did something to pick me up, and I needed it. Keeping up a gay front while they're throwing cold water on you really takes it out of you. And that after all that talk about marriage and eternal love. Cold water on top of a lot of hot air, enough to give any girl mental pneumonia. The hell with it! It wouldn't be the first big disappointment in my life. I had learned to take it. I went for a walk. Decided to go to a hairdresser the next day. Did so.

'When Al called me the next evening I was wearing a simple black cocktail dress and my pearls. Long black gloves up to my elbows. A mink cape and high-heeled shoes. He looked me over thoughtfully: "You look very European."

' "Is that meant as a compliment?"

' "No. Yes. . . . It's just that, uh . . ." he let it hang.

'It's only ten minutes' walk from the Waldorf to the Four Seasons. Taking my elbow to steer me around a group of people, he suddenly said: "Before I introduce you to my family I have to tell you something. We'll talk about it while we eat."

'At least he had taken the trouble to reserve a table. My spirits were rising a bit.

' "What'll you have to drink?"

' "Dry sherry."

'He shook his head just a bit. "You're not in Europe now", and he ordered two dry martinis. Sat looking around, fidgeting. I looked around and did not fidget.

' "Monique. . . ."

' "That's me."

‘ “Haha, yes. Before we get married I have to tell you something.”

‘ “I already got a message to that effect. Are you pregnant or something?”

‘ “No. You see, I am bisexual.”

‘His face was such a study in despair and embarrassment that I simply had to laugh. Part of my laughter was relief.

‘ “Is that all? I’ve heard worse.”

‘Now it all came out in a rush: “I have a boy friend, he is twenty-two. We are living together in New Jersey and if you and I get married I want it to be . . . the three of us.”

‘ “Ah, a ménage à trois. Do you think that would work?”

‘ “Yes. I’ve known you for years, Monique, and I think I know you very well. With you it would work, I feel pretty sure about that. With an American girl perhaps not, but with you . . .”

‘I was not sure how to take this. Then he popped the question:

‘ “His name is Maurice. Would you like to meet him?”

‘ “Of course I would.”

‘I had hardly uttered the word when he was out of his chair; “May I make a phone call?” and gone. I sat sipping my martini, looking at the clothes on the women. I had already noticed one thing: American men do not flirt. Perhaps they don’t know how, so they go straight for the hole in one.

‘Then Al was back, all agog and aglow. “He’ll be here in ten minutes.” He gulped his martini down. “Shall we have another one?”

‘ “Not for me. You can have this one. I prefer scotch on the rocks.”

‘I finished that in no time and asked for another. Al looked everywhere but at me. We did not talk. Lovely atmosphere—suspense. Then I saw him straighten, his whole face lit up. I looked over my shoulder and saw the most flagrant peroxided female faggot making for our table. Al pulled out a chair and began snapping his fingers at the waiters. I checked this child out: expensive rings, elegant watch, heavy gold bracelet, diamond tie clip . . . everything showy and overdone.

‘It looked me up and down: “So you are Monique.”

‘I glanced at Al, who was busying himself with the waiters and was obviously a bundle of nerves. Was this the same man who traveled around Europe with such self-assurance, doing business with tricky stinkers in Paris, Milan, and Frankfurt?

‘The waiters went away and Al looked at his Maurice beseechingly:

"Honey, I would have preferred to . . . to break it gently. But all of a sudden she was here."

'The waiter brought two dry martinis. Maurice took one sip and made a face; "not dry enough."

'There was a colossal to-do. Finally the martini was sent back, Al downed his fourth one, and began to study the menu. Maurice leaned back and said to me:

' "Can understand why Al should want to marry you. Good for him socially, probably in business, too. Perhaps. But"—he pulled out a diamond-studded platinum lighter—"we'd better have a talk about this first."

'This was getting really amusing—if you have the right sense of humor.

' "You see, every year Al gives me a new Jaguar."

' "I have a Mercedes 190 SL."

'He conceded: "That doesn't sound too bad."

' "No. And I pay for it myself."

'He tossed his lighter in the air and caught it again. "All right. I'll allow him to marry you. But I don't want any scenes when he prefers my bedroom to yours. And get this straight: it's my house. Al put it in my name."

'I glanced at Al. He sat studying the menu with bowed head, and by then I'd had it. I extinguished my cigarette in Maurice's martini, looked him straight in his arrogant face, and snarled: "You stupid ass peddler. Wait until you are ten years older and have to pay people to sleep with you. Who the hell do you think you're talking to? In Europe we use babies like you to sharpen our carving knives with!" Got up, slung my mink over one shoulder, and walked out.

'Next morning at eight Al began to telephone, almost in tears.

' "Sweetheart, he doesn't mean that way. He is just a little spoiled."

' "Then unspoil him."

' "But I can't, darling. I need you. Please try to understand, for God's sake. You can handle him. Please, please marry me, Monique. He drives me completely nuts. It's gotten so I can't work any more. He's ruining me."

' "The best thing that could happen to you. The faster you run out of money, the sooner you'll be rid of him."

'He wailed with anguish: "Monique, don't say things like that."

' "Listen, Al. I'll be around. Stop calling me. I won't have anything to do with you as long as you keep that cock- and bloodsucker around."

' "Monique—"

'I hung up and told the desk I want no more calls before noon.'

'Next day was Saturday: Larry's party. He had a two-room apartment, and at nine o'clock I did a head count and arrived at a total of sixty-seven queers. I was the guest of honor and there was only one other woman: Mary Sue, rumored to hail from Texas, about forty-five, drank straight from two bottles (one in each hand (which she only put down long enough to pull up her skirt, showing a colossal bush of black hair that began to peter out halfway down her thighs. She insisted on showing it to everybody in the room, evoking horrified squeals and yelps, and she simply could not understand why no one there wanted to make use of it—one way or another.

'I told Larry and his private friend Timmy about Al and Maurice. I simply had to tell someone. Larry said:

' "Why don't you go ahead and marry him, Monique? In about two months run out on him and hit him with a divorce suit. Then settle for cash."

' "No, I won't do that. I may be old-fashioned that way, but I still believe in fair play."

' "You're nuts. Did he play fair with you all that time in Europe? But it's your own business. What are you going to do now?"

' "I'd just as soon stay here in the States."

' "First thing you need is your own apartment. I'll come to your hotel tomorrow and we'll talk about it. I think I have exactly what you need." '

'We found a penthouse at 333 East 75 Street. Large living room, a bedroom, a bathroom, a kitchen with dishwasher, and a large terrace for two-hundred forty dollars a month. Within two days my telephone was connected. Larry was a naturally gifted interior decorator and had me settled in a week.

'Texas Sue rang me up: "Honey, I've got an old friend of mine here. Director of one of those oil companies. Will you hop over and have a drink with us?"

'When I got there she was already as drunk as a beldame and kept lifting her skirt in front of my nose, yammering at me to lick her slit.

When I kept refusing she said: "Dammit, I thought you European broads went for everything. . . . Show me your cunt then."

'Well, if that would keep her happy. . . . I took off my panties and spread my legs. She sat looking at me, masturbating with her tongue hanging out. Then her oil-well friend got down on his knees, sucked my clitoris like an eager puppy, and then lay down on the floor and tossed himself off. I went home richer by two hundred dollars.

'Sue asked me hopefully: "If I shave off some of this hair, then will you lick me?"

' "Shave it off?" I said. "What you need is an electric hedge-clipper."

'Sue kept ringing up. I soon found that she had money of her own, and lots of wealthy, bored friends. She drank night and day, but she was a good sport and seemed to like having me around. When I allowed her to kiss my cunt while some of her men friends watched she seemed quite happy.

'What with one thing and another I soon had a lot more money coming in than the total of my expenses, penthouse and all. I met enough men who were mad to lick my cunt and be tossed off (here I didn't need a massage table—they were perfectly happy being masturbated on the floor in front of the TV) that I had a steady stream of customers. It was obvious that I would not have to go back to Holland for lack of funds, so I wrote to Amsterdam, instructing them to send me my dog Pierre and some furniture that I was especially fond of.

'For some time I had been taking elocution courses, mainly to get rid of my rolling European *r* and while I was doing that, they sold me on a course in television commercials. A decent racket, of course, but, improbable as it may sound: through those silly and useless lessons it all started. Life has a way of finding its own improbable channels—just as rivers do.

'Part of what they taught us at that institute was how to approach a talent agency and how to compile a portfolio of photographs of ourselves. There was a lot of talk floating around about talent scouts, but I was agreeably surprised when I was called aside one day by a quiet, diffident man of about thirty, who gave his card, introduced himself as Lon Jenkins, photographer, and asked me whether I would be interested in modeling for him in what he called "unusual costumes".

'He did not strike me as being on the make. I liked him on sight, but I wanted to be sure what I was getting into.

' "Does that mean in the nude or something?"

' "Nonono! I've been looking around for a girl to do a complete series with. I have an order for several photos of a certain type of girl wearing cat masks, high boots, leather suits, etc. No, this is strictly business, no funny stuff. Come and look over my studio."

'I went there the next morning at eleven, and at twelve we were at work. He had a large collection of all sorts of stuff: rubber dresses and leather bathing suits, etc. Well—I suppose you tumble to what kind of market the photos were meant for. I did not tell him much about myself, but I kept my eyes open. He paid me fifty dollars a day, and after a week he asked me, as he was paying me:

' "Miss Von Cleef, we are running out of background here. Would you mind posing at my apartment tonight?"

' "Oh, no. Not at all."

' "I, uh . . . I wanted to do some whipping scenes. I keep most of that stuff at my apartment."

'I said nonchalantly: "Shall I bring some specialities of my own?"

' "Do . . . do you have any?"

'A couple of days before some suitcases with some of my things had arrived from Holland. "Yes", I said. "I've always had a weakness for exotic costumes."

' "Anything like that is welcome", he said, and I felt him looking after me as I left . . . smiling to myself. I now had his number.

'That evening I unpacked some of my own stuff: leather corsets, a black leather waist cincher, and several pairs of handmade boots of soft black leather, slit on the outside. These drove some people wild, for when I raised one leg to put a foot on a chair, the supple leather fell open and showed one thigh from the hip down. I had a whip, too, that I had bought a couple of weeks before from a Negro who ran Uncle Sam's Umbrella Store on the West side.

'The leather corsets and cinchers had to be tightened and the photographer insisted on doing that himself, leaving the lighting and focusing to his assistant. I felt his hands tremble and his breath come faster and faster.

'We ran through the usual poses for about two hours and then he closed up shop, sent his assistant away and nodded toward a leather-covered bar in the corner.

' "That was very good, I think. Shall we have a drink to celebrate?"

'As he went behind the bar he was so nervous that he nearly dropped the bottles and glasses—twice.

' "I've been wondering . . . Do you like high-heeled shoes?"

' "Of course I do. That's rather obvious, isn't it?"

' "I, uh . . . I have quite a collection of them myself. Would you like to see them?"

'He preceded me into his bedroom, stood fumbling with his key ring, and finally got the double-doors of his cupboard open. It was lined with flannel to which lines of loops had been sewn. These loops held fifty or sixty pairs of very high-heeled shoes; some of them with six or seven-inch spikes. I took one of them out.

' "Handmade?"

'His eyes were all aglow now. He nodded eagerly: "Oh, yes. All of them."

'I looked from the shoe in my hand to his feet. "Put a pair of them on and let me see how you walk in them."

'He couldn't get out of his flat suede pumps fast enough. Slid into the black spikes and began to parade up and down the room, swinging his hips, but very expertly. By now I knew more than enough.

' "You fool!" I barked. "Don't you know better than to do that with those stupid trousers on! Get into something more suitable!"

'Trembling all over with excitement, he unfastened his belt, let his trousers drop, tore off his shirt and stood there in a black satin corset with garters holding up black nylons.

' "That's better. Step out of those ridiculous pants, turn around, and walk in front of me."

'As he turned coquettishly around, I saw a long run in the back of one of his nylons.

' "What's that!" I screamed with a voice full of fury. "How dare you insult me, you lazy, slovenly slattern! There's a run in one stocking. I'll teach you a lesson you won't forget in a hurry! Run back to the other room and get that whip I brought with me."

'He ran there and back on those high heels as if he was born to the art. He probably was. With trembling hands he handed me my whip, and at once fell to his knees, raising his folded hands.

' "Please, dear Mistress. Forgive me just this one time. I swear to you it was an accident. I never have runs in my stockings."

'I raised the whip and his voice rose to a more desperate pitch.

' "Not with the whip, I beseech you—I have paddles."

'I kicked him in the side with one of my slit boots. "Since when does a slave have any choice of his own? I never heard of such a thing! Get over to that bed and bend over the side. Fast . . . faster!"

'With trembling knees he hurried over to the bed, bent over the edge, and stretched his arms full-length.

' "Count to ten! I'll teach you to wear stockings with runs. I'll whip them to shreds!"

'I put the heel of one boot on his prostrated neck, raised my whip, and waited.

' "Start!"

' "One . . .!" I let the whip whistle down, not too viciously, for if he was really used to paddles (ping-pong paddles) I didn't know how much of the whip he could take.

' "Two . . ."

'At ten I had him sobbing and weeping nicely. "Get up, you worm, and kiss my boots!"

'He groveled on the carpet and didn't just kiss my boots—he licked them. He paid me double, with tears of happiness in his eyes. When I worked him I felt a nice, hot tingling in my pussy. It made me think back to the first time I had whipped a man . . . at Gonda's place. And I had found my first American slave.'

'I heard nothing from him for two days. Then he rang up with stuttering voice: "M . . . mistress, may I introduce you to a friend of mine? He is the publisher of the S & M magazines I make my photos for."

'I met Martin that same afternoon. We had quite a conversation. He told me about the incredible needs and frustrations of the American male and the near-impossibility of finding truly dominant females. I looked at him with astonishment. Honest astonishment.

' "What do you mean? I had thought that there were too many dominating women in this country."

' "Yes", he said sadly, "but not in that sense. They dominate with yakkety-yak and wanting bigger cars, and then they still want to be treated like tender teenagers who never grow up. I've seen all your photographs. You've really got what it takes. I'll make you a business proposition. You can place ads in all our S & M magazines free of charge. We cover the whole country. Our coverage is 80,000 mailing addresses seven times a year. Everybody who replies has to enclose one dollar in his letter. The letters are sent to our box numbers and we send them on to you. You open them and no one knows who you are. You start with a code number."

'Within an hour we had come to terms and agreed on two ads to begin with. I remember them clearly:

DOMINANT FEMALE 38–24–36
WANTS SUBMISSIVE MALES

The second one ran:

BEAUTIFUL BLONDE FROM EUROPE WANTS
MALES TRANSVESTITES, RUBBER, LEATHER
FETISHISTS

'Within three months Martin was bringing me a big leather hold-all full of letters three times a week. Some figures are simply etched in my memory. For instance, on January 15, 1965, I had 8,734 letters in my files. Getting them was nothing. Reading them took a bit more out of you, especially when you let them accumulate for a week. Taking the dollars out became a bore, the dollar a letter just paid for the wear and tear on my collection of letter openers. It was the replying that killed me. But once I'd picked the right ones and built up my network . . . Oh, boy!

'I received letters from every state in the union and at first I could not get over my astonishment at the recklessness with which important businessmen and officials wrote the most intimate things on letter-head paper, complete with passport photographs and personal details. At first I refused to believe most of them. I thought they were playing tricks on me. Or trying to compromise someone else. But Martin assured me that these people were so sexually desperate that they were prepared to run any kind of risk. And pay any price.

' "They are nuts", I said. "I'll give each of them a code number, and write them by that number. All I have to do is keep a central register telling me who each number stands for."

'This was only necessary for those who became regular correspondents. But all the letters were answered, So they at least got something for their dollars. The answers had to be fairly short, or we would have needed a battery of slave-typists. Not that we couldn't have gotten them. . . . The first answer usually went something like this:

SLAVE,
GET DOWN ON YOUR KNEES NOW, AT ONCE, AS A SIGN OF RESPECT FOR YOUR MISTRESS!
FROM NOW ON YOU DO NOT HAVE A NAME, AND YOUR NUMBER WILL BE—
IF YOU RING UP YOUR MISTRESS YOU WILL ANNOUNCE YOURSELF BY THIS NUMBER, THEN AWAIT MY INSTRUCTIONS. CONSIDER YOURSELF LUCKY. YOU ARE ONLY PERMITTED TO CALL BETWEEN 5 AND 6 P.M.
MISTRESS MONIQUE

'This type of letter at once separated the real, natural slave material from the larger mass of those looking for an ordinary lay and the other usual stuff. Their second letter (in reply to mine) showed me at once the sternness of their stuff, for within fourteen days after mailing my first answers, things were already getting out of hand. The telephone rang all day and half the night, from all over the country. Flowers began to pour in, and bottles of whiskey and wine arrived. Long cables disguised as sentimental love messages.

'But once you start this tough-MISTRESS business, you have to maintain your role. If anyone, no matter who, took it into his head to ring at any other time, I poured such a load of invective through the wires that it might have burnt out the exchange. But the trouble with that was that some slaves so loved hearing me cutting loose that way that I had to threaten to cross them off my list entirely unless they obeyed the rules.

'Soon they were coming for "treatment" in ever-increasing numbers, and that necessitated running on a tight schedule. Furthermore my penthouse "office" was never intended to handle that heavy traffic. There was not nearly enough room and I began to look around for something roomier.

'Through my photographer-publisher connection, I got acquainted with Yvonne, a big-chested, good-natured French whore with flaming red hair and cow haunches. She had a thriving business on Staten Island. Through her I found a real doll's house there with three small rooms on the ground floor, four rooms plus bathroom upstairs, and above that a long, narrow garret, which I equipped as a torture room. From the beams and rafters I hung all my masks, boots, chains, handcuffs, whips, and canes. As the *pièce de résistance*

I had a real pillory made that was really something. Three steps led up to a wooden platform. The victim put his neck and wrists in three semi-circular holes cut into a heavy oak board. A second board with corresponding holes was bolted over the first, making it impossible to withdraw either head or hands. Leather straps fastened both ankles to iron rings on the platform, and the customer was ready to take his punishment. The only movement he could make was to throw his butt around while being beaten. The other piece of furniture there was a rusty iron bedstead with bare springs but no mattress.

'The stream of customers began to reach such proportions that I had to weed them out, keeping only high-quality trade, such as judges, doctors, senators, priests, big businessmen, film-and-TV executives, etc. Lawyers seemed to be a dime a dozen. Some customers came once a week, some once a month. Some of them knew exactly what they wanted and others simply said, "I want to be your slave. Do to me what you want. Knead me, kick me, humiliate me—I don't care, as long as you do not discard me." Important businessmen often told me. "Lots of people look up to me but I know that I often behave like a sadist and a bastard because I have no safety valve. Now that I have you, Monique, I am more relaxed and not only do my work better, but people like me more."

'Number 271 was an important judge in the Middle West. Whenever he was to sit at a murder trial he had me fly out to him one or two days before it started because otherwise he felt incapable of giving the accused a fair trial. He often told me so. He especially wanted me to witness part of the trial as an unknown member of the public. Watching him sitting there with his impassive face no one else knew, as I did how difficult that feat must be for him after the whipping I had dealt him the evening before in his hotel suite, tied down across the arms of an overstuffed chair, a washcloth in his mouth. He was strictly a flagellantism addict and wanted nothing else. I once gave him—believe it or not—five hundred strokes with a cane from his heels up to his neck, and his only complaint was: "Mistress, you send me home completely black and blue and for some days I can admire my back in the bathroom mirror, but after a week all discoloration and pain is gone and all the satisfaction with it." He related in detail how easy it was for him to "sit in judgment" completely relaxed and unprejudiced as long as he felt the vestiges of pain but how, as soon as the pain had gone, he became restive and irritable again. He was a brilliant man and often, sitting at the back of his courtroom, I could not help thinking: "May the Good Lord have mercy on the poor saps who get him as a judge if I should happen to be sick." '

'Of course I had my usual share of transvestites, and then I would call upon my priceless Eric to handle their clothing and make-up, for that bored me to death. Because Eric was part Chinese, part Indonesian, he always tried to give them an oriental aspect, which was sometimes a great success, but often led to the weirdest results, as in the case of "Elisabeth" (I have forgotten his code number, we got so used to using that nickname).

'Elisabeth was a small and ugly Jewish man who sometimes came to stay for an entire weekend, bringing a suitcase full of female clothing. Eric's oriental make-up on that Jewish face created a sort of Halloween mask, but Elisabeth himself preened and pranced around from room to room and mirror to mirror.

'The remarkable thing about transvestites is that the moment they put on female clothing, they walk like women, talk like women, think and feel like women. They can fool even an expert. Elisabeth worked in the White House (yes, THE White House), and was always sad when Sunday evening came and she had to put on her men's clothes. Once, when I was rummaging around in her suitcase, I found a box of Tampax tucked away in a corner, but when I confronted her with it: "Elisabeth, are you having your time of the month?" she got all nervous and distraught. "Please, Mistress, not so loud—I don't want Eric to know!" The rest of that weekend she was coy and prim in turns, and on Saturday, during dinner, Eric asked her:

' "What's eating you, Elisabeth? Anything wrong?"

' "My tummy aches", she replied curtly.

'I gave Eric a frown. "Don't ask such stupid questions, Eric. Don't you know that girls are unwell at certain times of the month?"

'Eric gaped at me. That was a new one even to him, but when I winked at him he tumbled to it and nearly choked on his pineapple. We later found out that our Elisabeth actually tried to use Tampax three days a month—anally.'

'While we are on the subject of transvestites, let me tell you about Miss Reverse. To me her story still beats them all.

'Miss Reverse had once been a boy, and told me that she had peddled her butt as such since she was twelve. But she had always dearly wished to be a girl, and finally found a wealthy old sucker who fell head over heels in love with her (at that time still a him). He offered to pay for the surgical transformation. All in all it took half a year and almost twenty thousand dollars, but the result was truly fantastic. She now called herself Kinky, and after hormone injections and silicone treatments and God knows what not sported a couple of tits that would have turned Brigitte Bardot green with envy. I sat talking with her in an expensive bar and the men who passed our table didn't give me a second glance, they all went for Kinky with her long, shiny blond hair and luscious mammaries. She was twenty-one, and she had eyelashes that could fan the ash off our cigarettes.

' "Monique", she told me, "all my life I've been sucking cock at ten dollars a trick, but now the bastards will really pay!"

'She hated wearing stockings or panties or any lingerie. She was usually completely nude under her dress and when she had a date in a hotel she went there wearing nothing but high-heeled shoes and a mink. She never drank liquor, for all those injections and hormones, neuroses and problems had loused her up so much that two weak martinis were enough to make her completely crazy; she would throw glasses and swear like a stevedore at any and everyone. I had met her quite accidentally through Larry, my homosexual friend, who did not know Kinky's astonishing history. Kinky and I soon became friends, and she began to confide in me.

'During one of our kaffee klatsches in my house on Staten Island she told me the damnedest story I've ever heard. I had a chance to check on it later and found that it was completely true.

'Not long after her final operation she had an offer for a five hundred dollar straight trick in San Francisco as a call girl. But when the fatal day arrived she became so nervous that the client might notice something amiss, that in the plane, halfway to California, she sat bent double with stomach cramps. She was tenderly taken care of by two stewardesses and three fatherly men. By the time she arrived in Frisco she was so completely hysterical that she rushed to the nearest phone booth, got hold of her client, told him she would be a bit later than expected, and wildly began to telephone doctors. When she finally struck one who was at home she blurted out an incomprehensible rigmarole about urgent symptoms, rushed out of the booth, frantically hailed a taxi and sat in the back, biting her nails all the way, thinking: "If my trick finds out I had myself changed down there he'll kill me! I have to talk to a doctor first."

'She paid for the taxi with shaking hands, dropping money all over the sidewalk. Rang the wrong bell, was finally admitted, and saw a gray-haired, white-coated physician, who soothingly took her by the elbow.

' "Are you the nervous young lady who rang up from the airport? Well, now you just sit down here, my dear child, and relax. Sip some ice water first. . . . It is never as bad as it looks. Are you in pain?"

' "Oh, yes, doctor", Kinky groaned. "I have the most horrible stomach cramps. You must examine me, doctor, I'm really ill."

'The doctor patted her, gave her some more water and told her to take her clothes off. Kinky started to do that, but then flew into a fresh panic and blurted out:

' "Doctor—before you look at me I must tell you that I am . . . I had . . . I am a sex change."

' "Of course, of course, my dear child", said the doctor. "We all have that now and then, but that's nothing to worry about. Don't be so nervous. You just lie down here. Do you ever have nightmares?"

'Kinky became frantic: "Doctor—please, please believe me. I have had seven operations . . . to change my sex."

'The doctor grabbed her elbows and tried to push her down on his examination table, but now Kinky flew into a rage, spread her legs, tore up her skirt, and pushed her synthetic cunt under his nose:

' "Why don't you listen to me, goddam it! I keep telling you they cut away my cock. Look for yourself, you quack!"

'The doctor stared at her for a second, turned red, walked to the wash-basin in the corner, filled another glass with water, walked back to her.

' "I am a general practitioner, but I know a hysteric when I see one. What you need is a psychiatrist", and he threw the glass of water full into her face. And with that he pushed her out the door. This was such an enormous relief to Kinky that she rushed downstairs, hooting with elated laughter, completely rid of all her nervous fears, and delivered her goods to the customer's complete satisfaction.

'She lived in a large and luxurious apartment where I stayed several times, so I got to know her pretty well. In the mornings she lay in her bath for hours on end and afterwards sat around completely naked, sucking her thumb, talking about herself and her psychological problems.

' "Monique", she said to me, "they fixed me up physically, but inside I'm still so mixed-up that I sometimes don't know what I really am: a lesbian or a faggot."

' "Or just a plain, straightforward whore."

'That got a laugh out of her. "Yeah. That's part of the make-up." Suddenly serious again, she added: "Would you like to meet my new fiancé?"

' "Fiancé? What have we now? Are you . . . thinking of getting married?"

' "Yes. To a Jewish surgeon. I've known him for some time. He knows absolutely nothing about my past and all that. But the trouble is that he's from a very strict and old-fashioned family and I told him I've always been a photographer's model. He gave me my mink coat and this bracelet. His family is very wealthy and he loves me to death. I've been playing it one hundred percent straight and by now he's boring me to death. I am really trying to think of a good reason to give him his walking papers. But—she stretched like a lazy cat—let's have one last fling together. The three of us. Are you game?"

'Well, why not? One thing about Kinky: it was damned difficult to get bored with her. Mad, yes, dog-tired, yes. But not bored.

'She grabbed the phone, had her surgeon paged at his hospital, and informed him that she felt in the mood for an evening on the town.

'So that night sees us having cocktails (orange juice for Kinky) in a posh lounge, when Kinky suddenly bursts out weeping, her head in her lovely, slender hands. Our surgeon whips out a handkerchief, deeply upset, and tries to find out what he has on his hands all at once. It's easy to see that this highlight of the medical profession may be able to cut women up, but he's never found out what makes them tick (quite apart from the fact that it would take more than a bevy of doctors to find out what makes Kinky tick). I sit looking on in fascination, and I swear I have never seen such a fantastic piece of acting.

'Plucking nervously at that handkerchief, with an occasional involuntary sob, Kinky tells him:

' "Oh, darling . . . I haven't dared tell you but I talked it over with Monique this afternoon, and she insists that you always have to be completely frank and honest with the people you truly love. . . .”

‘Her true love shoots me a nervous, questioning glance, and I nod affirmatively, although I don’t have the foggiest idea what Kinky has up her tricky sleeve.

‘ “Boohoo . . . I’m boohoo p . . . pregnant”, Kinky wails, and real tears come popping out and run down her perfidious cheeks.

‘Our surgeon nearly has spontaneous heart failure and shoots panicky glances at the nearby tables. “Hush, baby. Not so loud, darling. Try and control yourself, my sweet. . . . You? Pregnant? Oh, no! Kinky. . . . What will my family say? . . . How could this have happened to me, to us, I mean . . . It would be all right of course, once we had gotten married, but now . . . unthinkable!”

‘Kinky gives him a vicious look and hisses:

‘ “You cowardly louse! You should have thought of that before you fucked me!”

‘He turns as white as one of his hospital sheets.

‘ “Darling, please! Does everybody here have to hear about it?”

‘Kinky turns to me with the most tragic and heart-rending expression since Garbo died in *Camille.*

‘ “What did I tell you this afternoon? Did you really expect any other reaction from a man? It’s the girl who always pays in the end. When the going gets rough the worms try to wriggle out from under.” She has changed her mood instantly, swings around to confront her by-now frantic lover and spits at him:

‘ “And if you think that I’m going to let myself get messed up by an abortion, forget it!”

‘We are beginning to attract attention. But after this last lethal broadside Kinky falls silent, brooding over her glass of orange juice. No one says anything for a while, and we begin our meal with Kinky as a sort of live bomb that no one wants to tinker with. Kinky eats nothing, only shakes her head when her plate is taken away, and occasionally tears a cigarette into shreds. What an actress!

‘When, after a while, it begins to look as if the Kinky-bomb might be cautiously approached, Jack ventures a tentative:

‘ “Darling Kinky . . . please listen to me. No one is going to leave you in the lurch, sweetie. But please remember that I’m a doctor. How many weeks is it?”

‘ “Two months now. Eight weeks.”

‘ “For heaven’s sake! That long! You . . . you poor girl! And you’ve been worrying all this time without saying anything?”

'This gives Kinky an opening as wide as a barn door. She starts sobbing heart-breakingly but discreetly.

' "Y . . . yes. B . . . but I couldn't get up the courage to tell you. . . ."

'When Jack takes us home she does not allow him to come up with us.

' "Frankly, I'd rather be by myself. Monique is leaving soon and I would like to talk it over with her. At least she understands me. I'm sorry, Jack."

'He gives me a helpless and appealing look, takes off his hat and stands gazing after us as I help Kinky up the steps.

'We have hardly closed the apartment door when Kinky bursts out in wild laughter, kicks her shoes left and right and drops into an armchair. I pour myself an adult whiskey. Then I say to her:

' "You tricky trollop. Why didn't you tell me beforehand what you were going to pull?"

'She fell into another mood and sits there, gnawing her thumb.

' "You just wait. I'm going to get into that bastard for a thousand dollars cash and that's the last time I want to look at that sentimental dog face!"

'Next morning Jack rings up and Kinky informs him in a suffering voice that she and I have been up talking all night. Talking! The damn girl (?) snored like a bulldog.

' ". . . and Monique says that even if you were willing to marry me right now, that's no sound start for a lasting marriage. And also that I shouldn't be egotistic and think of only myself but I also should have some regard for your position and your family. So all right—I'll agree to have something done about it. . . . No, you cannot. I have to see Monique off at the airport. Come here at ten tonight."

'She drops the horn and sits grinning at me:

' "He'll cough up, all right, I've got him by where I can twist them."

'I took the plane back to Staten Island and picked up my old but ever-varying routine. But a couple of days later my telephone rings and keeps ringing at a very unusual hour. It is Kinky, sounding almost hysterical.

' "Is that you, Monique? . . . Monique, I simply have to tell you. . . . I'm so wild-mad furious . . . if I don't tell someone I'm going to break the windows or commit mayhem . . . you're the only one who . . . Know what that bastard pulled on me? . . . Jack, that weak-bellied slug, couldn't leave his bride in the hands of some quack. After the louse promises me a thousand in cash to get it seen to, he turns chicken and comes up with this story that he can't let his bride . . ."

' "Kinky—have you been drinking?"

' "You bet your fucking cunt I've been drinking! So the bastard finds a colleague who is prepared to do it, Because the chicken-livered shitbag, that rat, sits whining that he doesn't trust *himself* to perform an operation on his lady love. Monique"—she is fairly screeching—"you WON'T believe this—"

' "Kinky, hold it a minute. I want a drink and a cigarette."

'While I am getting them I hear the horn spluttering. I pick it up again.

' ". . . try what I might, and then he gives me some pills to quiet me down, he says, and in my nervousness I slap them into my mouth but they must have been some special drug that those bastard doctors will never give you when you really need them, for pretty soon I don't have the sense to resist when they talk me into getting into a car and drive me to his hospital. He's holding me by the arm and talking all the time, he justs keep talking at me and I was so . . . so mad and drugged and panicky at the same time they got me into a sort of examination room before I knew what to do. And . . ."

' "But, Kinky—why didn't you scream, or kick?"

' "That's what I'm so goddamned mad about. You know these nerve jags I get? When I get all jittery and jumbled up? They had me in one of those. I tell you I was simply paralyzed, I tell you. The craziest ideas kept whirling through my head. One moment I was sure they were going to murder me right there and dispose of my body in the morgue and the next moment . . . See what I mean?"

' "I know what you mean. But what did they do? I mean, how did they, you know what I mean. . . ."

' "That's what I'm trying to tell you, dammit. That other doctor . . . I was lying there with my legs spread and my feet in those stirrup things . . . that other one started pushing a sort of rubber tube down there inside me and I felt him pushing and prodding and then I panicked some more because on top of everything I was sure they were going to find out about—"

' "I don't need a blueprint of your insides. Tell me what happened!"

' "I saw them mumbling together like those bastard doctors always do—mumbo-jumbo—and then I distinctly heard the other one say: 'I can't seem to get this catheter to go any farther. . . .' And then Jack got mad at him and called him an idiot. Asked him didn't he know how to handle one of those things and then all at once the thing must have folded up inside me or spiraled or something like that, for I felt it slide in a way and heard him say: 'I've got it done.' He taped the end of the tube against the inside of my thigh. . . . I've got the fucking thing there now . . . and Jack wrapped me up in a rug and drove me home. And right there and then I told him I never wanted to clap eyes on him again, neither here or in the hereafter. . . . Jesus, Monique, I—"

' "And they never found out?"

' "Found out? Those quacks never noticed a damned thing!"

' "But, Kinky, what are you so mad about? It must give you a lot of confidence and besides, it's an ideal way to have gotten rid of him once and for all."

' "Rid of him?" she yells, and I hear the noise of shattering glass. "Yes, I'm rid of the rat all right, but the bastard conned me out of a thousand dollars!" '

'At the rate I was going it didn't take long before my house on Staten Island became tight under the arms. By now I was in a position to buy a house and pay cash. Late in 1964 I heard about a suitable house for sale at 850 Lake Street, Newark, New Jersey. I bought it and began to operate from there.

'And then the whole business exploded in my face. Shortly before Christmas 1965, a tough-looking yet hesitant customer suddenly identified himself as a Newark police detective-lieutenant, and the whole place was suddenly overrun by policemen—and women.

'*And that's when I got the treatment.*'

THE DAILY NEWS, June 12, 1967, Newark, New Jersey

A statuesque platinum blonde and her 'business partner' go on trial today in Newark, N.J., on charges of operating a sex-and-torture mill that already made headlines when police raiders broke up the operation December 21, 1965.

Assistant Essex County Prosecutor John Noonan said he is

prepared to expose a card file of the thrill house's clintele that lists 'several names prominent enough to be recognized.'

The blonde is Monique von Cleef—who was arrested when an Essex County deputy sheriff, posing as a businessman, arranged for an 'hour of discipline' at Miss von Cleef's plush home in an exclusive Newark neighbourhood and then brought along a carload of detectives.

*Neurotic Erotica*

Inside the 16-room house raiders found a torture chamber complete with whips, handcuffs, chains and leather cat-o'-nine-tails allegedly used by Miss von Cleef and her 'associate' James Beard (38) to satisfy the erotic whims of customers.

According to Noonan, the confiscated card file lists the names of 15,000 persons from across the nation and at least four foreign countries who paid $50 or more for an hour's entertainment. Noonan declined to release any of the names, although he said he will offer the list, plus other seized files and letters, as evidence at the trial.

*Several Occasions*

Authorities said clients with sadistic and masochistic tastes were accommodated not only at Miss von Cleef's home at 850 Lake Street, Newark, but also at locations chosen by the clients. Ads listing some of the 'special' services available ran in several magazines . . .

'Sitting there in that courtroom, listening to that dry voice putting into bad English what occasionally had been uproariously funny and always exciting, my thoughts shot back to the days when it all started.

'One of the first letters (at that stage still unbelievable to me) came from Dallas, Texas.

'For some things I have almost total recall. This letter read:

Honored Queen of my Dreams,
When I finally found your long-expected letter in my post office box and tore open the envelope with shaking hands and

read your Order I fled into a telephone booth, went down on my knees and said a prayer of thanksgiving. When I glanced up I saw a woman waiting impatiently outside and I got simply stuck there. I did not have the courage to get up again . . . she must have thought I was a dwarf and finally she went away. . . .

'I relived the vivid impression of the first live client who came to the penthouse for treatment. He had been given the number 36. I already had a houseboy then—not a Filipino, but a truly beautiful part-Indonesian boy with a colossal sense of humor and a very high I.Q. He could do anything he put his mind to, play any kind of role. When he was male I called him Eric, and when he dressed up as a girl he became Erica. We were expecting number 36 and at exactly the appointed time the doorbell pinged. We had arranged for Erica to stay in the kitchen as my maid and when I rang she would come tripping in to serve drinks or coffee.

'I opened the door myself and saw nothing but an enormous bunch of roses. "Dammit", I thought, "not another dwarf." And I tiptoed to see over the top of the bush. There, on his knees, lay 36, a slender blond young man, psychiatrist at a large New York hospital.

' "Stupid—come in!"

'He came hobbling in on his knees and I rang for Erica to put the flowers in vases. The eyes of 36 bulged when Erica came mincing in dressed in a tight black satin jockstrap (to flatten her male apparatus) an over-tight black satin corselette with red frills, black nylon stocking, and pumps. And falsies.

' "Mistress!" 36 stammered, "this has always been the wildest dream of my life. To belong to one single Mistress, and then be her personal maid."

' "Well, your luck seems to be bad," I said indifferently. "Erica suits me perfectly. If you behave you can clean the floors, for that's something Erica hates."

'I said no more and let him sit there on his knees. I filed my nails until Erica came back with two vases full of 36's roses.

' "Get us two scotches with ice", I told her, and when 36 attempted to say something I snapped at him: "You keep your trap shut. You may talk when I give you permission, and not before."

'Erica returned with two glasses on a silver tray. One of Erica's many talents: she was unbelievably fast in everything.

' "Now bring me that letter on my desk. Yes, that one."

'Erica handed me the letter and silently vanished. I began to read, and then, with a mocking laugh, read aloud:

> . . . although I sit in front of a mirror often and cannot honestly say that I think myself handsome, I know that many of the nurses in the clinic think me a real doll.

'I walked over to him, put one hand under his chin, and looked down on that thin face with the watery blue eyes.

' "But . . . Are you quite sure they don't say 'an ugly doll'?"

'He stammered: "I, uh . . . I am sorry you don't like my face."

' "How you yourself can look at it without a shudder beats me. Tell me about yourself."

'Hesitatingly our psychiatrist began to stutter about his youth, his school, his studies . . . the frustrations of his profession. Then about his desire to dress as a woman and have long, very thick blonde hair. "Like you have", he sighed, ". . . and then be raped. But not by a man," he added fearfully. "I am entirely free of homosexual inclinations. That is to say . . . unless I should be forced, against my will. . . . Bound, shackled, helpless . . . and if you would torture me. Then, yes, in such a case I naturally would have to submit. But that would be violation and rape."

'I rang the table bell.

' "Erica—bring me Lola's costume."

' "*Oui, madame.*" (With a heavy fake French accent.)

' "Is she really French?"

'I nodded and Erica returned with a large cardboard box.

' "Take 36 to the guest room and dress him up."

'Erica and I knew that Lola's Costume was the most humiliating one in my collection.

' "Get up and go with her!" I snapped.

'Number 36 got to his knees with difficulty and stiffly stumbled out of the room. I watched him: he was completely fascinated by Erica's well-shaped Balinese buttocks. I sipped my whiskey and dreamed of hundreds of slaves to bring me money, flowers, and jewels.

'Not long afterward Erica led in the most ridiculous human being imaginable. It stumbled along on heels of unequal height. The stockings were far too short—a limp little penis peeped from under a frayed garter belt. The brassiere had one full and one empty tit, and the wig was made of frayed rope.

' "Erica!" I said in astonishment, "is this the best you could do?"

' "*Oui, madame.*"

' "Bring me a pair of bloomers."

'She came back like a flash with one of those ridiculous victorian articles of female clothing: heavy cotton with little bands around the legs under the knee and a flap that could be let down at the back.

'Number 36 was put into the bloomers and Erica fitted two clothes pins to his earlobes. I looked it over and shook my head.

' "Really, Erica. . . . I must say this is still cheap-looking. The lowest Marseilles streetwalker looks like a princess compared to this. It makes me sick just to look at it!"

'Number 36 fell to his knees and began weepingly to wring his hands: "Oh, my goddess—my Mistress. It is her fault. That French maid of yours. I look much better when I do it myself. I sometimes put on my sister's clothing and it suits me much better. I swear."

' "Aha . . . so this is not the first time, 36?"

' "No, Mistress, no. I am sure I can look better. I look so well in my sister's clothes that I can walk down the street and men turn and whistle at me. I could earn a lot of money for you on Third Avenue, but this . . . this . . ." he shot Erica a dirty look "she is envious of me."

'I stamped my foot and shouted: "WHAT? Are you trying to insult my personal maid?"

'He twisted his body like a live corkscrew and wrung his hands: "Oh, no, Mistress . . . not really. . . . But . . ."

'I gave him a push in the direction of the guest room: "You stupid third-rate whore! You want to earn money for me? We shall see."

'I threw him down on the bed, which was covered with a white rubber sheet, fastened his wrists with leather straps, spread his legs, and fastened his ankles. Then I laughed mockingly.

' "We shall see if you are of any use to anybody. Do you really think anyone in his right mind would want to touch something as ugly and ridiculous as you?"

'I went to the kitchen, where Eric sat shaking with laughter:

' "Good God Almighty! Imagine being a patient in that man's clinic!" Eric mimicked in his unique way: "Doctor I have homosexual tendencies. Do you think you could cure me?"

'I shook him: "Listen, you. There isn't much light in that room. The patient is tied to the bed. Go in there and insult him as much as you can.

'Eric took off his shoes and slunk to the guest room. I listened near the open door. Eric was great. He shuffled up to the bed, bent over, and muttered angrily:

' "They call this a cathouse? Is this old bag the best they can do? Dammit, THEY should pay ME to fuck a wreck like that! Here, I don't want your dirty cunt. Suck my prick!" and pushed his tool into the readily opening mouth of number 36, our psychiatrist.

'When Eric had shot his wad we got out of there and left him in peace for a quarter of an hour. Then I went back, untied him, and made no comment about anything. I took him back into the room and rang for Erica.

' "*Oui, madame?*"

' "Help 36 to get his own clothes back on."

' "*Oui, madame.*"

'Five minutes later our psychiatrist came back in.

' "Put the money on the desk", I said, "and ring me up tomorrow at eleven. Exactly eleven, understand?"

' "Yes, Mistress."

'He was still a steady customer when Lake Street was raided. . . .'

ESSEX COUNTY COURT
CRIMINAL DIVISION
INDICTMENT NO. 1952—65

*Newark, New Jersey*

**Transcript of Proceedings**

Monday, June 12, 1967

*Opening Statement by The Prosecution.*

Mr. Noonan: May it please Your Honor, my colleague, Mr. Durkin, Mr. Foreman and ladies and gentlement of the jury:

The State contends that from October 1, 1965 until December 21, 1965, when something happened, that Miss Von Cleef and Mr. Beard conspired in the following manner: They came over here to Newark, New Jersey, and Miss Von Cleef purchased a piece of property, specifically a one-family house at 850 Lake Street in the City of Newark and that she and Mr. Beard then went to this house, stayed there, furnished it, equipped it, and among the equipment they had whips, chains and other devices that I believe you are going to see and I hope to offer into evidence. It will be described that an office was maintained there with mailing lists, file cards, records, and that this office was in furtherance of a magazine known as FLAIR, which, I believe, you are going to find was operated by Mr. Beard and Miss Von Cleef for the reception of advertisements by persons all over the country, and I believe that you are going to find that the nature of these ads and the nature of this magazine was designed to appeal to persons who had an interest in the deviant matters of sex. I think you are going to find from the testimony that such matters as transvestism, voyeurism, homosexuality, sadism and masochism are rampant in this magazine, which was operated, we contend, by Miss Von Cleef and Mr. Beard, that there was a checking account maintained and fiscal records, and letters were addressed here from people. I believe some of these letters are going to be offered, and they may be received by you in evidence. This is the belief of the State. You can read the contents of the letters. . . .

The Court: A little louder.

Mr. Noonan: I'm sorry, Judge. You may read the contents of the letters should they come into evidence and of correspondence from Miss Von Cleef. One of these letters at least, I believe you are going to find, is postmarked right here in Newark, December 10, 1965, and was addressed to a person here in New Jersey, and it came into the possession of Inspector, John Kallies of the United States Post Office Department assigned to a section known as the Pornographic, Indecency and Obscenity Section, and he undertook to investigate this letter, and he contacted Lieutenant Arthur Magnusson of the Essex County Sheriff's Department some days later.

In the letter was a telephone number, and Sheriff's Lieutenant Magnusson on December 20, I believe you are going to find from his testimony, telephoned this telephone number and asked for the person who signed that letter as 'Monique'. There was a return address on the letter, 'Monique Von Cleef' with a box number. I believe you are going to have before you the records of the Post Office Department with respect to the maintenance of this post office box, who maintained it, as you will with the financial records of FLAIR.

Detective Magnusson had a conversation with the

defendant Von Cleef and—this is what the State contends—as a result of said conversation he received an invitation from her to come to the premises at 850 Lake Street on December 21 at about one o'clock for a one hour period in discipline for a fee of $50. Detective Magnusson on December 21, accompanied by Detective Mueller, Policewoman Mason, Inspector Kallies and Detective Gearty did, in fact, go to the premises known as 850 Lake Street. They, of course, did not accompany him. They stayed in the nearby area.

By prearrangement, Detective Magnusson went to the premises, and I believe you are going to find that the door was opened and that there were workmen there, and he asked for 'Monique', whereupon the defendant James Beard came downstairs. Detective Magnusson had a conversation with him. Mr. Beard, who is the defendant here in the courtroom, the State contends, escorted Detective Magnusson up to the second floor and then to a third-floor apartment where Monique Von Cleef was waiting for Detective Magnusson and then, up on that third floor there was another conversation, and as a result of this conversation between Detective Magnusson and the defendant Marianna or Monique Von Cleef, the State contends, ladies and gentlemen, that the only purpose that she allowed Detective Magnusson on the premises for that day was specifically to have him take off his clothes, according to the gist of their conversation back and forth . . . and then she said she was going to give Detective Magnusson the discipline which he sought; specifically, she was going to flog his buttocks. And Detective Magnusson asked her if she were going to do that until he achieved a sexual climax as a result of whipping or flogging. She said that, yes, she would, and I think you are going to find there was talk of sexual gratification on his part and on her part.

Testimony will be produced to help enlighten you with respect to these acts which we claim were going to take place on that day and on those premises, acts that are defined as sadistic on the part of the person doing them and masochistic on the part of the person receiving them. We hope to bring testimony before you in the person of Dr. Chernus. . . .

I think that you are going to find that Monique Von Cleef placed advertisements, and the tenor of those ads, I think you are going to find, is directly appealing to persons of this deviant sexual group: masochists, flagellants, persons who like to have physical pain inflicted on them, as in this case, while in the nude until an orgasm, a sexual climax, takes place. That is what this house of theirs was there for. That is why all of those things were done such as getting the house and putting in a telephone, doing the things that have, of course, to be done to live in a house in the wintertime, putting in gas and electric, things of that nature, mailing letters and receiving letters, thousands of them, putting all of this equipment in such as chains, leather garments, rubber garments, high heels, exotic, bizarre costumes, whips, the physical objects which I think you are going to hear referred to as dildoes which are, frankly, artificial penises. . . .

ESSEX COUNTY COURT
CRIMINAL DIVISION
INDICTMENT NO. 1952—65

*Newark, New Jersey*

**Transcript of Proceedings**

Wednesday, June 14, 1967

*Examination of Lieutenant-Detective Magnusson by the Prosecutor, Mr. Noonan.*

Mr. Noonan: Selecting the first ad, for example, Lieutenant, Z-262 and reading the ad.
Magnusson: Z-262 in the FLAIR publication reads:

> NEW YORK CITY. FEMALE, BEAUTIFUL, BLONDE AND DANGEROUS. DEMANDS RESPECT AND OBEDIENCE.

Q: From your experience does this ad, Z-262, connote anything to you?
A: Yes, it would.
Q: What is that?
A: This connotes an appeal to people who are masochistic.
Q: Lieutenant Magnusson, I show you a letter which has been marked S–1 for identification, and I ask you when you first saw that letter. Excuse me. I ask you if you recognize that letter.
A: Yes, I do.
Q: Where did you see it?
A: It was given me by Postal Inspector John Kallies.
Q: After seeing the letter, what if anything did you do?

A: As the result of having this letter and other objects in my possession, I decided, after a conference with Postal Inspector Kallies, I made a phone call. I must say we first ascertained the telephone number from the New Jersey-Bell Telephone Company as to where the phone number was located, corresponding with the geographic location.

Q: I show you S–1 now received in Evidence, Lieutenant Magnusson, and I ask you to excerpt therefrom the letter . . . would you read it to us?

A: It starts with an initial. It says: My new telephone number is 201 484–0840.

The Court: Give that to me again.

Magnusson: This is the area code, 201.484–0840. 'The charge for a consultation is $50.' It is signed, 'Superior, Monique.'

Q: Did you make an investigation with the New Jersey Bell Telephone Company of that telephone number on the 20th of December, 1965?

A: Yes, we did.

Q: You learned to whom it was subscribed?

A: Yes. It was registered to, I think it listed, Marianna Von Cleef, 850 Lake Street, the City of Newark.

Q: After getting that information, did you do anything?

A: Yes, I did. I had a short consultation with Inspector Kallies, and I decided to make a phone call to that phone call to that phone number.

Q: Tell us what occurred.

A: I picked up the phone, and I set up a Dictaphone alongside the ear, and I dialled 484–0840. The telephone rang and a voice, a female voice with an accent, answered. 'Hello', I said. 'Hello. Monique?' She asked who was there. I said, 'This is blank Sullivan.' She said, 'Yes?' I said, 'I've got your new address. Where is that?' She said, 'In Newark.' I said, 'Oh, in Newark. Are you doing anything this afternoon?' She said, 'Oh, yes. I have to work in town.' I said, 'In town?', I said, 'Well how about this morning?' She said, 'This morning? Well, this morning is over, isn't it?' I then said, 'Well . . .' She said, 'No. I've got to be in town.' I asked, 'Well—could you tell me a good time for an appointment?' After this she said that she would be free tomorrow afternoon. I asked, 'What would be a good time?' She said, 'Well, after one.' I said, 'After one. Yeh. You told me your fee. Miss Von Cleef answered, 'Yes.'

I then asked, 'Could you tell me what you do for the fee? You know.' Miss Von Cleef answered, 'Oh, just an hour and a half of discipline.' I asked, 'Yeh. Do you think I could get it without clothes on, just the high heels?' Miss Von Cleef replied, 'Oh, we'll talk about that later', and I used the term, 'Heh?' Miss Von Cleef said, 'I would want to talk with you first.'

I then said, 'Well, I'm so excited now, you know.' Miss Von Cleef answered, 'It's stupid to talk on the phone.' I said, 'Why, don't you have a private line?' Miss Von Cleef said, 'Does that mean you have a private line but everybody else can't listen to your telephone? So does it make any sense to talk on the phone?' I said, 'Yeh.' She said, 'It's quite stupid.'

I then said, 'Well, I can hardly wait though, you know.' Miss Von Cleef said, 'Oh, well—you waited all your life, you can wait another few days.' I asked her, 'Would tomorrow morning be all right then?' 'No—not tomorrow morning,' replied Miss Von Cleef. 'I can't make it until after one o'clock.' I said, 'Okay. Well, I'll be there—oh, where is it?' Miss Von Cleef said, 'You'll be there. What time you come, at one o'clock?' I answered, 'It will be one o'clock, yes.' Miss Von Cleef said, 'Okay. The address is 850 Lake Street.'

Q: As a result of that telephone conversation, what if anything did you do?

A: I had another meeting with Inspector Kallies, and I appraised him of what I intended to do the following day, to keep the appointment. I further informed Lieutenant Tom Mueller and Detective Gearty of what I was going to do, that I was going to go into a house at 850 Lake Street in the City of Newark and I was going to portray myself as a masochist and to go there for a whipping, and I said that, not knowing the circumstances surrounding this particular home, I appraised them that I was going to enter promptly at one o'clock and their role was to enter the house, regardless of what happened, at 1:30 p.m. on the same date. I also apprised Inspector Kallies of the same procedure that would be followed and asked him to accompany Detective Gearty and Tom Mueller. I also went to the Investigation Division of the Newark Police Department and requested the services of a policewoman, Detective Helen Mason.

Q: After recruiting these people, did you go somewhere?

A: After assembling them, yes. I was in my own car and they and I proceeded to the area of 850 Lake Street. . . .

Q: Upon your arrival, what if anything did you do?

A: I parked just a little bit down from the house at 850 Lake Street. I checked my watch. Our watches were synchronized for this and exactly at 1:00 I walked up onto the porch and rang the doorbell at 850 Lake Street. A man who was working right behind the door—he was doing something that I could not observe—opened the door and said, 'What is it?' I said, 'I'm here to see Monique.' He said, 'Oh, Monique,' and he called upstairs. When he called upstairs a gentleman who I now know to be James Beard came down the stairway and asked me what I wanted. I said, 'I want to see Monique.' 'Oh," he said, 'for Monique. Come on upstairs.'

Q: Do you see James Beard here in court?

A: Yes, I do. . . .
Q: Where on the premises did you first see him?
A: He came down the stairway and I was standing in the vestibule of the house. When I told him I wanted to see Monique, he said, 'Oh, come on up,' and I followed him upstairs and he took me to a little room . . . and he asked me to be seated in a chair, and he said that Monique would be with me in a minite,
Q: By the way, how was Mr. Beard attired when you first saw him?
A: He had on I believe they were some sort of slippers. I don't think he was wearing socks. He had on sort of a turtle neck sweatshirt and casual slacks. I might say that I forgot to mention that as I came through this door or up the stairway . . . there were two huge dogs lying in the hall, and they were huge. He brought me into the room, and then I sat down and, of course, waited for Monique to appear. . . .
Q: Do you know what kind of dogs they were?
A: No.
Q: How long did you stay in the room waiting?
A: Well, there was a certain degree of tension on myself, and it seemed very quick from the time he asked me to sit down and wait for Monique. It might have been minutes, only maybe one or two minutes.
Q: Did you identify yourself to him by name when you first saw this Mr. Beard? Did you give Mr. Beard a name?
A: Yes.
Q: What did you tell him?
A: Mr. Sullivan.
Q: When you left that room, where did you go?
A: I was in the room, and then Miss Von Cleef came into the room. She was dressed wearing a black leather skirt and a white blouse, and she said, 'Hello. You are Mr. Sullivan? 'I said, 'Yes.' She then said, 'Come with me', and she walked me down the hall and to a doorway leading to a third floor. She preceded me, and I followed her upstairs. We went through a bedroom and into a sort of sitting room in the front of the house. . . . Miss Von Cleef asked me to sit in the chair that was there.
Q: Did she say anything else to you at that time?
A: She asked me to be seated, to take off my coat, make myself comfortable and then asked me if I would like to have a drink. She said, 'Scotch or rye is all I have here.' I said that scotch would be fine. At this point Miss Von Cleef said, 'Here's something for you to read,' and she handed me a copy of a publication called SPANKERS MONTHLY. At this point I asked Miss Von Cleef who those people were downstairs. There were some working men there. I said that I was just a little bit concerned. Miss Von Cleef told me, 'Don't worry. There's nothing to worry about. You're as safe here as if you were in the Bank of England.' And she told me that the people who were

working downstairs were a plumber, an electrician and a carpenter and that she was having the house decorated. Now, at that point she said, 'Let me get you your drink,' and she said, 'You can read that publication. It will excite you.'

Q: Then what occurred?

A: Well, Miss Von Cleef left the room and I was sitting there looking at the publication. She came back in three or four minutes and she had what would be at least a ten-ounce glass that had about five or six ounces of scotch in it and some water, and she gave it to me and told me, 'You know, this will help you to relax,' and she seated herself on a couch that stood there. Miss Von Cleef then asked me, 'Now tell me about yourself.' I said, 'Well—I can't say too much because I have to be discreet.' She then said, 'How can I help you if you won't tell me about yourself?' I then said that I understood what she meant, but that I hadn't had too much experience at being the servant of a professional sadist and then she asked me, 'Well then—when did you first start liking to be whipped?' I said that I had had an experience with a girl who I knew and went out with and that this girl and I had engaged in flagellation, where she would whip me to a point where I would be sexually aroused, and then we would consummate the normal sex act and Miss Van Cleef at this point said, 'Well—let's get this straight. I am not going to have intercourse with you.' I said, 'No. I realize that you're just going to whip me until I have an orgasm,' and Miss Von Cleef said, 'Yes.'

Q: What occurred after that, if anything?

A: She asked me more questions and I stated that you can't find too many people who know about this or who really understand it and she acknowledged that. 'Yes—I can see that' and she made a reference then that in Europe this practice is quite common and that she herself thoroughly understood it. I did make reference also . . . I asked her. I said to her, 'I notice you do have an accent.' She said, 'Yes, I'm Dutch. I'm from Holland,' I also made a reference to Mr. Beard. . . . Then I asked her, 'Will you get any enjoyment out of this or are you just a professional sadist?' She said, 'No. I experience gratification also with the right sort of person.' Then I told her that I would enjoy it more if I knew that it pleased her, too. We talked for a while about the publication she gave me . . . and then Miss Von Cleef suddenly asked if I was married. I said yes. She said, 'Then how do you hide the marks on your body at home?' I said, 'Well—I've never really had any noticeable marks on me. This is my first experience with a professional sadist.' She asked at this point if I would like to try some bondage and I said, no—that I did not want to do that right now, that I would rather get to know her a little better first. . . .

She told me not to be nervous and asked if I would like perhaps to dress in women's clothes and I replied well, no—that I had tried that once, but that it didn't mean anything to me. In that context I then referred back to my story about the flagellation with my so-called girl friend.

The Court: What is meant by bondage, Detective?

Magnusson: This is where you would be tied in some sort of restraining device or some chains, but actually it can be utilized in any way. I don't know what specifically Miss Von Cleef had in mind, nor was I about to find out.

Q: Tell us what you then said and what she said.

A: She asked me what I did, where I worked. I told her I was a department store executive, and then asked her how long I could stay and she said, 'Oh, about a half hour or so, depending on how I like you, and so on.' Now at this point Miss Von Cleef got up from the couch and went to a closet and brought out a pair of women's high heeled shoes which she brought over and dropped on the floor. She then ordered me, 'Now take off all your clothes and then put these on', and she went on, 'When I come back I want to see you up on that couch in a kneeling position. I mean all your clothes off. I am the boss.' I then asked Miss Von Cleef what she was going to wear and she said, 'You'll see,' and left the room.

After Miss Von Cleef had left, I started looking around and I took off my tie, shirt, undershirt, shoes and socks and that's as far as I intended to go. I then started to look around some more. I opened a door into some sort of hall and . . . through another door I saw Miss Von Cleef in the process of putting on this special costume.

Q: What stage of dress or undress was she in?

A: She was undressed and dressing herself up.

Q: What kind of a costume did you observe her putting on?

A: It was black. It was, I would say, eh . . . it was maybe 16 feet away and, of course, I couldn't make a direct observation, but Miss Von Cleef spotted me out in the hall and she said, 'What are you doing? Why aren't you undressed? What the hell takes you so long?' So I said, 'I'm sorry. I'm a little nervous and I have to use the lavatory, the bathroom.' She said, 'Well, there's one over there.'

As Miss Von Cleef finished dressing herself, I walked down the hall, went into the bathroom and tried to kill a minute or so and then, after I was finished there I walked back into the sitting room and there was Miss Von Cleef, dressed in these black high-heeled shoes, net stockings, and a rubber suit—a tight fitting rubber apparatus which would resemble a bathing suit. Looking at my watch I saw I still had a few minutes to go, so I sat down and asked her if I could finish my scotch, that it would further help me to relax and take it easy.

Q: What did she say, if anything?

A: She said, 'That's fine. I understand.'
Q: What then?
A: Well, while we're sitting there Miss Von Cleef had either one or two phone calls which she took in another room and I could not hear the conversation. When we were together again—it seemed the time was just 1:30 or 1:31, I started to hear a noise, a banging, and I asked Miss Von Cleef what was that noise and she replied, 'Oh, that's nothing—just the workers and carpenters.' Then the banging got louder and Miss Von Cleef got up and went into another room, a bedroom, where I followed her and at this point I heard shouting, 'Art, Art, where are you?' I hollered, 'In here!' and Detective Tom Mueller came around apparently up through the hall and Detective Mason came in by a second door. Of course Miss Von Cleef then said, 'What is this? What's all this?" and Detective Mueller told her, 'This is the police'

She then said, 'Police? What have we done?' and she looked at me. 'We haven't done anything!' I pulled the badge out of my pocket, showed it to her and said, 'I'm sorry, Monique. It's all over. I'm from the sheriff's office.' Miss Von Cleef then looked at me and said, 'You're a nice guy to do a thing like that right before Christmas.'

By then the telephone rang in the room where we were standing. I picked it up and it was a long distance call apparently, because it was a toll call, and the operator said, 'There's your party', and I heard a fellow say, 'Hello Monique?' and I replied, 'No.' He then asked, 'Is that you, Jim?' and I said, 'Yes.' So the coins started to go in, and I heard the plunking of the quarters going down and then, all of a sudden, Monique jumps up and over and hollers into the speaker, 'Hang up! It's the police here. The police are here!' I heard Mr. Beard on the extension also telling the guy who rang up that the police were on the premises, so I asked her not to do that again and she said something to the effect, 'Don't get anybody involved in this.' Maybe I shouldn't say that. I don't remember exactly what she said at that point, but she did say something in regard to my answering the phone . . . I don't know what it was and I'll just have to forget it.

Noonan: Judge, we still have a long narrative to go on with.

The Court: Yes. This may be an appropriate note on which we might take our luncheon recess.

ESSEX COUNTY COURT
CRIMINAL DIVISION
INDICTMENT NO. 1952—65

*Newark, New Jersey*

**Transcript of Proceedings**

Friday, June 16, 1967

Prosecutor
Mr. Noonan: I thank Your Honor for the time afforded Mr. Durkin and myself. Your Honor, I have a series of letters. When I say 'a series of letters', I mean a number of letters. . . . Lieutenant Magnusson, where did you first see . . . these letters.
Magnusson: They were on the premises at 850 Lake Street on December 21, 1965. . . . They were with other mail in the storage room on the second floor. . . .
Mr. Noonan: Now from your experience and training, Lieutenant Magnusson, do you have an opinion as to these letters?
A: Yes, I do.
Q: What is that opinion?
A: They are solicitations for various types of sexual activity.
Q: Can you give us an example from any of the letters?
A: Do you wish I should read one?
Q: One or more. . . .
A: The first one is entitled, 'Mistress Monique'.
The Court: Would you keep your voice up, please?
A: MISTRESS MONIQUE: You would never believe one little slave could love one mistress so. The things you order number 35 to do . . .'
The Court: Not so fast.
A: . . . things you order number 35 to do and especially the way Mistress trains 35 to carry out her orders. Thank you very much, Mistress.

Last Sunday, Mistress, you had 35 in such great pain. Number 35 felt as if he were dying. Honest, Mistress. Your little slave is always truthful to you. Mistress, when you wanted to gag 35 to keep him from making too much noise, oh, Mistress, how could you tell when 35 had more than he could stand?

Mistress, 35 is too dizzy, too faint, if that is what Mistress had on her mind. Please, Mistress, 35 isn't trying to be funny or even a mind reader. Mistress, 35 is thinking out loud at that precise moment instead of three days later after most of the soreness subsided. The Preparation H which 35 had to use helped a great deal. Oh, Mistress, please don't laugh. It does sound funny now, but at the time it was no joke to this little slave who had to experience this punishment at the hands of his Mistress.

Oh, Mistress, 35 is pleading on his knees to his Mistress please be lenient to 35 when he is to receive the same punishment in the future.

Oh, Mistress, 35 is begging for mercy on his knees in front of you. Please, please, have mercy on your little slave, my wonderful Mistress. Mistress, what would you do to 35 if he had said he was calling you from the hospital just to see if he could worry his Mistress? Yes, Mistress, you told 35 before that he is an insignificant little slave and he means absolutely nothing to you. To 35, my wonderful Mistress, you are my heaven on earth, as beautiful as a flower, the best thing that ever could enter this life of a little one called 35. Mistress, you are so magnificent 35 is overjoyed knowing you and proud to have you as my mistress to lead 35 in the beautiful ways of life.

Mistress, your little slave was a lost soul on this earth until Mistress Monique found 35 to bring happiness into his life. Mistress, thank you very much for taking 35 by the hand to help him find his way. Oh, Mistress, 35 loves and worhips you so very much. You would not believe it possible that such a little slave has that much love in him.

Thank you, Mistress, for allowing 35 to share part of your life. Thank you so much. It's beautiful. Your little slave worships the ground his mistress walks on. Oh, Mistress, you are such a goddess on a pedestal for 35 to look up to and to worship. Your little slave needs you, Mistress, to guide him and experience the beautiful things in life.

It is signed,

your obedient slave, 35.

Q: Do you have any other letters which you wish to read into the record?

A: DEAR MISTRESS MONIQUE,

Yes, mistress, already I feel your slave, feel under your spell, your dominating aspect. You asked about my training. Well, most of my actual training has been in New York, but I have been ordered to dress as my mistress wishes, rubber diapers and bra, corset, stockings, and if I am good, occasionally a pretty slip and panties. When I visit her in New York, I arrive not having been allowed to drink anything for hours. Sometimes I stand outside the door, facing out. She pulls a rubber cap over my eyes, and then I'm let in and told to undress. Then my wrists are strapped together behind my back. She says: 'Kneel down, slave. Repeat after me: "I am your complete slave. I will obey your every command. I will accept every humiliation your darling fancy directs. I will maintain always an attitude of respect."

'You will address me always as Mistress Monique at the beginning and end of every sentence and you will not speak a word at any time except to answer questions. If you do, you will be sorry, I promise you. Your life is going to be tough, and when I whip you, you will say,

"Thank you, Mistress", and when I give you something to drink that is too humiliating, likewise you will say, "Thank you Mistress, for the delicious drink".'

Well now, let's say that it is time for Betty to go to bed. Into the bedroom or call it the punishment room, if you wish. Betty has disobeyed so many times and that means lashes, so she is stretched out on the rubber sheet on the bed face down, bottoms up, feet strapped apart to the bed posts and wrists also strapped to the side legs of the bed, and the whipping begins in earnest.

Betty cries and remonstrates. This causes fierce lashes and you remind her that she was not to speak a word, so you say, 'Betty, you rinse your mouth out', and you do. Again Betty remonstrates and you feed her another punishment drink. Well now, to get along, finally you turn Betty over. She meekly accepts the turn. Her face is still covered. There she lies helpless before her pretty mistress. She repeats: 'I will try my best to satisfy you, pretty Mistress. I will follow your every direction. Yes, Mistress Monique, I will suck, kiss, fuck and suck as long as you feel like coming in my enslaved mouth with your adorable kissable pussy.'

Mistress, when I opened, thrilled, your letter, I was wearing black rubber diapers and a white rubber bra and pretty black panties. I couldn't comply with your order right away but I have now, to kneel and respect you ten times. Mistress, please accept me as your slave. I am just dirt. Mistress may send any instructions to your Betty that you please. If you send me your girdle, I will wear it whether it is too small or too big and send you a new replacement plus a very lacey bra. How is that?

You are a pretty mistress, and I love the name. Please do accept me as your slave and make me your slave. Strict orders and severe punishment. I want you to have fun and, of course, at Betty's expense. So write, pretty mistress, and make Betty obey and submit. Your obedient and most affectionate slave, Betty.

Am I too presumptuous to suggest ideas rather than to await your instructions? I hope not, but you have asked me my training and experience. Thank you, Mistress, and thank you again.

Q: Do you have an opinion as to that letter?

Magnusson: Yes. In my opinion it would be written by a male masochist who is probably a transvestite and uses a female name and is writing down the experiences that he would like to experience and descriptively giving information as to what he would like, involving sadomasochism and possibly fetishism. . . .

ESSEX COUNTY COURT
CRIMINAL DIVISION
INDICTMENT NO. 1952—65

*Newark, New Jersey*

**Transcript of Proceedings**

Friday, June 16, 1967

Defense lawyer
Mr. Durkin: I would just inquire, Your Honor, I have no objection to the letter, but I don't know whom it was addressed to, or to what address. We have a date on it—that's all.
The Court: Well, it was taken (came from) 850 Lake Street.
Mr. Durkin: Yes.
The Court: On December 21, 1965.
Mr. Durkin: Yes, Your Honor.
Prosecutor
Mr. Noonan: I think the jury should hear and get the benefit of it.
(*He reads*):

MY DEAR MISTRESS MONIQUE,

I sure hope you remember me. I'm a truck driver from New Jersey. I was over to see you one evening and never have forgotten it. I have been very busy and travelling quite a bit. I am looking forward to another appointment with you in the very near future. As I said, I've done quite a bit of travelling and have also made a few contacts around the country. I have found the treatment which I really enjoy, and it really sends me wild. I will describe it to you in detail, as I find it easier to write rather than spend the time with you talking. I will let you decide as to whether you could give this treatment or not.

First let me go back to the night I was with you. To me, the most exciting part of your treatment was when you put me on the floor and I had to look *UP* at you. At this point I felt as though I was *completely* dominated by you. As for standing up and being whipped, nothing for me. Now let me describe this treatment I wish.

To begin with, this girl, Princess Sue, was a great deal like you. She was dressed in a skirt (short), very high heels, and had a very sheer nylon blouse with long full sleeves on. This blouse was buttoned up the front, very revealing, so that when she bent over me her breasts, which were very full and beautiful, were about exposed. She had no bra on, and the sheer nylon blouse, heavily scented with her perfume, nearly drove me wild. Sue then took me to a room where I was strapped on a table, sort of spread-eagled on my back. I was stripped of all my clothes at this time. She had about three nylon scarves, which were heavily scented with a wild scent, and these she moved around and over my face as sort of a blindfold. It was thin enough so that I could see. I was wild from the feeling of nylon and the scent of her perfume.

At this point Sue took some lotion and began to massage my body. First she began on my face. I was *forced* to take her breast in my mouth. She would open her blouse just open enough so that I could have it.

As I said, the massage began with my face and worked down over every part of my body, spending quite a bit of time on the thighs and inner thighs. Sue then took my organ and genitals and massaged ever so slowly. She then rubbed me down with some alcohol, which was soothing. More treatment with her breasts and the nylon scarves, and then I was gagged and blindfolded so I couldn't see, and I waited with anticipation. I could see just a little bit, and I saw her take a small whip with three fine strands. She came to the table and began to work with this whip around my thighs and inner things and gradually the tempo got faster and stronger until she was punishing and I was reacting. This kept up for quite some time, Finally she stopped, rubbed some more alcohol, which felt good. I was then released and told to turn over with my back facing up again strapped in the spread-eagled position. Again the teasing with the scarves. Also I saw her put on a pair of rubber gloves and move them around my privates. The rubber really excited me. I had been lying on a rubber sheet. I wondered what the odd feeling was. Then Sue told me about 'rubber'. She took a thin rubber sheet from the cabinet and covered me completely and it was wild. Then she went to work on my rectum with her rubber covered fingers. I almost went out of my mind. Then more and more complete massage, especially the rectum, thighs and so forth. Finally I was turned over and more breast feeding. Oh, yes, I had received my punishment with the whip on my back also.

After much teasing with her breasts and scarves, I believe it was, I was blindfolded. Then she slipped out of her clothes and got on top of me. She sat on my thighs and gradually worked me into a frenzy. When she got it into her she moved back and forth and up and down until it was over. Finally she got off and, after slowly dressing, she releases me. It was quite a treatment. . . .

Mistress Monique, I would like to duplicate this treatment with you as my mistress. From what I can remember you have a beautiful and domineering body with which to do this. Please, mistress, do you have a full-length photo of yourself you could send me? I could take it with me when I travel and be completely dominated by you. Please send a full photo if you are able to. I will make an appointment with you as soon as I hear from you. Anxiously I await your reply and photo. Till then I am your obedient . . .'

Then it is signed and it has the post office box number and the city in New Jersey.

Mr. Durkin: That was the basis of my objection. I think you now understand why. Here's a client of mine supposedly the recipient of that particular letter, written by somebody who tells her about an experience he has with somebody else. I think that is clearly inadmissible before this jury and was only used for the purpose of enabling them to hear it.

The Court: The objection is denied.

ESSEX COUNTY COURT
CRIMINAL DIVISION
INDICTMENT NO. 1952—65

*Newark, New Jersey*

**Transcript of Proceedings**

Monday, June 19, 1967

Mr. Durkin: Oh, Your Honor, I received a phone call this morning at my house at approximately a quarter to eight, wherein I spoke to both Mr. Beard here present and Miss Von Cleef, and I was advised she fell last evening and struck her head and she had put in a call to a Dr. Karl Shaw on East 58th Street in New York and was waiting for the doctor to come.

Mr. Noonan: Mr. Durkin and I, Your Honor, have been attempting to verify certain aspects of this information and, as a result of our discussion, we would inquire for this limited purpose only, merely as to what has occurred with Miss Von Cleef through Mr. Beard.

The Court: I think the record should also show that an attempt was made to reach Miss Von Cleef by telephone this morning at the place where she was supposed to be living on East 76th Street in Manhattan and that there was no answer, and that an effort was also made to reach her physician, Dr. Karl Shaw, who maintains his office on East 58th Street, and he is not available at the present time. As a matter of fact, the Court made the call and was informed by a lady who apparently is employed in the same building that the doctor is expected to be back about eleven-thirty. . . .

WITNESS ALBERT JAMES BEARD IS SWORN

Question by
The Court: Mr. Beard, we are only concerned with this incident that was reported by Mr. Durkin with respect to the condition of the defendant Von Cleef, and it was felt that you might be able to shed some light on this matter, and that is why you were called to the stand. When did you first receive intelligence concerning this episode which is alleged to have occurred last evening?

A: I was in her apartment late last night when she arrived from a dinner date. I said, 'You look dreadful.' She then said, 'I had an accident.' I said, 'How do you feel?' She said, 'I think I'll be all right.'

The Court: When was this? Around what time was this?

A: Around eleven-thirty or twelve. I arrived in my apartment around twelve-thirty, so it had to be around twelve when I left her apartment.

Q: Were you in her apartment when you arrived?

A: Yes. I was waiting.

Q: What apartment does she occupy in that building?

A: One D.

Q: Did you observe any injuries of any kind?

A: Nothing other than that she did not look well. She was dizzy.

Q: Were there any marks of any kind of injury?

A: No. I didn't see any, She had her clothes on. She was wearing her clothes, naturally.

Q: Did she complain of any visible sign of injury?

A: She didn't feel well and she was very dizzy.

Q: I am not talking about subjective symptoms, I am asking you whether or not objectively you saw any signs of injury.

A: No, I did not.

Q: Do you know where this occurred?

A: No, I don't. I think it was with friends of hers.

Q: You told us she was with friends of hers. Did she indicate to you where this happened?

A: No, she did not.

Q: Did she tell you how it happened?

A: She fell on the last four stairs of a stairway.

Q: Well, was this some commercial building?

A: I don't know, sir. It could have been a private home. I don't know.

Q: You never inquired as to where this happened?

A: I was not concerned with where it happened, only that it did happen. I was concerned about her.

Q: The only complaint she made to you was that she was dizzy?

A: She didn't feel well. I said, 'Well, you look dreadful.'

Q: Do you know who the people are she was out with?

A: I'm not sure. I think it was the Orensteins.

Q: This happened in their presence?

A: I would imagine so, sir. I don't know.

Q: Now, is there anything else you can tell us that we have not covered?

A: That I arrived this morning and she could not get out of bed. She attempted to get out of bed and fell and I put in an emergency call to Dr. Shaw, and they informed me that he wouldn't be there until one, and I gave the phone to Miss Von Cleef. She said, 'This is an emergency. He's been my doctor since I've been here.' Then I called Mr. Durkin at once. I left the apartment, and I left the front door open so that the doctor could enter. Then I came here.

Q: There is a telephone there, isn't there?

A: Yes. The nurse did say she would put in an emergency call to his home. That's the only knowledge I have of it.

Q: Did you try to reach her by telephone since you arrived at this building?

A: No. I've been sitting here waiting to do something.

The Court: You heard me say that there was no response at the other end of the telephone. Anything further?

Prosecutor Noonan: No, sir.

The Court: We will take a short recess.

THE JURY COMES INTO THE COURT ROOM

The Court: Good morning, ladies and gentlemen. I am sorry for the delay, but unfortunately it was reported to the court early this morning that one of the defendants, Miss Von Cleef, was ill and that she was confined to her home, and we have been trying to ascertain the nature and extent of her illness so that I might be in a better position to guide you ladies and gentlemen as to what steps should be taken with respect to the continuation of this trial and we are still trying to ascertain the nature and extent of Miss Von Cleef's illness and so, in the meantime, it has been decided to excuse you ladies and gentlemen until tomorrow morning at nine-thirty. We trust that Miss Von Cleef will recover in the meantime sufficiently so that she will be present in the court tomorrow morning.

So now you are excused and you will return here at nine-thirty to-morrow morning . . . and you will remain in the courtroom to give the sergeant-at-arms your home telephone numbers, please.

ESSEX COUNTY COURT
CRIMINAL DIVISION
INDICTMENT NO. 1952—65

*Newark, New Jersey*

**Transcript of Proceedings**

Tuesday, 20, 1967

Prosecutor Noonan: Pursuant to Your Honor's instructions yesterday, a party from the Prosecutor's office, including the defense counsel, and I, proceeded to New York City where we obtained the services of a physician, whom I shall not name for the record, whose report was submitted to you in writing, sir. We arrived, I believe, at about one-thirty . . . at the defendant's apartment in New York City. Mr. Durkin arrived almost simultaneously or a few minutes later. We were in two different cars. Mr. Beard was already at the apartment, and the doctor and Lieutenant Magnusson and I waited in the lobby.

Mr. Durkin—this was pursuant to his request—went into the apartment and some few minutes later came out and then the doctor went in and examined Miss Von Cleef, and you have the results of his report, sir.

Mrs. Helen Mason, the Newark police woman, and myself went into the apartment and spoke to Miss Von Cleef. She was, in fact, in bed. I had a few sentences with her. I asked her how she felt. She said she did not feel good. Of course, I am not a physician and I did not attempt to either examine her physically or by testimony. That is about the status of it, Your Honor. All I can say is that as a result of certain developments this morning, I am continuing my investigation and inquiry into the matter, and I shall have some report for you later today.

Mr. Durkin: After I left Mr. Noonan yesterday in New York City, I went to the office of Dr. Earl Shaw, who had been to Miss Von Cleef's apartment. He told me he had spoken to you on the telephone and had given you the findings that he had at that particular time. He also told me that he had recommended that Dr. Abraham Umansky, an orthopedic surgeon in New York City, see Miss Von Cleef and that he would make the arrangements. I understand those arrangements were made and Dr. Umansky did see Miss Von Cleef last evening somewhere between the hours of five and seven, as I understand it.

The Court: At his office?

Mr. Durkin: That's right. Mainly because, Your Honor, from what I gather and from what Dr. Shaw had told me, it was rather difficult to X-ray in her apartment. Dr. Umansky made the X-rays and, as the result of his findings, indicated that hospitalization was in order. He was unable to locate her in the Joint Diseases Hospital last evening. He was unable to do so this morning, and suggested that she go elsewhere with the expectation that she would be subsequently transferred. I have no other information, Your Honor.

The Court: Well, under the circumstances, I am obliged to continue this matter, and I will excuse the jury until two o'clock. I trust that between now and that time we will have some further information. As the Prosecutor has indicated, the investigation is continuing. We are attempting to ascertain whether or not Miss Von Cleef is, in fact, suffering from an injury or whether or not this is just an attempt on her part to escape her responsibilities. Very well. We will take a recess now until two o'clock.

THE JURY ENTERS THE COURT ROOM

THE ROLL IS CALLED

The Court: Good morning, ladies and gentlemen. Apparently there is no change in the report which we received yesterday. It is alleged that Miss Von Cleef is still incapacitated and unable to appear here. However, the Court desires that a further inquiry be made in this matter, and I am going to ask you if you would be good enough to return here at two o'clock this afternoon. We may have some further intelligence with respect to her condition at that time. May I suggest that you might go downtown and do some shopping perhaps. This gives you an extra dividend, in any event. So you are excused now until two o'clock. If you will return at that time, it will be appreciated. Thank you again.

THE JURY LEAVES THE COURT ROOM
(*Recess*)
THE JURY ENTERS THE COURT ROOM

The Court: Good afternoon, ladies and gentlemen. I regret to say that I will have to ask you to return again at nine-thirty tomorrow morning. During your absence, of course, the Court in conjunction with others has conducted an investigation into this matter, and I am not at liberty to indicate to you exactly what has taken place, but I would ask you to return at nine-thirty in any event tomorrow morning, and we hope at that time to proceed with the trial of this case. In the meantime, I would ask you not to read the newspapers concerning this incident because it has no bearing upon the guilt or innocence of the defendants. As I told you repeatedly, the guilt or innocence of the defendants in this case must be determined by you solely upon the basis of the evidence as you hear it from the witnesses in this courtroom and not as a result of any extraneous occurrences of any kind. . . . So now until tomorrow morning at nine-thirty I will say good night.

THE JURY LEAVES THE COURT ROOM

The Court: Mr. Noonan, during your absence the jury was recessed until tomorrow morning at nine-thirty. Do you have a report that you desire to make in court?

Mr. Noonan: Yes, Your Honor, I do. Pursuant to the Court's instructions to investigate this matter, Your Honor, Lieutenant Magnusson and I proceeded to Saint Barnabas Hospital, where we picked up Dr. Peter Gianquinto, Chief of the Radiology Department. We then proceeded directly to New York City, to the office of Dr. Umansky at 115 East 70th Street. We identified ourselves and spoke to a Mrs. Pollock, who apparently is the nurse in charge of his office. She showed us the X-rays which were taken last night and about which I will have Dr. Gianquinto testify at the conclusion of my report. I spoke with this Mrs. Pollock, and she advised us that Miss Von Cleef had come to the office on 70th Street, apparently from her home at 76th Street, and to the best of her observations, she did not come in any sort of a hospital vehicle or ambulance or anything of that nature, but that she came in unaided and unassisted. In fact, Mrs. Pollock commented that she was dressed very nicely. . . .

Lieutenant Magnusson, Dr. Gianquinto and I proceeded to the street address where Miss Von Cleef presently resides. We left Dr. Gianquinto in the car. Lieutenant Magnusson and I proceeded first to the residence and then, noting a brass plate with the name of the superintendent being two doors away and with her telephone number, we walked to the address of that house, which is 203 on the same street, two doors away, and we rang the doorbell. A young man answered, and a Mrs. Perry, who is the superintendent of the apartment where Miss Von Cleef is presently staying, came to the door. We identified ourselves with our official identification and advised her that we wanted to have her accompany us while we rang the doorbell to see if Miss Von Cleef was in the apartment.

Mrs. Perry let us in the hallway to the door, to the immediate door, of the apartment, which had previously been identified as 1–D, I believe. Mrs. Perry rang the bell several times. There was a long pause between each long ring of the bell. There was no answer and, as Mrs. Perry was about to open the door, she being the superintendent and having a key, a voice answered: 'Who is there?' Mrs. Perry, being in front of the peephole, advised that it was the superintendent. The door was opened. Miss Von Cleef stood in the doorway, and Lieutenant Magnusson and I stepped forward and advised her that we had been sent there merely to check on her well-being and report back to the court. She was dressed, as I recall, in a black high neck shirt that she had on here the other day, and I believe a skirt of gray color with a houndstooth check or something of that sort. She appeared to stand straight and not to be in any difficulty or pain. There did not appear to be anybody else in the apartment. She came to answer the door and opened the door herself. Her only conversation with us was that she wanted no pictures, no photographers and in ten minutes she was going to the Lennox Hill Hospital to be admitted.

Lieutenant Magnusson, Dr. Gianquinto and I proceeded to the house office address of the doctor whose name I furnished to Mr. Durkin and which I will furnish to the reporter for the record, where we had a conversation with that doctor. He stated he is on the staff of the Lennox Hill Hospital and that he knows Dr. Umansky who is not on that staff. Dr. Umansky had called him. . . .

I posed the following questions to him, Your Honor. One, was hospitalization absolutely necessary even considering the nature of her subjective complaints? His answer was equivocally and categorically no . . . she could be treated at home.

I then asked him if she would be able to attend the trial. He said, well, of course, if you really believe her or if you believe her story or believe her complaints, it would be uncomfortable for a person with low back pain to sit; that's the most uncomfortable position.

I asked him if Miss Von Cleef could travel. He said absolutely she could travel and, in fact, he reiterated several times there were good doctors in Essex County and if she needed treatment, in his medical opinion, she could be treated here. . . .

The Court: I should like to supplement the report by the Prosecutor for the record and indicate that Mr. Harry Durkin, the attorney for the defendant Von Cleef, reported to this court on Monday, June 19 at nine-thirty a.m. that his client had suffered an injury the previous night, Sunday, due to an accident and was confined to her apartment because of the disability which she sustained. The Court thereupon requested and arranged for a physical examination at her home by a qualified physician of the City of New York . . . with negative findings. Do you desire to be heard? First I will call on Mr. Durkin. . . .

Mr. Durkin: I presume, Your Honor, you were aware of the fact that yesterday I accompanied Mr. Noonan, Mr. Magnusson and others to New York City. I certainly take vehement exception to be informed by the Court at ten-thirty this morning that we, and I took that to mean everybody at counsel table, were excused until two o'clock. I arrived back here at two o'clock only to find that no one was here and that people were making investigations in New York, including going to my client's apartment house. I certainly take vehement exception to that, Your Honor. I think I should have been also part of your instructions to be there, more particularly since we have a medical doctor from New Jersey who went for a specific purpose and, I represent to this court, I would have had no hesitancy whatsoever in asking the doctor to look at Miss Von Cleef, notwithstanding his particular specialty, since he is certainly a physician. . . . I further recite to the Court that I made a call to my client about forty-five minutes ago and got no answer. Prior thereto, I had been told by her that she was going to be admitted to either of the two hospitals.

The Court: Mr. Noonan?

Mr. Noonan: Well sir—

Mr. Durkin: Your Honor. . . . I might also say when we adjourned at ten-thirty allegedly until two o'clock, I asked Mr. Noonan what was going to happen and how could I assist in getting this medical information, and I was told at that particular time, 'All we're going to do is make a few phone calls', and the next thing I know I was excluded from going to New York, although I was not excluded yesterday, and I certainly, for the third time, take exception to this. . . .

The Court: Well Mr. Durkin, I think the Court and you, both of us, were imposed upon because you reported yesterday that this lady had been admitted to the Lennox Hill Hospital or at least this morning. I'm sorry.

Mr. Durkin: Your Honor, when I say 'admitted', she was in the emergency room. I understand you checked with this gentleman who is the director of admissions, and she was there. Now, if it was represented that it was an admission it was absolutely, in my opioinn, an admission because I thought she was in the hospital in a room as opposed to waiting to get a room.

The Court: In any event, Mr. Durkin. . . .

Mr. Durkin: And, Your Honor, I might also add this for the record about any imposition: I don't mind any imposition when it comes to my clients, and I certainly would have liked to be there this morning with this Mrs. Pollock, who was only an agent of Dr. Umansky. I now ask the Court whether the Court has spoken to Dr. Umansky. Have you, Your Honor?

The Court: No.

Mr. Durkin: I also say if I am not entitled to go there I don't know how the State's chief witness, Detective Magnusson, can. What position has he in going on this? I have no idea whatsoever, and I think it is totally improper.

The Court: It is the considered opinion of the Court on the basis of the investigation with respect to the defendant's behavior and the medical reports . . . that Marianna Von Cleef is a malingerer and she had, without just cause, deliberately impeded the progress of this trial and by her conduct subverted the administration of justice. Mr. Noonan, what is your pleasure with respect to this matter?

Mr. Noonan: I move that bail be forfeited, Your Honor, and that a bench warrant be issued to secure the appearance of Miss Von Cleef at this trial, sir.

The Court: It is so ordered. And since the Court has determined that the defendant's absence on Monday and Tuesday, June 19 and 20, constitutes a voluntary act on her part, the trial of this case will proceed tomorrow morning at nine-thirty with or without her presence and in accordance with Revised Rule 3:5–4, subdivision a. All right. . . .

Now, there is one other thing that I, of course, desire to mention, and that is that, on the basis of my determination, this lady who has placed herself in this position is a wrongdoer by absenting herself, and I regret this very much, but I have no other alternative except to follow the recommendation made by the prosecutor to forfeit her bail and issue a bench warrant for her arrest. The rest is up to her. You get in touch with her and tell her she better be here tomorrow morning at nine-thirty.

Mr. Durkin: Just for the record, she is going to be admitted into a hospital and, that being so, I do not intend to convince her to be here tomorrow morning.

The Court: Very well. She is not going to play fast and loose with the Court.

[Oh . . . isn't she?]

ESSEX COUNTY COURT
CRIMINAL DIVISION
INDICTMENT NO. 1952—65

*Newark, New Jersey*

**Transcript of Proceedings**

Wednesday, June 21, 1967

*Examination of Lieutenant-Detective Magnusson*
*by Prosecutor Mr. Noonan.*

Q: Detective Magnusson, I show you a red notebook, a two-ringed notebook, containing ruled paper, received in evidence as State's exhibit No. 59. Have you seen this?
A: Yes, sir.
Q: Where did you first see this?
A: This was found in the office of Miss Von Cleef at 850 Lake Street on December 21, 1965.
Q: What does it contain?
A: It contains an indexed list of individuals, alphabetically, of their names and addresses. There are certain notations made alongside of the names. Some incorporate photographs that are attached to the page, and others seem to be pertinent information or details that are alongside their names.
Q: Directing your attention to the item I am pointing to, what is that?
A: This is a numeral, 50, with a circle around it.
Q: How many times does that appear on that page?
A: Twice.
Q: So that we may protect individuals whose names appear in here, we will refer only to the cities. Where the number 50 appears, what city is it?
A: It has the name of an individual in Staten Island, New York.
Q: And the next one?
A: Long Island City, New York, 50 dollars. Or rather just fifty.
Q: Do you see that again on the page I just turned over?
A: Four times.
The Court: You mean the number 50?
Magnusson: No. Two 50's and two 25's.
Q: Is there some writing, handwriting, next to the one from Los Angeles, California?
A: Yes. It says there, 'Mild discipline and tight clothes'.
Q: What does that connote to you from your experience?
A: This person would be a masochist and probably also a transvestite.

Q: Does the name of a naval vessel appear here in the one I am pointing to, with a fleet post office address?
A: Yes.
Q: What does that say?
A: Likes to cross dress, docile, a novice.
Q: Does that connote anything to you?
A: Yes.
Q: What does that connote?
A: That this would be a passive type of person who was a masochist and he is new at it.
Q: And the next one?
A: The next one is listed in New York, and alongside of it there is a phone number, and it has 'Slave' and 'TV'. )
Q: What does that mean?
A: A 'Slave' would be a masochist and 'TV' is a transvestite.
Q: What cities, states or countries are listed on this page?
A: Chicago, Illinois and Brooklyn, New York.
Q: Does the writing opposite the New York address connote anything to you?
A: Yes. It has: 'Generous for right girl. (Not bright yet. Is a novice)'.
Q: What does that mean to you?
A: 'Is a novice' would mean that he wants to be a slave and he's new at it as far as the training or discipline may be concerned. The other thing is that there has been no price set on it, yet and on the top it has, 'Generous to the right girl.'
Q: Directing your attention to the one opposite the Hollywood, California, address, is there a photograph attached thereto?
A: Yes, there is.
Q: What are those three words here? Would you read them out?
A: It describes him, and then it has: 'Not priced yet.'
Prosecutor
Noonan: The jury will have this, Your Honor, but so that the record will reflect it I am attempting to get a random sample. Detective Magnusson, here again we have a New York address for another person. I am going through this alphabetically. I am now in the section under E.
A: It says: 'Likes racing and a slave' with the circled 50.
Q: And the one in Arlington, Virginia?
A: It has his age, 'A slave' and then it has the figure 16 a lesson.
Q: New York, N.Y.?
A: A slave.
Q: Middlesex, New Jersey?
A: Age, height, weight, price, a figure of 40. 'Posing in unusual costumes. Excitement.'

Q: Do these connote anything to you?
A: Yes.
Q: What do they connote?
A: That he apparently would be a transvestite and possibly a masochist.
Q: San Francisco, California?
A: 'Shoes, Said he sent them.'
Q: Does that language mean anything to you from your experience and training?
A: Yes. It could have been sent possibly by a person who has a fetish and is a possible masochist.
Q: Directing your attention to the Syracuse, New York address, do you see two words written opposite that address?
A: Yes. Bondage, a slave.
Q: The one opposite Louisville, Kentucky, with a picture?
A: There's a circle around 100 and a notation: 'Just a fat, ugly slob who doesn't know if he is a lover or slave.'
Q: The latter part, does that connote anything to you?
A: Either he doesn't realize whether or not he's a masochist or is just interested in being a lover as far as straightforward sex, as far as using the term 'straight sex' would be concerned.
Q: Sacramento. What does that word say here?
A: 'Exotic panties' . . . Or it could be: 'parties'. With the circled figure 50.
Q: Bridgeport, Connecticut?
A: Slave. With the circled figure 40.
Q: Flushing, Michigan. Read us the figure and the language.
A: The figure 50 is circled and it says, 'Meek Male', I think.
Q: Sherman Oaks, California.
A: 'A tall Texan living in California. Sounds like a normal trick. Anxious to meet Monique.'
Q: How many times does a number appear with these four ads on the next page?
A: Four alongside of four names, three 50's and one 40.
Q: How about the one 40, Linbrook, New York?
A: 'Wants to be a slave. All man.'
Q: Cincinnati, Ohio. What does it say there?
A: 'Likes men and women. Has to call.'
Q: Is his sex apparent from the name?
A: That's a man.
Q: Croton-on-Hudson, New York, with a phone number, complete with an area code.
A: 'TV—satin doll.'
Q: Are there any circled figures on that page?
A: Yes. A 50 and a 40.

Q: Detective Magnusson . . . have you gone through this book completely?
A: Yes, sir.
Q: Will you tell us what cities, states and countries are encompassed in here?
A: Just about all of them, all the states in the country, or quite a few of them. I couldn't tell you if any states are omitted. But there are the states and some are out of the country.
Q: Foreign countries?
A: Yes.
Q: I read what appeared to be F.P.O. with the name of a ship. Do similar ads appear in that book?
A: Yes.
Q: Any others related to the Armed Forces?
A: And the military. Yes.
Q: Bethlehem, Pennsylvania, again with a picture. What does that say?
A: 10 D. a lesson.
Q: San Francisco, California, with a circled figure.
A: The circled figure is 50. The caption is, 'Slave, a novice, would like to bathe a woman with his tongue.'
Q: Opposite the one from Hartford, Connecticut—don't name the individual—what does it say?
A: 'Friend of Ralph Blank. No prices yet.'
Q: Detective Magnusson, from your experience, what is this book?
A: This would indicate a master file of possible correspondents and contacts, prices and agreements of individuals who have been in contact with the owner of this book.
Q: You saw the filing cabinets with the file cards, did you not?
A: Yes, sir.

ESSEX COUNTY COURT
CRIMINAL DIVISION
INDICTMENT NO. 1952—65

*Newark, New Jersey*

**Transcript of Proceedings**

Wednesday, June 21, 1967

*Examination of Lieutenant-Detective Magnusson by Prosecutor Mr. Noonan.*

Noonan: Your Honor, I am going to ask Lieutenant Magnusson to read just two more letters so that the record will reflect the physical evidence. . . . Lieutenant Magnusson, I show you . . . exhibits S–73. Will you, for the record, read those two letters, please?

Magnusson: My adored Mistress,

It is hard to imagine a man of my age and presumed intelligence writing a mash note, especially to one who is most certainly a professional courtesan. If nothing more, I do not yet entirely buy the story of the M.D. degree in psychiatry, and so forth, although I confess that spending a few minutes with you in sober conversation convinces me that such is not impossible. But no matter, you are adored and are most certainly mistress of poor me. My first experience of your training is hard to describe. It certainly leaves me wanting to call again for another session, which I will most certainly do when next in New York.

'Was it pleasant?' That's a hard question to answer. Is pain ever pleasant? I guess it is when you receive it at the hands of a person such as you. Certainly I was in a most excited state from start to finish. Your lovely figure and imperious air thrilled me. The excitement you created was sensational and it was pure ecstasy to lie supinely across your knees while you expertly applied that wicked whip. But this is only part of the whole, and it leaves me to dare to make one protest. I think you would agree that only a base and worthless man would accept commands and chastisement from a woman who is not attractive. Maybe once, but not twice, and only once because an appointment had been made and had to be kept.

I believe in an earlier letter I indicated that you might well be a person who could command obedience with an order or a look, and you most certainly are. I found you personable, pretty, well formed and over all most attractive. As I stated at the outset, I was willing to submit myself to you to do as you would, and you did. The sting of the whip and even the most unpleasant hair pulling was more than compensated for by the sheer joy of having one so lovely in command. Here I protest the urinating. It did no harm, but it does detract from your otherwise effective performance. It brings a sour note into your effective training. I beg you to omit next time. Am I being presumptious? Do I need further training and of what sort? I am sure you know the magnetism you have for me as for so many others, I am sure. My desire is overwhelming.

I said I am too old for mash notes, and I doubt if they are so rare in your life as to have much meaning. But believe me when I say I desire you intensely. I desire to be once again on my knees before you and over yours and to do your bidding to the best of my ability. And I desire much more. Happily and hopefully,

S–31

Noonan: Now, Lieutenant, will you read the latter dated April 7?

Magnusson: Dear Mistress,

I cannot tell you how excited I am about the prospect of visiting you next Wednesday. As I mentioned yesterday, this will be my first actual experience of physical face-to-face subjugation of myself to a woman for the purpose of being disciplined. I have corresponded with several during the past three years and have submitted to their remote control but I have never before had the opportunity or obligation to present myself, and now I must to you, like a slave to his new mistress who will direct and train him in the ways of servitude and reverence.

The four or five women who dominated me from a distance and by letter succeeded in getting me to do many humiliating and degrading things and required me to write regularly long and very descriptive letters to report in detail and without reservation exactly how I carried out their instructions. The two carried this out so far as to make me take photographs of myself undergoing the ordeals which they prescribed. For example, they would send me every week or so a small package of their soiled underwear with instructions to launder it the French way, as they described it. Perhaps you know what is meant. If not, you can make me tell you, and perhaps you will demonstrate the method when I visit you.

Not only did I have to do this, I was also required to take photos of myself while doing it and then send them along with detailed written descriptions of my experience so they could be sure that I had been obedient and also that they could enjoy as vividly as possible the knowledge of my humiliation and suffering. I mention this so that you will understand that although I have never experienced the intimate personal control you have consented to exercise over me, I am prepared for the strictest and most severe disciplining. Indeed, I believe you will find it very difficult to make me beg for mercy or to think of a humiliation which will fully test my obedience. That, my mistress, if you will permit the boldness, is a challenge to you from your lovely slave. . . .

Your photos would indicate that among the etceteras must be leatherwear, high-heeled boots, restrictible garments and devices, whips and other instruments of corporal punishment and control. I hope so. I am no less interested in all of these. I have a few such items and may bring them with me.

I have obtained a room at the New York Hilton for the night of April 14th. I will check in at the hotel and call you upon my arrival there. I hope you will be able to meet me, for the first time at your home, since I am totally unfamiliar with the big city and will not know how to avoid chance meetings in public places with the many people who will converge on the Hilton to attend the Education Convention which I shall be expected to attend during the week following Easter. I am known by hundreds of them and have the distressing reputation of being a woman hater, since I am never seen in public with a woman. Perhaps you will want to correct this or at least punish me for it, but please, for our first meeting, let it be private. Please, dear mistress, I hope to speak to you again by phone before this reaches you, but I want to get this information into your hands as an aid to you in your plans of how most effectively to bring me to heel, as you would say in referring to the control you must exert over your two big dogs. Do you think you can train me as thoroughly as you have trained them? I wonder. And I wonder most of all what it would be like to have you try. I can hardly wait to find out, although my eagerness is strongly mixed with fear

It is signed: 'Yours'.

ESSEX COUNTY COURT
CRIMINAL DIVISION
INDICTMENT NO. 1952—65

*Newark, New Jersey*

**Transcript of Proceedings**

Wednesday, June 21, 1967

THE FOLLOWING TAKES PLACE IN THE JUDGE'S CHAMBERS

The Court: During the course of the dialogue which ensued yesterday between the Prosecutor and the Court and also the attorney for the defendant Von Cleef and the Court concerning the defendant's absence from the courtroom on Monday and Tuesday of this week, reference was made to the fact that she had been examined by a physician at the Court's request. I desire to identify that doctor for the record as Dr. Jacob L. Oberman, whose office is at 2 Sutton Place in the City of New York, and I have his written report, which, I think, was made available to you. . . .

I have not been furnished with any written certifications by any physician on behalf of the defendant and, since ordering her arrest on a bench warrant last night . . . it was reported to me this morning that the defendant was admitted to the Hospital for Joint Diseases late yesterday afternoon by Dr. Umansky. I immediately communicated wtih the hospital and have requested a copy of the record of her admission, and I am still waiting for word from the hospital as to whether or not this record will be made available to me. I am satisfied that the defendant continues to absent herself on a voluntary basis and, for that reason, I must reaffirm my determination to proceed with the trial of this case today.

Mr. Durkin: May I be heard, Your Honor?

The Court: Well, of course, I don't think it's necessary, Mr. Durkin.

Mr. Durkin: I have just a few comments I would like to put on the record. First of all I am happy that Your Honor has taken the opportunity to state what you have stated in chambers. Monday prior to the trial I believe at ten or ten-thirty you were going to go out to the courtroom, and I asked you not to go as far as issuing any bench warrant. I think, in view of the publicity that has been in the papers this morning regarding your comments last night, that I will make a motion for a mistrial, Your Honor.

The Court: The motion is denied.

## HOW TO KEEP PEOPLE'S NAMES OUT OF COURT
(but slip them to the FBI)

ESSEX COUNTY COURT
CRIMINAL DIVISION — *Newark, New Jersey*
INDICTMENT NO. 1952—65

**Transcript of Proceedings**

Thursday, June 22, 1967

*Cross-examination of Detective Magnusson by the Counsel for the Defense, Mr. Durkin.*

Durkin: I understand, Lieutenant Magnusson, that you observed a man leave the premises of 850 Lake Street shortly after your arrival. Is that correct?

Magnusson: When I was seated in the room that Mr. Beard had taken me to, I observed Miss Von Cleef escort some male unknown to me. I saw the back of him as he was going down the stairs.

Q: I see. Now I am going to talk about the 1965 appointment book of Miss Von Cleef.

A: Yes.

Q: And I understand that your name—the name you used—name of Sullivan appears next to one o'clock. Is that correct?

A: That's correct.

Q: Were there names above that, of Sullivan, in time, on that particular day, sir?

A: I don't believe there were.

Q: Well . . . did you check any of the names in that book against the file cabinets which were brought in, or the red book which you described to us yesterday?

A: No.

Q: Or against names in any other books on the premises?

A: No.

Q: So there was no investigation made regarding any names in that 1965 book. . . . Is that correct?

A: Yes.

Q: And none of those names were checked against the catalogue or file card listing or any other book found on the premises. Is that correct?

Noonan: Your Honor, may I just say that it is not really—I will have to put it in the form of an objection. It was not checked *by this witness.*

Durkin: Yes, of course. By this witness.

Magnusson: No, it was not checked by me, sir.

Q: Do you know anything about that, Lieutenant? Can you give us the name of anybody who did check this, sir?

A: I will have to tell you this: that I made all of this available to the Federal Bureau of Investigation, and whatever they did, sir, I don't know.

Q: You don't know . . . but can you give us the name of anybody who checked the names of the appointment book against . . .

The Court: He has answered it. Mr. Durkin. I mean, you can't have six different kinds of answers to one question. I think he made himself very clear.

Durkin: He said he didn't know. Then he mentioned an agency. He said he turned it all over to the FBI. I'll ask him this way:

Q: Well, as a result of the appointment book I just mentioned, the red book, and the card catalogue or any other name or address found on the premises that day, did you personally, as a result of finding said names, go to any of those people?

A: I personally did not. With one exception.

Durkin: I think I'd better see Your Honor at side bar.

(*The following takes place at side bar out of hearing of the jury.*)

Durkin: I believe I should have this conference at side bar, because I now anticipate what his answer would be to my next question: that an individual by the name of Roy Chisholm was arrested by the post office sometime after this raid on Miss Von Cleef, and had told the authorities that he had met Miss Von Cleef on Staten Island. Is it our understanding that he never had anything to do with Miss Von Cleef in this jurisdiction? We have a juri-dictional problem here.

Noonan: My understanding is this: As a result of one of the letters which was read into the record—he's the truck driver from Westfield—Detective Magnusson spoke to him and he was arrested. We don't have to go into the arrest.

Durkin: But I don't think he arrested him pursuant to this case. He arrested him as the result of something that happened in the post office.

Noonan: As a result of this letter.

Durkin: I don't know if it was as a result of this letter.

The Court: You are going into a rather dangerous field, it seems to me, as far as your defendants are concerned. How is it going to help you to show that this man was pursued and arrested, even for a Federal violation?

Durkin: I do not want to go into that, but what it would lead to if, say, we didn't have a jury here, is that this man Chisholm supposedly had an appointment, or whatever you want to call it, with Miss Von Cleef out of this jurisdiction.

The Court: What do you mean by 'out of this jurisdiction'? This is a conspiracy charge.

Durkin: I understand that. But this happened a long time ago in Staten Island.

The Court: What do you mean by 'a long time ago'?

Durkin: A few years ago.

The Court: I thought it was within the period of the . . .

Durkin: No, no, Your Honor, positively not. This is when Miss Von Cleef was still living in Staten Island. I want to show this jury that, as a result of all those names in the appointment book, the State has not produced one single one of those people to assist the jury in determining whether or not there was maintaining etcetera etcetera. I only requested this conference at side bar to avoid a mistrial. I don't want Lieutenant Magnusson saying, 'I spoke to Mr. Chisholm and he said he committed a lewd act with her', when, in fact, we know said lewd act, if committed, was a long long time ago in Staten Island and has nothing to do with this case.

The Court: What question do you want to ask him?

Durkin: My question was: Did you, as a result of reviewing all these names and addresses, go to talk to any of these people for the purpose of ascertaining whether they actually ever were at 850 Lake Street? I think if I add that last phrase that may help it, because we know that Lieutenant Magnusson did not speak to Chisholm at 850 Lake Street.

Noonan: But they were tipped on to Chisholm by finding the letter on the premises.

Durkin: I understand that, but I can ask him that, as a result . . .

Noonan: I have no objection to that question as you ask it.

The Court: You'd better be careful about one thing. This is opening the door to something.

Durkin: I don't want to open any doors. I will be guided by it. I think you know what I am trying to do as far as assisting the jury. We have one charge here of maintaining a house etcetera. If we are to show maintaining, we must show some activity. I want to ask him this question: As a result of all the names and addresses which you found on the premises, did you locate any individual named therein who told you that he was ever at the 850 Lake Street address between October 1 and the time of the arrest.

The Court: Ask him if he interrogated him.

Durkin: If I say 'interrogate' he'll answer yes: One Chisholm that he did interrogate him, and Chisholm . . .

The Court: Can't you just stop there?

Durkin: If Magnusson says yes he interrogated one Chisholm and then stops, the jury will get the impression: why doesn't he pursue that further?

The Court: Why can't he answer: 'Yes, I interrogated Chisholm', and stop there? 'I interrogated a man named Chisholm.'

Durkin: Well—then we may run into a problem. Let's go off the record.

(*Discussion off the record entirely.*)

The Court: You see, this is the danger, that you may open the door to something.

Durkin: What I want to say is: do you have something to say in summation? They are all charged with maintaining here and you have all these names and addresses.

The Court: But I can't, after all, tell you how to try your case.

Durkin: I understand that, Your Honor. Now, as I understand it, Mr. Noonan has no objection to this question.

Noonan: No, sir.

Durkin: I will then ask this question: 'Detective Magnusson, as a result of finding all those names and addresses in various boxes at 850 Lake Street, did you contact any of these people and find out whether or not any of them had ever been to 850 Lake Street from October 1 until the day of the raid?

Noonan: I have no objection. I would even add the words: 'books and papers found there'.

Durkin: Yes.

(*The following takes place back in the hearing of the jury.*)

Durkin: Now, Detective, directing your attention to all the books and papers where names and addresses appeared, which you found at 850 Lake Street on this particular day, will you tell the jury whether you contacted any of these people and ascertained the name of any person who was at 850 Lake Street between October 1 and the day of the raid? Did you ascertain the name of any individual, sir?

Magnusson: Who was at 850 Lake Street?
Durkin: Yes.
Magnusson: No, sir.

ESSEX COUNTY COURT
CRIMINAL DIVISION
INDICTMENT NO. 1952—65

THE STATE OF NEW JERSEY
*versus*
MARIANNA VON CLEEF
JAMES ALBERT BEARD

Volume IV (page 43)

*Thursday, June 22, 1967* and
*Friday, June 23, 1967.*
*Newark, New Jersey.*

**Transcript of Proceedings**

Prosecutor Noonan: Q. You were asked by Mr. Durkin on cross-examination whether you investigated the names and addresses of people whose names and addresses were found in the letters, lists, and file cards. You mentioned that you turned these materials over to the FBI.

Lieutenant Magnusson: A. Yes.

Prosecutor Noonan: What else was done?

Magnusson: I made a complete file copy for the United States postal authorities. I made a complete file copy for I think it was military intelligence. Partial files were taken by Naval Intelligence. The Internal Revenue Service. There were other Federal agencies. It was disseminated that way.

ESSEX COUNTY COURT
CRIMINAL DIVISION
INDICTMENT NO. 1952—65

*Newark, New Jersey*

**Transcript of Proceedings**

Friday, June 23, 1967

THE FOLLOWING TAKES PLACE IN THE JUDGE'S CHAMBERS

The Court: Mr. Durkin, I think, in all fairness to yourself, some statement should be made for the record with respect to the posed picture which appears in the daily press. I refer to the identical photograph which I saw in the *Daily News* and also in the morning *Ledger*. It carries the AP wire legend . . . does it not?

Mr. Noonan: Yes, sir. I believe it does.

The Court: I know what you told us previously with respect to the difficulties which you encountered in communicating with your client during the time that she has been confined. . . . In this *Ledger* copy which I have before me the photograph is entitled: 'MONIQUE VON CLEEF RESTS IN HOSPITAL' . . . I am certain, Mr. Durkin, that you did not participate, either directly or indirectly, in arranging for this posed picture. However, I think for your own protection a statement should be made.

Mr. Durkin: I agree with you fully, Your Honor. I appeared at the Hospital for Joint Diseases last night, approximately six-thirty, in the company of William Gearty, an attorney in Newark, New Jersey. We went to room 701D and spoke to Miss Von Cleef. After being there approximately 20 minutes, I was informed, that an individual—she described him as short—had appeared with what appeared to be a telegram, signed by Harry F. Durkin, indicating that I gave permission for a photograph to be taken. . . . Mr. Gearty then asked her whether she had the telegrapm, and then she said, 'No. I probably should have kept it, but he just flashed it in front of me, showed me your name and said that you gave permission and then a picture was taken.'

A few minutes thereafter she called Dr. Umansky and spoke with him for approximately three or four minutes and said to Dr. Umansky, 'My attorney is here at the bedside. Would you speak with him for a minute or two?' The answer was no. . . .

I have attempted to contact Dr. Umansky on at least six occasions, calling both his office and the hospital and I had hoped to speak with him last night, and on each and every occasion my attempts have been futile.

Mr. Noonan: I think there is something that I want to add for the record, Judge.

Judge, this is Mr. Gene Spagnoli of the *New York Daily News*. Mr. Spagnoli conversed with the defendant Von Cleef yesterday.

The Court: Relate in narrative what occurred yesterday with respect to Miss Von Cleef and any interviews and photos.

Mr. Spagnoli: When I called at our office yesterday, they said that Miss Von Cleef had called me. This was in the morning at perhaps ten-thirty. I'm not sure of the time, but it was in the morning. They said Miss Von Cleef had called with the number TR7–6000, with Room 701D. My call was screened by a Mr. Green who was the administrative assistant.

The Court: At the Hospital for Joint Diseases?

Spagnoli: Yes. My call was put through. I talked to her and she said, 'It would be all right to have my picture taken today.' She said, 'If you can come up and have the photographer come up, you can take a picture.'

I asked, 'How about an interview?' She said, 'There's a lawyer, my lawyer', and I am not quite sure what the connection was. She mentioned her father in Switzerland had contacted a lawyer, gotten a lawyer, a fellow named James Siff, and she said, 'The lawyer must be present.' I said, 'How do you feel?' She said, 'I don't feel too good.' I said, 'How did the accident happen?' She said, 'Well, we'll have to wait until you come up and the lawyer is here.'

So I hung up and called our desk and gave them the two numbers she had given me for the lawyer and then I believe they assigned someone to go up to take the pictures.

The Court: Do you have the numbers you were given?

Spagnoli: Surely . . . CAnal 6–5454 and PLaza 1–6592.

The Court: Those are the telephone numbers of Mr. Siff?

Spagnoli: Mr. Siff, yes. Then from there our office took it. They evidently contacted him, and I guess you saw the picture in the paper today. That's how they got it.

The Court: Mark the picture in the *Star Ledger* as an exhibit . . . do you know whether or not she was paid for this?

Spagnoli: No, I do not know. If you want an assumption, I would assume not, but I do not know.

Mr. Durkin: Let me put on record what I was told last night. First of all, I will very briefly relate that two or three nights ago I received a call from James Beard while I was in my office, telling me I was going to receive a call from an attorney that Miss Von Cleef had decided to consult. However, he was not in New Jersey. He wasn't a New Jersey attorney, and he would only participate to assist if it was necessary, and I would receive a call from him, which I did and I spoke to him for about forty-five minutes.

The Court: When was this?

Mr. Durkin: I am quite sure it was Tuesday night. He then went on to tell me there was some connection between Miss Von Cleef's father and him. I spoke with Miss Von Cleef last night and asked exactly what the story was, and I was told that she never knew James Siff until a few days ago, when she left the court last Friday and was all upset about the possible penalty of nine years and she called her father in Switzerland and said (I am quoting her): 'Papa, I don't think it is going too well.' Her papa then said, 'I'll put Mr. Bernstein on a plane and send him over.' This Mr. Bernstein in Switzerland is well known in International law. He came to New York and deemed it advisable to contact a New York lawyer rather than get supposedly my slanted views as to how the case was going, and consequently. . . .

The Court: You don't mean your slanted views?

Mr. Durkin: That's what she told me last night. He wanted to get the viewpoint of a lawyer who was not involved in the case because he admittedly, I understand, is not familiar with criminal law, particularly criminal law in the United States. So he contacted this James Siff. James Siff, by the way, informed me he is thirty years old and has been practising just a few years. . . . Last night in the presence of Mr. Gearty . . . she assured me that I was the only attorney as far as the case was concerned, but because she was nervous she called her father. Her father got in touch with Mr. Bernstein. This Mr. Bernstein got in touch with Mr. Siff, and Mr. Siff got in touch with me and that's how this other attorney situation came about.

The Court: Did Bernstein actually come to New York?

Mr. Durkin: Yes, Your Honor. Actually, he's staying until tomorrow. Miss Von Cleef indicated surprise that he had not contacted me, but I state for the record that he has not.

The Court: That's quite a story.

Mr. Durkin: It even goes back further with Mr. Von Cleef—strike that—I don't think that's his name—Mr. Mohr supposedly saved Mr. Bernstein's life during the war, and he told his daughter that Mr. Bernstein had owed him a favor for a long time and he would get him to go to that extent, to come to New York on her behalf.

The Court: Well, this about does it. All right. . . .

Mr. Durkin: I would like to put this on record: We spoke about His Honor's ruling that the case is going to proceed and she indicated, 'Well, I just cannot be there presently', and that was the extent of the conversation. She did not request, nor did I suggest that she appear Monday, Tuesday, Wednesday or any other day, because I understand Dr. Umansky has not told her or indicated to her any day when he intends to release her. . . .

ESSEX COUNTY COURT
CRIMINAL DIVISION
INDICTMENT NO. 1952—65

STATE OF NEW JERSEY
*versus*
MARIANNA VON CLEEF
JAMES ALBERT BEARD,
Defendants.

SENTENCE

*Tuesday, September 12, 1967*
*Newark, New Jersey*

Before:
HONORABLE LEON W. KAPP, J.C.C.

Appearance:
HARRY P. DURKIN, ESQ.,
Attorney for the Defendants.

*Filed, October 9, 1967.*
NICHOLAS V. CAPUTO, *Clerk.*

ANGELO J. CARDENUTO,
*Official Court Reporter.*

Mr. Durkin: Good afternoon, Your Honor. I am certain of the fact that you have a comprehensive probation report before you and consequently I will limit my remarks.

One interesting point, among others, should be called to the Court's attention at this particular time, namely, sentencing, and that is that, unlike most crimes, as we look back we find in this very, very bizarre case that we do not have a victim and we do not have these particular persons having committed fraud on anybody. Consequently, no one was victimized, as is true in the typical situation on sentence day.

I also call to Your Honor's attention, and without going into detail because Your Honor knows as well as I it is not necessary, that these individuals have fully co-operated with the powers that be.

It was testified throughout the case, Your Honor, and

more particularly by Dr. Chernus, that persons engaged in this type of activity are sick, sick, sick.

Benjamin Franklin said a long time ago, 'There are no gains without pains.' And whatever these people may have gained, Your Honor, in respect or in the opinion of anyone else, they certainly have sustained pains throughout. They lost their house. Their property was confiscated by breaking and entry, and numerous other harassments were sustained by these individuals.

Very succinctly, Your Honor, I have no hesitancy in saying, as an officer of this Court, that these people have paid the price. You know as well as I that sentence is for the purposes of paying a debt to society and for the purposes of rehabilitation. You are familiar with these people's background and their record, or I should say the lack of a criminal record, and for those and other reasons, Your Honor, which I am familiar with or which are in your file, I respecfully ask that you extend leniency on behalf of Marianna Von Cleef and James Albert Beard, and that you eradicate from your mind everything that has happened, although it is rather difficult to do so as far as publicity, as far as image or lack thereof, and render a sentence here which is commensurate with the facts and, consequently, Your Honor, I am sure you will deem it advisable not to inflict a custodial sentence. Thank you.

The Court: Miss Von Cleef, do you have anything to say in your own behalf?

The Defendant Von Cleef: No, sir.

The Court: Mr. Beard, have you?

The Defendant Beard: No.

The Court: Of course, you realize that you are privileged to be heard if you desire to do so, Miss Von Cleef and Mr. Beard.

Mr. Durkin: I have advised them of that, Your Honor.

The Court: Each of you is convicted on multiple counts by a jury in this Court. One, for conspiring to violate the criminal laws of this State in maintaining and operating a building at 850 Lake Street in the City of Newark for the purposes of soliciting, procuring and engaging in acts of lewdness and assignation; two, for permitting the premises in question under your control to be used for the purposes of lewdness and assignation; and, three, for the purpose of unlawful possession with intent to utter and expose to the view of others obscene and indecent books, publications, pictures and other representations.

The Court has had the benefit of a thorough and painstaking pre-sentence investigation conducted by the Probation Department of this county and the reports of psychiatric examinations performed at the Menlo Park Diagnostic Center and by Dr. Samuel Martin, the director of the Psychiatric Clinic here in Essex County. The Court has also considered the report by Dr. Frank S. Caprio, whom the defendant, Marianna Von Cleef, consulted on May 29, 1967, at his office in Washington, D.C., prior to trial of this case. The Court is satisfied, based upon the opinions expressed by the specialists, that in your case, Marianna Von Cleef, there is no evidence of psychosis, mental deficiency or of a deep-seated mental or emotional disorder. A consideration of all the evidence elicited at the trial, including the numerous exhibits and the information, contained in the pre-sentence investigation, indicates an awareness by you that you were engaged in a sordid business for financial gain. Indeed, it is a sad commentary on human behavior in a civilized community to learn of the existence of an establishment where flogging and acts of bondage are performed by the quote master unquote upon her quote slave unquote as a way of life.

Through the publication, *Flair*, which both of you caused to be circulated, a pamphlet characterized as a quote sex club unquote, which contains a listing of quote services unquote, such as homosexuality, sadism, masochism and transvestism, you solicited sick people who cannot relate in a normal manner sexually and are sometimes referred to as sex perverts or deviates because of their emotional illnesses. Your sadistic acts were motivated solely on a mercenary basis of a fixed fee of fifty dollars an hour. These unfortunate sick individuals were your prey.

You have failed to evince a feeling of remorse or contrition. On the contrary, I find that you have not been forthright and initially that you failed to co-operate with the authorities. Your conduct, by furnishing misleading information, has thwarted the expeditious disposition of your cases.

In my judgment for the record, you, Marianna Von Cleef, are a cruel, calculating and wicked person and I sentence you to serve a term of eighteen months in the Essex County Penitentiary on the first count of Indictment

> No. 1952 of the 1965 term. However, the execution of the sentence is suspended only to the extent that you shall be confined for a period of four months and upon your discharge from the penitentiary that you continue on probation for the remainder of the term herein imposed and that you pay a fine of $1,000. The sentence in your case on counts three and four will be suspended.
>
> In your case, Mr. Beard, it is the sentence of this Court on Count No. 1 of Indictment No. 1952 of the 1965 term that you serve a term of six months in the Essex County Penitentiary. However, the execution of that sentence is suspended and you are placed on probation for a period of eighteen months and directed to pay a fine of $500. The sentence in your case, Mr. Beard, on Counts three and four will be suspended.

'Yes, when Magnusson, who arrested me, said that in court, I recalled saying to him: "Don't get anybody involved in this." Well, they didn't. They must have had a whole series of fits when they got a good look at the names and addresses in my files. They did their damnedest, too, to keep those names out of court and out of the newspapers. I kept my own trap shut, and that's one reason why they let me off fairly light. They could have thrown several books at me if they had really wanted to play rough.

'Take the case of Richard the Senator. If I remember right he was number 417. He really was a big wheel in American politics, and those boys have a lot of pull. He was a chubby, jolly little man with one of those rosy barbershop faces, you know the type. About fifty years old, and his greatest wish was to be a baby again. Or at least two, two-and-a-half years old. That would vary, But never, never over six.

'There simply are no diapers for grown people, so in his case I used white tablecloths, and those large safety pins they use to fasten camping blankets. He lay quite contentedly sucking his thumb on a rubber sheet, wetting his diaper, and would begin to cry if I did not change and wash him soon enough. I would then dry him, powder him, and I swear his prickie was no larger than my little finger. He then got his bottle of milk, which he happily sucked empty through an old-fashioned nipple. When he needed me he rang up the evening before, left his home early, took a plane to Newark, rang me up from the airport, took a taxi, and was at my place shortly after nine. He came so regularly that I had one room furnished with baby equipment. I had bought a playpen with some animals and when he felt in a bad mood he threw everything out, then began to weep loudly until I came and threw it all back in. Sometimes I tried to give him a doll:

' "Here, Dickie, a nice doll to play with."

'He crawled to a corner of his pen and made a face.

' "I don't want no doll. Dickie is a boy."

'Then I prepared a bowl of milk and cornflakes, put him in a chair at the table, and said:

' "Here is a spoon. Now be a big boy and eat it yourself."

'Five minutes later I came back and discovered an unbelievable mess. Milk and flakes all over his face and sweater. I began to slap his face and he yelled as if he was being murdered. That was all in the game. Whatever we did, whatever I bought, the whole intention was to make me so mad that I would take off his diaper or his pants or whatever he was wearing and spank him until his fat little ass was blue. I knew exactly what he wanted. If he went on misbehaving after a handspanking that meant that I had to use a hairbrush. He sometimes sat talking to me quite normally after one of these "treatments" and then he talked like a normal politician . . . there was nothing he detested so much as a fag, etc.

'Came the day when he was up for re-election and his whole hometown was plastered with large posters: "Mr. X for Senator!" Jesus—if they had only known!"

COURT CRACKS ITS OWN WHIP,
RULES FOR PAIN-FOR-PAY Gal.

Washington, June 23 (NEWS Bureau)—

Ruling that Newark cops were carried away in their search for evidence against a buxom pain-for-pay madame, the Supreme Court has vacated the 1967 conviction of Dutch-born Marianna Monique Von Cleef.

In a 6–2 decision today, the Court held that police illegally seized thousands of lewd photographs, magazines, letters and drawings when they raided Monique's torture house in 1965. At the time of the bust, Monique was wearing a black rubber suit and was preparing to give a half-naked undercover detective a $50 whipping.

Overturning the convictions of both Monique and her 'friend', James A. Beard, the High Court said:

'We have no hesitation in concluding that the action of police here in combing a three-story, sixteen-room house from top to bottom and carting away several thousand papers, publications and other items cannot under any view of the Fourth Amendment be justified as "incident to arrest" . . .'

The case drew wide attention when it was disclosed that police had confiscated long lists of correspondents and customers throughout the country, some of whom were described as prominent.

In an interview today, Monique's lawyer (Herald Price Fahringer of Buffalo) said that, while his client's actions were 'terribly flagrant', the police brought the Supreme Court's action on themselves through allegedly shoddy search and seizure tactics . . .

Fahringer said that he spoke to Monique, 'who is somewhere in Europe', only hours after the Supreme Court ruling. . . . He said Monique illegally skipped the country last month, rather than appear at deportation hearings.

The lawyer noted that a tricky legal problem now surrounds his attractive client, since the basis for Monique's deportation hearings—the obscenity conviction—is no more. . . . It seems that Monique just might turn her considerable talents to publishing, Fahringer said, and write a book about her 'experiences with the law'.

(from *Daily News*, Tuesday June 24, 1969,
byline:
Frank Van Riper).

And here we are, back where it all started—in Holland. Many years later, with Monique now a big girl, and no longer in Amsterdam, but in The Hague. Monique stands with her back to me, looking through a plate-glass picture window. I get up, add some soda water to my Tio Pepe sherry and ask:

'Do you want to tell me how you got back from the States? You've never said much about that. Were you extradited?'

She drums on the windowpane with her fingertips, turns around, walks slowly back to her armchair and sits there, grinning at me, one hand sliding up and down, up and down a long, black, whore's stocking.

'I cannot give you any names, of course. We did it this way. I approached some good friends and told them I simply had to get out of the States, and as soon as possible. Sentence or no sentence, bail or no bail, appeals or no appeals. By this time I was really getting panicky, you see. I had a trapped feeling. As that trial dragged on I became more and more sure that I was an unimportant pawn in a far bigger game. A pawn? I felt like a prawn—among sharks. The only thing any of them were at all interested in was keeping the names of my clients out of the papers. No one gave a bloody hoot about what would happen to me. And conspiracy is a federal charge, carrying a damn heavy penalty. You see . . . I conspired with Beard. I began to see that I had to take care of myself.

'So my friends took a lot of my photographs—of myself, I mean—and then found a male homosexual of my height, general age, eye color and general likeness. An American, so his passport was genuine. And had been used, which made it look even better. And then they quote stole it unquote while he looked the other way.

'What did they need your photographs for?'

'For comparison. We did it the other way round. They reproduced several takes of my face passport-size. To—'

'Ah, I get it. Then they went looking for an honest-to-God American with a passport, who looked like you and was about the same age, etc.'

'To see whether I could be made-up to look like him, pass for him.'

'In man's clothing?'

'Yes, of course. They are a bit effeminate anyway . . .'

'While you—yes. You met roughly halfway.'

This strikes her as funny. 'Nice way to put it, But I'll confess to you: I've never in my life been in such a pants-pissing state of nerves as when I was finally in my seat on that plane on the runway.'

'Not while you were passing the checkpoints?'

'No, you see—as those things always seem to happen—the plane was delayed. And for no visible reason. I was so afraid that I literally froze where I sat, and it was probably a lucky thing, too. I was wearing sunglasses so no one could notice the expression in my eyes. And the rest of me—hands, feet, mouth, couldn't betray me because I was frozen with terror. Mentally and physically. You hear of people getting heart failure from fright. Let me tell you, buddy, that when that plane finally started moving, finally got off the ground, I nearly had a heart attack from sheer relief. Like when a very tightly strung wire suddenly snaps and the end hits you.'

I nod a bit. Then I say: 'Smooth going. There should be a medal for that kind of thing. Yes, by that time your nerves must have been pretty well shot.'

She obviously hates to admit it, then grudgingly says:

'Ye . . . es. I couldn't take much more.'

'Of course not, dearie. You are not really as tough as you pretend to be. I'll lay you seven to one that you are even afraid of guns even when you're at the right end.'

She sits looking at me with compressed lips. I sit looking back. For a long time we say nothing. Then I go on, airily sloshing sherry-soda around in that huge glass. 'Listen, sweetie pie. Long ago women thought up a brilliant piece of propaganda. They spread the story that women are eternal and unfathomable mysteries, while silly, stupid men are nothing more than transparent and slightly retarded children. In reality, of course, it's dead easy for a man to understand a woman once he's been through the propaganda. But it's impossible for a woman ever to really understand a man. Men are the real mysteries. And in her heart every woman knows that. You too.'

She still sits quite still, our eyes locking. 'Meaning what?'

'That every woman wants to be understood by a man—a little. But no woman likes to be understood too well. She can't afford it, because then she'll lose any game in three moves.'

'What are you driving at?'

'As a writer, I have to understand you or I could never have worked with you on this book. But that doesn't mean that you necessarily enjoy being understood by me the man.'

She shoots out of her low chair, takes the three steps that separate the two of us, bends over, and kisses me full on the mouth. Then straightens up, stretches, stands looking down at me with half-closed eyes, and says: 'You know, you're a real bastard. But, thank God, not a stupid one. . . .'

I bow my head. The door bell buzzes. Thirty seconds later an absolutely stunning girl comes in.

'Hello, Monique.'

Monique is suddenly all business. 'This is William Waterman. I told you about him.'

'Oh—the man with the book.' The girl flashes me a lightning-swift look. Her eyes barely flick at me. I remain low down in my chair.

Monique says: 'It's five to four. He'll be here any moment now. William, you know the rules: you can stay in that chair, but whatever happens you keep your mouth shut. Just watch.'

The girl gives an invisible sign. Monique nods. 'He's the only one of all of them who may do this.'

I'm watching, all right. I'm watching this new girl. One of those fantastic, true blonde, slightly perverse Viking faces, constructed from the cheekbones and jaw outward. She has a pair of legs that look six feet long, sewn into skin tight jeans. The buttocks of a twelve-year-old boy, and two perfect tits—not too heavy, not too small—that she seems to carry right beneath her collar bones. Monique calls her Femke. No, there's nothing French about it, it's as German as can be. One of those ancient girls' names from northern Holland. It means just what it sounds like: 'little woman'. I've known lots of beautiful, or sexy, or fascinatingly mad girls in my life. But this one is what they used to call a new departure.

I say, articulating clearly: 'To once fuck a girl like you and then die.'

She flashes a set of teeth like a wolf bitch. She smiles. But when she smiles, she draws the corners of her mouth back and shows all her teeth. Well—she can afford to.

'It's an idea, isn't it?' she says.

The buzzer buzzes. In comes a man who at first sight looks absolutely middling. Size, age, weight, neat gray suit, haircut. A man who appears to be trying not only to blend into his background and environment, but who may even be attempting to blend himself completely away. Except his eyes. He has overlooked his own eyes, behind those crystal-clear rimless glasses. I know those eyes. Brilliant engineers have them. And research chemists. And sometimes mathematicians. He sees me lolling on the small of my back in that enormous chair, but takes no further notice.

Monique and Femke are slowly retreating to opposite sides of the room, the man between them. Monique says, in an undertone: 'Femke . . . Shhhh . . . do you see what I see?'

'No, what? . . . Where?' Femke squats a little and looks around her.

'Over there—a rabbit!'

'Ah, yes! I see it now. Lord—a nice young juicy grass-fed rabbit. And I haven't had any food for two whole days. . . . My teeth are watering.'

'Shall we try to catch it?'

'Not so loud! He's heard us!'

At this the rabbit-man in the rimless glasses senses the danger. He ducks, moving his head from right to left, sniffing the air—now gets down on hands and spring-folded legs, rabbit-like.

'He's still too far away. We can't hop that far. Let's get closer.'

Both girls begin to slink up to their prey, but as they get near, the rabbit turns and hops away through the open door into the hall. With a snarl and a growl the girls go after him. I remain in my chair, and play around with the idea of getting my own teeth into the cunt of the wolf bitch. I'd give her something to yowl about. From where I sat I can hear the chase-game. Monique and Femke intersperse their dialogue with fantasies about what they're going to do with their rabbit after they catch it. How they are going to skin it, eat it—get their teeth into it.

The poor frightened rabbit is hopping all over the place, twisting and turning. The girls growl and snarl, and finally he escapes upstairs. The girls are getting furious now.

'That rotten rabbit, he's slipped away again! Jump him, Monique!'

I hear them yelping, growling and threatening all over the floor above me. This goes on and on and on, but I detect a gradually increasing note of fury and sadism in the girls' cries. I get up and pour myself some more sherry-soda. Then sink back.

Now the thumping and jumping stops—I hear threatening voices. Then a man's voice, raised in deathly fear:

'Nono! Don't eat me. Not in the hot pan!'

Now Femke's voice, raised to a mad, menacing pitch: 'Hold him, Monique! Hold him tight. I am coming . . . coming with the hot pan, full of hot oil! We'll put him into it alive and hear him scream and sizzle! Like a live lobster! We'll broil him. . . . In smoking hot oil! We'll broil him! Here's the pan. . . . PUT HIM IN!'

A man's voice, raised to a screech of insane terror—then slowly subsiding and dying away, in a long, sobbing moan.

The girls come back into the room. Monique has a wad of money in her hands. Counts off a few and hands them to Femke, who throws them nonchalantly on the couch.

'How does it work?' I ask. 'Is the terror enough to make him come?'

Monique is pouring two whiskies. Femke lies back in one of the club chairs, her hands behind her head.

'Not entirely. The moment Monique grabs him and I get close with the hot pan, Monique unzips his fly and gets hold of his penis. He needs the terror to get it stiff. When I am very close and start talking about the boiling oil, and he starts to screech, she gives him a fast toss or two and then he comes. That's all. It's just a matter of timing.'

'And without the terror he can't get his pecker up?'

'He can't even get a climax. No way at all.'

'And the game never varies?'

'Not basically. We vary our dialogue, of course. And he sometimes escapes downstairs again. Takes a bit longer, that's all.'

'What is he? I don't want to know his name, but his profession?'

Monique sips some whiskey, then says: 'He seems to be an internationally famous brain behind the Philips computer production.'

I had expected something like that. I turn my attention to Femke the Viking Princess.

'Is it utterly and completely out of the question to fuck you? Just once?'

'Of course not,' she says. 'Would you like to?' She doesn't even bother to get out of that low chair, but unzips one side of her tight jeans and stretches out her legs.

'You have to pull them off yourself.'

'Yes!' says Monique in sudden enthusiasm: 'I want to watch William fucking you. I'm in the right mood.

'Gladly, darling,' I say, get out of my chair, and begin to peel the pants off my wolf bitch, who still has her whiskey glass in her hand.

I get her pants off, she has nothing on underneath. She spreads her legs. I sink down on my knees and admire her, then get up and take my own pants off.

Very gently I push my tool between her so-available folds. I feel no pain. No pain at all.